THE MYTH
OF MATURITY

...TH
OF MATURITY

WHAT TEENAGERS NEED
FROM PARENTS
TO BECOME ADULTS

TERRI APTER

W · W · NORTON & COMPANY

NEW YORK   LONDON

For information about permission to reproduce selections from this book,
write to Permissions, W. W. Norton & Company, Inc.,
500 Fifth Avenue, New York, NY 10110

The text of this book is composed in Centaur with the display set in Donatello

Composition by Gina Webster

Manufacturing by Quebecor Fairfield

Book design by Margaret Wagner

Library of Congress Cataloging-in-Publication Data

Apter, T. E.

The myth of maturity : what teenagers need from parents to

become adults / by Terri Apter.

p. cm.

Includes bibliographical references and index.

ISBN: 978-0-393-32317-7

1. Parent and teenager—United States. 2. Child rearing—United States.

3. Adolescent psychology. I. Title.

HQ799.15 .A678 2001

306.874'2—dc21   00-069245

W. W. Norton & Company, Inc.
500 Fifth Avenue, New York, N.Y. 10110
www.wwnorton.com

W. W. Norton & Company Ltd.
Castle House, 75/76 Wells Street, London W1T 3QT

3 4 5 6 7 8 9 0

*for Julia
and Miranda*

CONTENTS

CONTENTS

ACKNOWLEDGMENTS

My DEEPEST thanks go to the young people and families who gave their time and energy to participate in this project. Without their generosity and dedication, this book would not have been possible. Teachers and counselors from several colleges and high schools were willing to give me intensive instruction in the problems young people face as they step over the threshold of adulthood. I have agreed to withhold naming them to protect the privacy of the young people whose well-being they work so hard to foster.

The process of shaping this book was a long one, and I had much help. The Delta Kappa Gamma Society's Great Britain Conference provided a responsive and useful forum for early presentations of my findings. The clear and critical eye of my editor, Jill Bialosky, helped establish a general framework for the individual stories I wished to relate. The enthusiasm of my agent, Meg Ruley, kept this project going when it seemed that nothing else would.

The Mellon Research Funds of Clare Hall, University of Cambridge, offered generous financial support.

THE MYTH
OF MATURITY

LIFE ON ONE'S OWN

HER situation couldn't have been better. At eighteen, she was starting college, having weathered the rough interviews and the rougher exams. She had come through, safe from disappointments, entitled to pride. As we packed and shopped for the things she would need as a college student, I felt a mother's thrill at a daughter's adult potential: her whole life ahead of her!

She dragged her feet about packing. Only at the last moment did she make a real effort and begin checking off items on her list. But I was too excited on her behalf to register her mood. We made the short but tense journey in a gear-stuffed car on a perfect autumn day, clear and golden, full of promise. As I maneuvered into a small space in the crowded parking lot, I felt elated. The sun butted up against the yellow stone. Geraniums and old English roses were still in bloom. Even the earth beneath them glowed. I ached with excitement.

"My room's in the new court," my daughter announced. "A cement block."

"This is a lovely room!" I exclaimed when we entered. "It has a stunning view." For though her room was in a recent development, its large window looked out on the older courtyard. The room was larger than many in college residences I knew and was, in any case, her very own. Here her new, her very own life would begin.

Her little sister at once set off to explore. She sized up the shared kitchen and bathroom. She opened the cupboards and measured the drawers, then sat on the bed, her back against the wall, hugging her knees. "I can't wait to go to college," she shivered with excitement, feeling the prospect of the best years hurtling toward her—but not fast enough. "I know," I concurred. "I wish I were going again, too." We felt full of fun, but I knew my older daughter was anxious to see us off, to establish herself in her grown-up world.

The car was now unloaded, and we were ready to leave. "No. Wait. Okay. Go." This was familiar: a request made and then withdrawn as she decided, "What's the point? They won't understand. They won't be any use." I tried to pick up her meaning: Did she want help unpacking? Having told us, five minutes before, that she didn't was no indication of what she really wanted now. "Okay, you can unpack," she allowed, "but *I* decide where things go." Did she then want us to take her for lunch? I suggested. What a terrible idea. What she wanted, she now said, was for us to leave. But, in an uncharacteristic movement, she lifted her cheek to be kissed and didn't squirm away from my hug, but simply muttered a pride-saving, "Yeah, yeah." (*There she goes, doing her silly mother-thing.*)

"Doesn't she like her room?" my younger daughter asked as we carried the now empty boxes and cases back to the car. "Isn't she glad to be here?" And then I focused on a question I'd been pushing aside: "Why wasn't she happy?"

This was a strange puzzle, given I'd had my own experience of college and given, further, that I deal day-to-day with problems my own college students bring to me. I'd had a similar leave-taking twenty-five years before. As I moved into the dorm in Chicago, when I was the age my daughter is now, I expected that I would be stepping out of my ill-fitting and unbecoming adolescence. Waiting for me in my new life, I supposed, was a sharp set of adult clothes. Yet when I arrived, I felt naked, helpless, terrified. Everyone else moving in had what I lacked: assurance, flair, personality. My father's presence made a bad situation worse. He spoke too loudly, breathed too loudly, looked silly when he carried my cases, all flushed and anxious. When, awkward and friendly, he spoke to another young woman on my corridor, trying to establish an acquaintance on my behalf, I felt branded by my association with him: "That's it," I thought, "that's that relationship ruined." I wanted to be free of him, but when he left, I felt abandoned.

There I was, left to start my own life, on my own terms, with my brand-new checkbook, blank notebooks, and a clean social slate. I marked all these with the utmost clumsiness, making mistakes I still blush at, striking poses that everyone (but me) could see through, and lurched toward goals that were either ill-conceived or utterly unrealistic. My mistakes were now my very own, and I had to handle them alone. Any admission of needing my parents or failure to obtain the prize ribbons of happiness would be an admission of shameful immaturity. "You're behaving like a child," could sting me to silence. "How adolescent!" would force me back into my mature facade. "Grow up!" was like a slap, leaving me shamed, because it declared that I was not as I was supposed to be. Like good parents, mine believed that independence was good for me. Now, they fervently believed, I should be standing on my own two feet. Trying to do the right thing, they wanted to let go. If I found myself in free fall, then I just didn't have what it takes.

Each day I try to reassure myself that my daughter will not have the tough time I did and that her declaration that she is "doing fine" is genuine—not the false bravado I felt compelled to display to my parents. Like most parents, I feel caught between my daughter's need to find her own way into adulthood and her equally strong need to remain connected to her family. As I try to calm myself with self-soothing words ("She's doing fine. She'll be okay.") there lurks an awareness of how difficult this early—this too early—phase of adulthood is.

The years bridging adolescence and adulthood are a testing ground for all the assumptions we have about ourselves. Every young person confronts a series of challenging questions: "How will I manage as one of *them*—one of the grown-ups? How do I measure up in a larger world-pond? Will I be able to learn what I need to know? Who will be my friends?" Wanting to go forward, many young people feel as clumsy and needy as a toddler.

When parents fail to understand the mechanisms and pressures of this phase, they are at a loss as to what a daughter—or son—needs when she says, "I have no future" or "There's nothing to look forward to." All too often, we fail to work alongside young people to address their doubts. Instead of being the safe containers for a young person's anxieties, parents, teachers, and employers often have a tin ear when it comes to hearing cries for help. However much they want to understand, advise, and support, parents stand as confused witnesses to such turmoil: "She's twenty-two, and I have more interrupted nights than I did when she was two," Faye said of her daughter. "She wakes up crying and needs me to hold her and talk to her." Her daughter Christa explained: "I've kept on track, I've done well at school, but now I just can't focus. Everyone expects me to glide off smoothly into a good life, but I can't even see what a good life would be—let alone decide how to go about it." The long road to maturity exposes young people to grave anxieties—especially in a culture that values independence so highly.

EXPECTATIONS ARISING FROM THE MYTH OF MATURITY

There is a common saying that when childhood and adolescence come to an end, life begins.[1] No longer bound by our roles as children, no longer legally under a parent's control, we come of age, independent, responsible, and free. It is now time to be our own person, keep our own hours, do our own thing, free from parents' demands, but not yet burdened by adult responsibilities. At the threshold to adulthood, promise and reality come together. We test our abilities, yet our mistakes are forgiven. Novice adults have the best of everything: youth and independence, confidence and challenge, opportunity and choice. The common image is of a bird stretching its wings and flying from the nest like a pro.

Yet few young people enter the adult world with ease and confidence. They feel awkward, odd, or even unworthy as they see and cannot meet the expectations of those around them. This was beautifully summed up in the landmark 1960s film *The Graduate*, as the young Dustin Hoffman, newly graduated from college, wriggles away, both irritated and despairing, from questions about his future, his interests, his "plans." Leaving adolescence, he has a one-way ticket to adulthood, but all the adults around him seem sleazy, money-oriented, and hypocritical. He wants, somehow, to become an adult—but his own person. It's like early adolescence all over again, but somehow it feels worse. This time, we are playing for keeps.

Putting together a viable adult identity in this complex society isn't easy. The generation of young adults who watched *The Graduate* when it was first released defended themselves against the demands to join the adult world by creating the cult of youth.

Young people made themselves the measure of the real world and accused the grown-ups of living by worn-out principles. Like the character played by the young Dustin Hoffman, they wanted to forge new patterns of adulthood.

This rejection of adult goals and habits gave a previous generation drive and energy. But there was another side to this that they often didn't show—especially to their parents and teachers. They carefully hid their lack of direction and low confidence. When parents of today's young adults look back to their own threshold years, there is inevitably a moment when they pause and turn pale, as they shudder at the memory of this dark side of their youth. To their parents they seemed supremely self-assured. Now they ask, with horror and amazement, "How could I have done those things/taken those risks/married that totally unsuitable guy/slept with those creeps/missed that golden opportunity?" As they pose these unanswerable and highly charged questions, they look back upon those years with the rage of someone betrayed: "Why didn't my parents support me? Why did my teachers let me get away with that? Why was so much expected of me, so young?"

For some of us in mature, midlife adulthood, the false roads and high pressures of early adulthood haunt us still. "I thought twenty-three was supposed to be grown up and so at twenty-three I thought I was too old to change track," Beth said to me. "Now I see my daughter coming up to that age, and I see how young she is and how mean it would be to ask her to fix on just one track. But there I was, seeing myself on the shelf, you know, seeing time fly and thinking it's time to be all settled. I spent so much time pretending to be mature, that I didn't grow."

We look back upon decisions forced upon us by expectations of our maturity—marriages made, children born, jobs held, apprenticeships declined under the force of a myth that in one's early twenties, one is supposed to have reached the magical state of maturity.[2] Time and again I hear people reflect on their threshold years: "My early twenties were such a rough time. My parents didn't give me the support I needed." As Lydia's father, Jim, forty-nine, explained: "My parents loved me, but thought they'd ruin my character if they gave me too much help. 'Spoiling' was their word for it. 'We'll only spoil you, if we keep helping you along,' they kept saying. My Dad argued that he'd given me more than his father had ever given him. And so I didn't deserve more, so it wasn't good for me to have things too easy." Rosa, fifty, looking back to her late teens and early twenties, said, "I was ashamed to show my parents how frail and unprepared I felt. I was supposed to be grown up, and so I tried to look grown up. If you'd asked my parents, they'd say my problem was I had too much confidence. If only they'd known how I really felt, they might have been there for me."

As these women and men see their daughters and sons struggle through the years between adolescence and adulthood, they say, "I know it's hard for them. But how can I help them? They don't need their mom or dad like they used to." Buying into false expectations, they think their children are ready to fly the nest, when they are simply moving away temporarily and are all the more in need of support. Parents assume their daughters and sons want to push them away—when they simply need a different kind of closeness.

WHAT DOES IT MEAN TO BE GROWN UP?

Children these days, it is repeatedly said, grow up more quickly than ever.[3] They reach puberty sooner—some at nine, most by fourteen, whereas only one hundred years ago the average age of puberty was seventeen. Though they grow up more quickly, however, they do not so quickly become grown-ups. Children may race into puberty, but they take longer than ever to reach adulthood. "My students get both younger and older every year," a professor at Berkeley's Business School observed. "When I started teaching fifteen years ago, my students were in their early twenties. Many of them were married, and most of them were settled. Now they are twenty-five, or over, and don't feel in a position to marry or have children. They're older in years, but they're at an earlier phase of life."[4]

It is taking longer and longer to prepare for the adult world. Education and training are now extensive. Leaving home is not a single event but a prolonged process. Forty percent of young women who leave home, and fifty percent of young men, subsequently return.[5] Leaving home is a stop-start transition and does not mark true independence from parents, either emotionally or financially. Young people, when they leave for college, or a job, or to marry, are at best "incompletely-launched young adults."[6] Setting oneself up as an adult in an independent household was once one of the taken-for-granted markers of maturity. It is now a distant, easily frustrated goal, given its high cost. More and more young people return home after college to live with parents, using home as a base for their first career steps: 58 percent of young people between the ages of twenty-two and twenty-four now live with their parents, and 30 percent of those aged between twenty-four and thirty are living with their parents.[7] It now takes a young woman or man between five and ten years to shift home base, fully, from a parent's home to one's very own.[8] While "self sufficiency" and independence and autonomy are more highly valued than ever, they have become increasingly difficult to attain. And so thresholders face a breach between their realities and their needs, on the one hand, and their hopes and expectations, on the other.

HOW DO WE MARK THE ENTRY
INTO ADULTHOOD?

What does it mean to be grown up? What marks the entry into adulthood? It cannot be defined by age alone, or even by specific events. Graduating from high school or college, leaving home and then making a home of one's own, forming a partnership, taking a job, are important signposts of being grown up; but these markers rarely come together before the age of thirty. Along the way, there are many possible pitfalls and detours. In previous generations, there was an expected sequence, set steps toward establishing oneself as an adult. In the 1950s, the average age of marriage was twenty. People typically had their children before they were twenty-four. Housing was relatively cheap. Employment was relatively secure. Salaries were intended to provide a "family wage," which meant one working person could support a household. At this time, young rebels criticized the predictability of maturity. The trajectory into adulthood was threatening because it was so well planned.

Now young people are threatened by a maze of diverging paths and by increasingly contradictory aims for material and personal fulfilment. Fewer and fewer young people today follow a neat path from college to job, marriage, and parenthood within a five-year span. As the space between adolescence and adulthood widens, young people are confused about what counts as maturity. They want to feel grown up. They want to make their own decisions, trust their own judgment, and go their own ways.[9] Yet all this is no longer feasible in early adulthood. Entry into adulthood is now less tangible and more individualistic than ever. Each thresholder will advance at her own pace, seek out her own vision, and suffer her own doubts.

During the past decade, psychologists and researchers and

writers have focused on teenagers' problems. They have shown how everyday pressures from ads, films, television, and magazines to have designer looks and celebrity personalities, to be successful, smart, and sexy, sap teenagers' energy and self-confidence. While there has been a lot of interest in the problems of adolescents, however, the growing turmoil in the lives of young adults has gone virtually unnoticed. Many young people between the ages of eighteen and twenty-four (whom I call *thresholders*) suffer a basic sense of being overwhelmed. As Daniel Levinson noted when he observed important life transitions, young people hit a "rock bottom time"[10] where there seems no viable way of living as an adult. More than half of all thresholders hit major snags during this time. There is an epidemic of waste and suffering among our most promising young adults. Compared with people born just half a generation earlier (who themselves felt unprotected during this phase), those entering their twenties today confront even more challenges.[11]

It is not surprising that these young people are showing signs of increasing anxiety, depression, and despair. Since 1940, rates of suicide, eating disorders, illicit drug use, and alcoholism have increased dramatically for each and every cohort of eighteen- to twenty-four-year-olds. And though adolescence has its own set of dangers, progress through the threshold phase has the serrated peaks and valleys of sharks' teeth. Among six hundred thresholders who were tracked both in the United States and Europe for a period of five years,[12] a full 28 percent had downsized their goals within that period, and 50 percent did not believe the goals they still had would ever be achieved. A quarter were suffering from depression and one third admitted to having considered committing suicide,[13] yet half of these young people had never experienced depression during the adolescent years. Over a third of the young people questioned judged their abilities to be significantly lower at twenty-one than they had thought them to be at age seventeen. This fall in confidence has a great impact on their ability to keep a steady course.[14]

What is so puzzling to me, as a parent, a teacher of college students, and as a psychologist, is how hard it is to predict who will glide through this transition and who will founder. Why does one young person stride forward, happily determined to get where she wants to be, whereas another, equally talented, equally privileged, loses confidence, direction, and control? Why does one young person shed adolescent anxiety or stabilize her sense of values and purpose, while another, starting with an equal mix of self-control and impulsiveness, become increasingly reckless and impulsive and irresponsible in her twenties? Why do some thresholders resort to binge drinking or drugs or fall prey to depression when they encounter difficulty while others persist in constructive efforts? How can we spot the fifty percent who have real trouble? How can we help them? And what can we learn from those who thrive?

YOUNG PEOPLE'S STORIES

The lives of the young people described in this book, with their struggles and disappointments and successes and resilience, provide windows through which parents can gain a clearer view of the young people close to them. Through the young people portrayed here, parents, teachers, and thresholders themselves can see what might help them and what is likely to fail them. These stories have come to me in various ways over the course of the past decade. The core stories have come from thirty-two young people I interviewed from 1994 to 2000.[15] Some of them were contacted when they were still in high school, and I was able to follow them into their college years. Some I contacted first in college and tracked past graduation. As will be clear from their stories, they come from diverse backgrounds. Most were college bound, and all approached the close of their teenage years with a sense that their futures held value.

This relatively small sample has been supplemented with my day-to-day work with college students, from freshman to graduates. I have also drawn on large, international studies that track the well-being and development of young adults.[16] Many of these people came through adolescence without problems above and beyond normal teenage bumps and bruises. These are young people with promise, capable of achievement and responsibility. Yet none passed the next stage—the threshold phase—unscathed.

Young people suffer instability from standing both in childhood and adulthood, part of each yet belonging to neither. In such a position, a sense of both opportunity and anxiety rage on. Thresholders are thrown off-center. Their judgment, control, and self-trust falter. As the various contexts in which they develop—neighborhood, school, family, employment—fail to work together, young people turn to counselors, therapists, gurus, to guide them. Crutches of all kinds—habits of distraction and denial—come into use and may remain in use throughout their lives. Thresholders often feel that there is no firm base of support and no one to help them understand themselves. Even when young people navigate this crossroads looking "just fine," even if they eventually come through "okay," a silent tragedy of unnecessary suffering is endured, which could—and should—be lessened. For this suffering gives rise to self-doubt and diminishes motivation at a time of potential turning points, points at which choices made can change forever the course of adult adjustment and success.

EACH disturbing story impacts on an entire life course. Carlos, at eighteen, was offered an athletic scholarship to a state university. Halfway into his first semester his coach put him on probation for breaking training. "It wasn't just one hard night out," he admits to me. "I wanted to go and blow my mind. There'd be all this pressure, and after a while I just wanted out. What people don't get is that after you win something, it's not like something's finished. It's like: what next? And the further you go the more you have to worry about people expecting you to do more, or people thinking you're moving away from them. I tell you, it feels good to mess up sometimes."

At eighteen, Carri, energetic and responsible, took a year out as an *au pair* in England to gain some adult experience before going to college. Three months into her year abroad, she is facing criminal charges for drunk driving as well as a civil suit brought against her by her employers who charge her with endangering their child. "I can't understand it," her mother told me. "She's always been honest and reliable. This is a blot on her record, and on her heart—and mine. We'll get over it, but it will take some doing." Carri, now twenty, says, "I was out of my depth. I was scared. Everything was so different. Nothing seemed real. I didn't know who I was, and couldn't learn the rules. I'm ashamed of what I did, but it was the weirdest thing. I suddenly had no judgment. None. I was both me and not me."

Ric was hospitalized for alcohol poisoning toward the end of junior year exams. "He's always been so reliable and sensible," his mother says. "I can't understand what's happened to him. He's now a young man and more trouble than he ever was as a teenager." And Ric says, "I just couldn't keep myself together. Then I broke up with my girlfriend and went wild."

Of course, some sail through the early threshold years untroubled by the tensions that beset so many others. But such ease does not mean they come through unscathed. Some thresholders crash after graduation, which they see as an awesome event that should automatically cast the mantle of adulthood over one's head. Emma said, "Leaving college and thinking about the whole rest of my life terrified me." From now on, she assumed, life was going to be for real. She felt incapable of planning her life and shamed by her knowledge that she had not achieved that magical state of maturity. Some thresholders find the entry into adult employment a terrifying affair. Tim, at twenty-two, is paralyzed with fear at the prospect of finding a job. He feels dwarfed by others' (apparent) confidence, by their grand and eager plans, by what he sees as their cutthroat competitiveness. Living on his own, in an unfamiliar city, he is kept awake with anxiety attacks, feeling that the whole world is closing in on him. This was what he describes as his "first run-in with the real world—the real world that doesn't love, doesn't support, and doesn't care."

Ned, twenty-three, seems to have lost little of the determination that marked him at sixteen. He works in a chic advertising agency that has promoted him twice in the last six months. His apartment is newly decorated, his clothes are elegant and up-to-date, and his social life is a whirl. His father is, initially, proud that "already he's earning more than me." His parents describe him as "having a whale of a time," but he tells me that he is "running on nervous energy. I feel like nothing inside. I'm always afraid and always running. Everyone expects something of me, and I rush to do it. Even when I look like I'm goofing off, I'm hard at work. There's no such thing as a rest. I keep pulling out the stops, but I don't know where I'm going. This is the life I thought I always wanted, and somehow it's all worth nothing. I know it's going to collapse in on me. But in the meantime, I just keep running. I look shallow and superficial to other people, but what they don't get is that I'd like to fight it, but don't know how."

Greg graduated with honors, having also worked as the editor of the college newspaper in his senior year. He thought the world would welcome him, see his virtues with the excitement and trust his teachers had. "I was twenty-one when it suddenly hit me that I wasn't what I thought I was. I wasn't mature. I wasn't talented. I wasn't marketable. What I am is a person who trips and falls on the first step. There's nothing special about me. I'm a nobody. No one taught me how to survive as a nobody." Unprepared for the difficulty of finding a match between his talents on the one hand and painstaking adult development on the other, Greg sees himself as a failure. Suffering unexpected disappointment, he gives up on himself, withdraws from even his closest friends. Helplessly his mother notes, "It's like a light has gone out in him." Both parents and young adults need further understanding of the two special bridges of the threshold phase—one from home to college, and the other from college into adult worlds of work and play.

REFRAMING IDEAS OF WHAT THRESHOLDERS NEED

Even when parents understand how difficult the threshold phase is, they are at a loss as to what to do. Too often, they are confined by the myth of maturity and the myth of the spoiled child. The myth of maturity is the assumption that being mature means being independent in the sense of being separate or autonomous. It is the myth that young people can only prove themselves by showing that they do not need or want their parents.

The myth of the spoiled child is that parents will harm a son (or daughter) by continuing to give him support and by continuing to care for him. It rests on the assumption that we under-mine a young person by giving him help. So intimidated are many of us by these myths that we feel we are in the wrong when we continue to nurture our adult daughters and sons. So biased are we against continued attachment that we think we are doing our children a favor when we let them struggle by themselves. So stunted is our understanding of young people's needs that we simply do not know how to be there for our grown-up kids.

Dealing with a young adult's impasse is very different from responding to and managing a child or teenager. Young adults do not respond to parents with a child's loving awe or with a teenager's passionate, minute criticism. Their responses are a potent mix of past experiences and present influences. Their hopes and fears for their futures color each human exchange. At no time in the life of a parent is listening and picking up on cues more important. At no time in the life of a parent is under-standing a daughter or son more difficult.

When parents are aware of the different shapes loneliness, loss, and confusion take and when they learn to spot the danger signs, they can address and help correct the problems that other-wise distort this transition. The first, most obvious tactic, is to help relieve a thresholder's fear that this crucial relationship will be lost. "Being there," and being aware that even an adult daugh-ter or son requires an active loving presence is essential.

But "being there" becomes an empty cliché if we don't under-stand what this means or when it is needed. I have heard parents ask, "Does it mean that I have to be at my son's beck and call?" "Does it mean that I have to give my daughter financial support or pay her debts?" "Does it mean that I'm forever going to be on call or that it's my responsibility to keep tabs on my kids, even when they're grown?"

The answer to these questions is "no." Being there does not

mean being physically present in the same home or even town. It doesn't mean being constantly on call for them. It doesn't mean giving in to every request or helping them out of every scrape. It doesn't mean trying to solve their problems. It means finding a variety of ways to offer emotional and psychological support. It means boosting their confidence in their coping skills. It means tracking their capacity to manage responsibility. It means giving them essential second chances.

While parents have a huge bank of advice, examples, social customs, and media images that guide them through their years with young children, there are no sources to draw upon when their daughters and sons pass into the threshold phase. Now the daily urgencies have subsided. The hands-on watching, listening, and scolding that were once part and parcel of a parent's life are no longer appropriate. What we need, instead, is to find new ways of relating and holding that meet their changing needs.

A good start is to remind ourselves of the different dimensions of this important relationship.[7] Through this, we can see the range of daughters' and sons' continuing need for their parents and the range of opportunities parents have to help them.

The first thing we think about when we think of the parent/child relationship is that both parent and child are *attached* to one another. The now familiar term "bonding" highlights a process that occurs early in an infant's life. It involves an active and mutual clinging. Most psychologists believe that early attachment is a fundamental building block of future mental health and development. Few people would be surprised to hear that babies and children who are well attached to a parent do better in life, but many are amazed to learn how persistent is the importance of this attachment. Thresholders who feel close to their parents are much better at dealing with stress and loneliness and academic or employment setbacks than are those who describe their parents as "distant." Those who describe their parents as "available" are more resilient than young people who describe themselves as "self-reliant."[18] Attachment to parents is not just for kids.

A somewhat different dimension in the parent/child relationship is *support*. If we think of the term "emotional support," we can see how ordinary speech shows that we depend on certain relationships to hold us up, to keep us from falling. Having such support is particularly necessary during transition periods. People are most likely to talk about their need for support when their life structures are changing. At the threshold stage, young people are trying to forge their own identities and find a path that may be very different from the one their parents had mapped for them. Yet, when they go their own way, they need someone important "behind them." Too often, parents assume that their college-bound children want to leave them behind.

We also need, from people who matter to us, a sense that they know who we are, that they see us and reflect something good back. *Focus* and *validation* are needed as much as bonding: we all have a need to be understood, to be acknowledged for who we are, by people who matter to us. An early form of focus and validation is mirroring. Parents mirror us as we grow. They focus on us with great intensity: on our early steps and speech, our play and work. What we do matters to them. They express pleasure and anxiety about what we do. They name our activities as achievements or transgressions ("What a clever child!" and "What a naughty thing to do!"). To a significant degree, we develop a sense of ourselves as good or bad, exciting or dull, creative or destructive, strong or weak, with reference to the language of their responses. As we grow, we seek new mirrors— friends who get to know us as we are today, stripped of all those old family stories and biases and expectations, teachers who discover unexpected talents, lovers in whose eyes we spring to a passionate new life. But well into mature adulthood, we need a continuation of the first eye-to-eye contact that helped us assimilate our experiences and our bodies into a sense of self. Without it, we don't feel real.

As a young child is mirrored by a parent, she seeks a very general sense of reassurance. In the threshold phase, however, a daughter or son needs a more complex understanding and appreciation. Validation now becomes an important form of mirroring. This is a response to the feelings and thoughts someone is trying to put forward—whether directly, by speaking them, or indirectly, by expressing a mood or need. It indicates, "I hear what you are saying and what you are saying makes sense to me."

Another dimension of a parent's love is *idealization*. The delight parents take in a child's first smile and first steps or in her improved reading or soccer skills feeds a child's confidence. The combined need for validation, which registers reality, and idealization, which registers faith, sounds like a paradox, but it is through a mix of a parent's validation and idealization that we come to know ourselves and believe in what we can be.

Parents' awareness of just how important their responses are to a daughter or son tends to be battered during the teenage years. A teenager fights so hard for a parent to understand her and to see how she has changed from the child she once was that she often rejects a parent's idealization: that parental adoration, that beaming smile, can make her shiver with irritation and rage. The thresholder, however, comes to need this idealization all over again. She needs the parent's heartfelt belief in her and the person she will one day be. Stepping away from her parents, she needs to be held up by their blind faith. But thresholders tend to be more muted than teenagers in their impatience with a parent who "doesn't see" or "won't listen" or "can't understand." Shadowed by the maturity myth, they silence their needs for a parent's responses. We have to help our young people voice their needs—which we can do by responding to them.

As young people work to establish their own identity, as they forage for and construct an adult sense of self, they need, as well as awareness of individuality and difference, a sense of belonging, of being included, of having an identity within a cultural or social or family context. The opposite of being uprooted—alone, ungrounded, exposed—is being *embedded*. Early experiences of this come as an awareness of oneself as a member of a family, and of a family as a member of a neighborhood, a culture, a nation.

During the threshold years, the context of embeddedness changes. We want to join other groups. We leave behind high school friends and the intimate, subliminal routines of living with our families. Thresholders want to belong to their new communities—but as they perform the daily acts of participation and communication that will weave the web of connection in a new context, they also need, still, to connect to their parents, their homes, and their culture of childhood.

Attachment, holding, focus and validation, idealization and embeddedness: these are the dimensions of the parent/child bond that can ease the passage from adolescence to adulthood. What this means, in practical terms, and how it needs to be adjusted to be useful to our nearly adult daughters and sons, will become clear as the stories of the thresholders in this book unfold. Through these stories, we will see what helps and what hinders them, what parents do to aid or impede their growth.

This book is for thresholders and their parents. My hope is to awaken adults' sensitivity to thresholders' lingering needs and to help thresholders gain a better understanding of their own experiences as they come of age. Along with the lengthening time it takes to reach maturity comes the lengthening time of parenting—a change that comes, ironically, just at the time we are having children much later in life. Parents have to take a new look at their realities and revise their expectations of when parenting ends. Children are forever, and, as one father in my study reflected, "forever is longer than it was for my parents."

Too often, while witnessing a child's marked but unnameable loss in the course of becoming a grown-up, a parent assumes that it is an isolated event and wonders, "What's wrong with my child?" or "What can I do to help her now?" These individual problems are part of a trend. There are no easy formulas to correct this trend, but as a psychologist and writer, I hold to the premise that insight is a key to change. With understanding, we can build forums at home, in colleges, and in the community to discuss these rites of passage and normalize these crises. We can alert parents and teachers and employers to the necessity of emotional and instrumental support. Most important, we can discover new ways of enabling young people to tolerate the frustrations of slow maturity and to develop constructive solutions to the life questions that press upon them. In so doing, the problems of growing up in today's society will engender new paths for the future.

FIRST SOLO FLIGHT

THE prospect of making one's own way in the world is exciting. Many parents are filled with pride as they see their daughters and sons fend for themselves, test their abilities, and seek their own truths. A recent and unforgettable image of this youthful flight occurs in James Cameron's film *Titanic*, when Jack (Leonardo DiCaprio) holds onto Rose (Kate Winslet) at the prow of the ship: Rose stands into the rushing wind, oblivious of the ship, rails, and arms that support her, and declares that she is flying, leaving the gilded cage of her past. Both Rose and Jack are on the brink of adulthood, exhilarated by their futures. But, like all exhilarated young people, growth requires not only individual courage but also a nurturing environment.

Any form of leave-taking is psychologically wrenching, and involves confronting difficult questions: "How close do I have to be to my parents? How much do I need them?" While young people have wondered this many times before, at many points during childhood and adolescence, thresholders register a new struggle. In leaving home, they are opening the door to adulthood and, therefore, closing the door to childhood. They fear that in creating this new distance between themselves and their families, between childhood and adulthood, they will never again be protected by their parents' emotional holding. In the early stages of this transition from adolescence to adulthood, the ambivalence (both wanting to leave and panicking at being away) is often intolerable. An acute separation anxiety unbalances thresholders. They stabilize only when they gain assurance that this separation is not, after all, a disconnection. A parent's ability to offer reassurance and security during the early months may determine the success—or failure—of their launch. To offer appropriate support, parents need to educate themselves about thresholders' complicated worlds.

THRESHOLDERS CONTINUING NEEDS

What is it to be grown up? We ask this of ourselves at each turning point: when we hit thirty, or forty, when we make our first presentation at a company meeting, when we first take charge of a class, when we have a child, when we bury a parent. But at no time does this powerful question strike as deeply as when we engage in the contemporary process of walking away from our childhood home and into the rest of our life.

Whether a parent or thresholder, we share cultural norms about what feelings and behaviors are expected and therefore what feelings and behavior are acceptable. We share assumptions about when adolescence ends and what we should become when it ends. Repeatedly parents describe children of nineteen, twenty, and twenty-one as "all grown up"—a term that is accompanied by a flick of the hand, indicating how the grown-up child has gone away. If being twenty-one means being an adult, and if being an adult means not needing one's parents, then it is humiliating to admit this need. A young adult continues to be dependent on his parents' love, admiration, and approval to define and stabilize his sense of self. When this dependence seems "wrong," he suffers a new version of separation anxiety.

The term "separation anxiety" was first used to describe the intense anxiety an infant feels when her mother leaves her, even for a short time. This anxiety emerges between six and eight months, by which time the infant has literally "fallen in love" with her caretaker (usually a parent, usually the mother). This love makes her exquisitely vulnerable to the loss, or the threat of loss, of the person the baby loves. By this time, too, the infant has learned to associate safety and comfort with this attachment. The mother's holding is as necessary as air.

As the child grows and develops her own skills, she delights in her ability to run from a parent, to startle and surprise with her newfound competencies. As toddlers delighted in our own antics, we crow. As toddlers aware that we can fall as we run, displease the people we love, and lose someone if we run too far, we become terrified of our own bravado. Episodes of proud rebellion alternate with desperate clinging. This pattern emerges again during the long and complex process we often call "leaving home."

Young people's anxieties about separating from parents are often hidden. They are hidden because so many of us—parents and thresholders alike—adhere to common myths about maturity. There is a cultural police force suppressing the needs of young people for family support. Mature young people, it is thought, are independent. Mature young people don't need their parents the way children do. The expectation is that detaching oneself from one's family is normal; therefore it should be easy. If it is not easy, then one is not "ready"; one is immature.

Thresholders give clear signals of separation anxiety. Many parents complain that a daughter or son has become particularly "obnoxious" just before leaving home. There is a throwback to earlier phases of adolescence, when interchanges between parent and teenager are full of "maturity reminders"—as a teenager reminds a parent that she is old enough to do what she wants to do, that she knows enough to look after herself, that she doesn't have to be told what to do or when to do it. During early and middle adolescence, too, warning signals are common: there is the "teenage eye-roll," as she looks to the sky for guidance as to how to deal with difficult parents; the "porcupine coat" that replaces the willing cuddle; the "adolescent lip thrust" in reply to a parent's suggestion. There is the familiar stretch of a parent's name: "*Mo*-ther" with the elongated vowel exhaled in a sigh, or the high-pitched squeal of protest, giving "Mom" or "Dad" two descending syllables. These adolescent techniques for expressing despair at a parent's "stupidity" or "dimness" dominate middle adolescence. They subside for a while, but then unexpectedly recur during the months before an event that marks a new adult stage, such as going to college or taking a job or traveling alone.

Sometimes, as this marker event draws near, the former rebellions and rude routines recur, too. Young people who have been delightful companions since the age of sixteen, once again begin throwing their weight around, showing off to younger siblings. Many parents interpret a son's or daughter's regressive behavior as a sign of readiness to leave home. Usually, however, it is a sign of *anxiety* about leaving home, of leaving behind childhood status.

This anxiety, which can impede a young person's development in the threshold years, comes in three forms.

1. Sometimes anxiety centers on a recognition of a deep-seated need for one's parents—alongside the belief that such needs are inappropriate, immature, or for some other reason demeaning.

Young people struck by this type of anxiety are likely to have trouble settling down in their new situations. They cannot concentrate. They suddenly become sluggish learners. They face a special risk of developing eating disorders, substance abuse problems, or other destructive coping mechanisms.

Reassurance that they are still attached to their families and that their need for attachment is not "immature" allows them to accept these needs.

2. Another anxiety is that in growing up and developing skills, one is being disloyal to one's family.

This anxiety is often linked with guilt about being "the successful one" in the family. These young people are uneasy about having opportunities their parents or siblings lack. They may feel more comfortable when they fail because they are afraid success will threaten their closeness to their family. However, they also bear the burden of others' expectations.

Parents can help these young people by assuring them that their differences are rewarding to the family, rather then threatening.

3. Sometimes the prospect of independence triggers fear as sharp as that of an abandoned infant. Thresholders in the grip of this anxiety can lose their ability to function on a day-to-day basis. They often develop physical symptoms of anxiety, such as breathlessness or dizziness. Each nervous symptom, they believe, signals the onset of a terrible disease.

This form of separation anxiety can turn a gutsy adolescent into a timid thresholder, locked into old childhood fears and unable to tolerate being alone—however much he longs to make it on his own.

These thresholders need patient parents who express confidence in a son's or daughter's competence, but also offer emotional refuelling.

THRESHOLDERS have grown up in a culture that places a high value on independence, but that is, without emotional support, a cold and lonely place. In this context, rough passages and incomplete launches into adulthood are extremely common. Feeling lonely, young people feel personally weak. Unsupported, they feel lost. As they fear life's demands, they withdraw from the creative engagements that will open up their adult potential. But the setbacks common to this phase need not be lasting. The thresholders described in this chapter—Peggy, Carlos, and JoAnnabel—negotiate this transition while the emotional charges of leave-taking rock their lives. To help thresholders like them, we need to change our expectations about their needs for both independence and attachment, and then bring these revised expectations into our relationship with them.

Leaving Home (Peggy)

Leaving home is a strange term for going to college, where regularly scheduled returns home, for holidays and term breaks, are already planned. For many students, their "permanent" address continues to be the family home. But going to a college has symbolic meaning. It is not just a temporary move from one place to another. It is a marker, a sign of moving on and moving forward. In this context, many thresholders, while leaving home only temporarily, nonetheless feel ambivalence about being uprooted.

At 8:30 A.M. on departure day, Peggy is in the kitchen, eating what her mother calls her "last breakfast at home." As Peggy spreads jam on her toast, her mother, Ruth, reminds her to look over the "things-to-take-list" they made together some time ago. "I'll look at it later," Peggy tells her, her voice edgy, as though this nagging about checklists has been going on for years. Ruth backs off. She does not want to quarrel. Peggy scoops three books from the floor beneath her chair, puts them on the table and, along with an empty glass, pushes them toward her mother. "These have to be back to the library by Saturday. Can I have some orange juice?"

They plan to leave at 10 A.M. The next job, after breakfast, is to pack up the car. Ruth goes to the back porch, where her husband, Kevin, is piling up the suitcases, boxes, music system, and computer. Kevin complains that everything is disorganized. "How can you tell what's where?" he wonders aloud. From the kitchen table Peggy shouts, "It doesn't matter. I'll unpack everything as soon as I get there." But Kevin continues to complain: there is no padding for the kitchenware, which will "rattle all over the place and bust to pieces" as soon as it is moved. Ruth wonders whether Peggy is taking too much anyway: "You won't have a lot of space in your room." When Peggy does not reply, Ruth adds, "I hope your room here is clean and neat before we go." Peggy clumps upstairs. Ruth sighs, and begins to stuff padding into the box of mugs and plates. Peggy then returns to show her mother a dry cleaner's receipt. At first her mother says, "These will have to wait until Thanksgiving." Peggy retorts, "They can't. There's my *bathrobe*. Which I need. And a silk blouse. It's my only one." Relenting, her mother suggests, "We can send them. You'll have them next week." Peggy barks, "No."

These exchanges are reminiscent of earlier chapters in the mother and daughter saga—of the teenager at thirteen, fourteen, or fifteen, burning with irritation at everyone, and of the mother's exasperation at a daughter's endless criticisms. A few months ago, these tense times were distant memories, as Peggy and Ruth enjoyed a summer of celebratory togetherness. Ruth usually came home an hour before Peggy; at her daughter's return Ruth would leave her gardening, wash her hands, and then, together, they would prepare dinner and chat. Sometimes Ruth met Peggy at the coffee bar in the mall, where Peggy had a summer job, and they shopped for "things for college," or took an aerobics class at the nearby gym. There is often a glow between parent and child during the months before college begins, when the hectic issues of college applications, grades, and SAT scores are over, and when the social whirl of the high school senior year has eased. The spring and early summer of "the last year at home" tend to be calm, as parents' and children's appreciation of one another is intensified in face of the anticipated separation.

But as leave-taking becomes imminent, this calm is shattered. Each assumes, with unnerving ease, roles they thought they had left behind years ago. Ruth remarks under her breath, "You haven't been this difficult since you were fourteen." Peggy hears this, as she was meant to, but clenches her teeth: she is "holding her tongue." Her red-brown hair has given her the reputation of "having a temper," which she now is controlling, albeit (in her view) against great odds. It is warm on the screened-in porch, where the last of the packing is being done; she is perspiring and flushed. "Don't tape that up yet," she instructs Kevin, and then runs upstairs again, while her stepfather calls after her, "It's time to go and this box is going now."

"I can't wait to get away from here!" Peggy exclaims. "Everyone's *always* telling me what to do. This place is like a prison!"

"I guess she's ready to leave," Ruth remarks for Kevin's benefit, hoping to soften the impact of her daughter's temper. "You bet," he responds tersely.

Peggy, now eighteen, lives with her mother, stepfather, and younger half brother. She is going to college and wants to study "something in the humanities." Though her test scores were impressive, her high-school grades "were all over the place," so college application time was tense, and her acceptance by the competitive state college was a relief for everyone. Both she and her mother describe themselves as being "very close." "It was only us until I was eleven," Peggy explains. "I liked that, but I was glad she had lots to distract her when I was in high school." Though she thinks of her stepfather, whose name she has taken, as "just my dad," the more passionate relationship is clearly with her mother. It is between mother and daughter that most conversation in the home occurs, and it is between mother and daughter that the quarrels are more likely to arise. In the few weeks before the start of college, the conversations have been dominated by quarrels: "She's constantly inconsiderate, and it's not just that she's not thinking about us. She'll be inconsiderate with *attitude*, like she's showing us she doesn't have to come home at a certain time, or tell us where she is. Basically she's such a nice kid and I hate to spoil the friendship we usually enjoy by coming over as the heavy mom. I hate for her to leave home on a sour note, but she's really been getting to me lately."

By regressing, Peggy is acting out her fear of leaving. In calling her home a "prison," Peggy is trying to talk herself out of her anxiety at leaving. She denies her positive attachment, repudiates the support home provides, and uses the image of a prison to persuade herself that she cannot wait to get away. This negative take on her home life screens her concern about what leaving will actually involve, and sets aside questions she cannot answer, and would rather not ask, such as: "What will it be like, separating from my family?" and "Who will take care of me when my mom or dad isn't around?"

REMAINING ATTACHED

Many thresholders do not take on board what freedom means. In leaving, Peggy focuses on her wish to be "free": "My mom always has to know where I'm going and who I'm with. I always have to check in, and just thinking about telephoning and time can be a real spoiler." Her conception of freedom is "not always having to explain where I'm going, or to answer to mom or dad about how I'm getting there and when I'll be back. I can just go where I want, without them picking apart all my plans. I don't have to plan, and I don't have to be bogged down, worrying about them worrying. I want my mind totally free of my parents. I don't want them anywhere in my mind."

But her profound anxieties about being separate emerge ten weeks into the first semester. We meet in a restaurant one block from the campus. From the window we look onto the wide avenue edging the university's main square. It is a warm October day, and muggy, but Peggy wears a heavy shirt that bunches like a smock in the front when she slouches. She has gained, she says, "maybe nine and a half pounds, but I think now it's all under control. If I eat too much I know how to get rid of it." She points to the inside of her mouth with her index and middle finger, miming the process of self-induced vomiting.

Her red-brown hair, which was long and held back in a clip at the nape of her neck when we first met, is now cut severely short. "I chopped it off myself last week and then went to a hairdresser yesterday. This was the best she could do after I'd messed it up." I ask her about her courses, her teachers, her friends. Her answers are curt, giving the message: "I'm not interested in this conversation." I ask her about her family. "Oh, them," she says, scooping up the ice cream in her rootbeer float. "I really feel cut off from them."

She notes my surprise. I tell her that her mother has said that they "talk on the phone all the time and exchange emails." Ruth had gone on to say, "We get all kinds of news that she ran a blackout on when she was in high school. She even wants to talk to her little brother now. For years she'd belittle everything he said. Now she asks him everything—little things, like what he's planning to do for his birthday, whether he's still friends with Pete, how he's coming along with his Rollerblades. I can't see why she says she feels cut off."

Peggy does not contradict her mother's account, but she has a very different experience of their communication:

Yeah, I guess we talk a lot. But I still feel lonely, and it's worse after I phone them. It's like I can't tell them anything. There's this rush of "Hi! How are you? Everything okay?" And it's like they just want to hear the good news. So I'll tell them about my classes—as long as it's not too humiliating. Sometimes I start telling them I'm having trouble with a course, and my mom says, "Don't worry, it's only your first semester," and my dad says something real grim like, "College is supposed to be challenging." But I don't feel challenged. I feel totally lost. It's not like I'm working hard, but not making it. Most of the time I can't work. I can't concentrate. I'm in this history course. We have to write an essay. "Discuss the real causes of the Civil War." And I have this reading list, and I sit reading a chapter for one hour, and for the life of me I couldn't tell you a minute later what I read. And sometimes my mind just closes off after a sentence. I can read words, but I can't read sentences. I can't learn what I need to know to stay here. I don't know—maybe I never learned to learn? You know, like maybe I was just spoon-fed stuff in high school. My mind's emptier than anyone else's. It's not—I'm not—I don't think I'm stupid, but my head's empty. If things don't start moving soon, I'm going to be out on my butt.

When I ask Peggy if she enjoys anything about college, she says that she enjoys being left alone. She also enjoys being able to eat when, what, and how she likes. She says that eating is a way of keeping her hands busy and letting her mind work. As for many people with eating disorders, food takes on a primitive symbolism.

Peggy engages in a bizarre play on words: she thinks that perhaps she cannot learn without being "spoon-fed," so she feeds her stomach, spooning food in, long after her appetite has been sated. But the substitute she makes—food for knowledge—does not work; eating doesn't help her learn. So she wants to purge herself of the useless food. After purging, she feels comfortable in her emptiness: "After a knockout binge and purge, my head buzzes, and I get this peaceful drained feeling." She develops a way of dealing with her anxiety about learning—but not one that will in any way help her learn. What's worse is that this habit becomes a comfort and a pleasure; and so she feels less urgency to find creative outlets.

EATING ANXIETIES

The proliferation of eating disorders in early adulthood is linked to separation anxiety, as thresholders try to fill themselves with mother love, which is sometimes associated with food. All too often, eating disorders are referred to as a condition of *adolescent* or high school girls,[1] but a close look at the numbers of such cases shows that eating disorders do not peak during adolescence. Instead, it is during what I call the threshold phase that these problems are most prominent. On college campuses, it is estimated that 20 percent of women students are anorexic. If we ask when anorexia is most likely to occur, we find that it is most likely to erupt around a major separation from home.[2] On some college campuses, 20 percent of women binge and purge two or three times a week.[3] (The definition of bulimia is binging and purging at least twice a week on a regular basis.) Bulimia reaches its peak not during adolescence but in early adulthood, when pressures to be independent mount and family support declines.[4] In other words, the greatest risk is during the threshold phase, not adolescence.

The desire to be thin and the attempt to diet do not create eating disorders, but they offer golden conditions for eating disorders to thrive. Eating disorders are not just bad habits. They are symptoms of psychological problems—usually conflict over one's needs and desires. Some young women (90 percent of all people with eating disorders are women) feel ashamed of their own needs for love and attention. Sometimes the feelings that confuse them are sexual: they may feel bad about having sexual desires (even if they are sexually active). But they can also feel bad about needing to be close to a parent and needing a parent's love and approval and validation. These needs are as powerful and as confusing as sexual desires. They are also desires that many young adults feel pressured to deny.

The desire for food comes to symbolize the needs a young woman may be ashamed of having. Food, initially the nurturing gift of a parent, comes to be associated with a parent's love and care. For a young person suffering from anorexia nervosa, food— inextricably linked with emotional needs—becomes repulsive, and she thinks her own urge to eat is repulsive. She therefore suppresses her appetite and actually seems not to experience hunger. (Indeed, "anorexia" simply means having no appetite.) A young person suffering from bulimia cannot control and deny her appetite as the anorexic does. She is a sort of "failed" anorexic who also finds her appetite repulsive. Yet a bulimic woman tries to meet her needs by filling herself with food, which symbolizes the love and attention and care she craves. Then, repelled by her indulgence (she feels she's bad to have these desires and even worse to give in to them), she induces vomiting, thereby rejecting food (which represents her need for love). All this occurs in a context in which she believes that being thin is good. Being thin is good because it shows she is not indulgent, not a person with strong desires and appetites. A person who can triumph over her appetite, cannot—according to this distorted logic—need her parents. Instead, she is what she should be: independent and separate.

HOW EXPECTATIONS ABOUT MATURITY AND SEPARATION ARE FORMED

Peggy, Ruth, and Kevin would not describe themselves as holding to a special theory of adolescent development, but they nonetheless share ideas about what is appropriate to various ages. Both Peggy and her parents have expectations about teenagers and thresholders that shape their sense of how Peggy is doing. Ruth expresses impatience with Peggy's adolescent behavior. Kevin thinks that an eighteen-year-old should take on the mantle of adulthood and "stand on her own two feet." Peggy thinks that, as a college student, she should not be homesick, that she should have the independence and self confidence of a "real grown-up." She believes that she should be able to learn on her own, without being "spoon fed."

This "maturity policing" is also done by Peggy's fellow students, who think her "a drag" for feeling so anxious and depressed. Her family, too, enforce this norm. Ruth thinks Peggy should be "over adolescence." The fact that she's still moody and surly strikes her as a sign of "immaturity." Kevin says he "doesn't mind her calling home, but she calls too often, and wants to talk about every little thing. She should be standing on her own two feet now." Such casual remarks, when backed by cultural endorsements of independence and autonomy as high personal goods, carry a hard punch. Ashamed of that depression and neediness we call "being homesick," Peggy does not express her feelings in ways that can be addressed by others. Surrounded by people who think her needs are "wrong" (a sign of immaturity), she avoids rejection by hiding her feelings. In this context, Peggy's bid for growth reaches an impasse: "I shouldn't still need my family," she tells me. "But I can't seem to keep myself together. I don't want to think about who I am or what I'm supposed to be doing. I'd love just to lie in bed, and veg out, do some serial film watching."

HOW PARENTS CAN ADDRESS PEGGY'S PROBLEMS

As parents see their daughters and sons mature, they hope that their parenting work is winding down. Realistically, however, they need to do the following:

1. Accept some regressive behavior.

Regression can be both aggressive and passive. In its aggressive form it emerges in quarrels, irritability, and criticism. In its passive form, it emerges as withdrawal, lethargy, or whining. Both styles are most effectively countered with a neutral response. A parent's anger will provoke more quarrels and more withdrawal. Any accusation of being "immature" or any instruction to "grow up" will increase a thresholder's unease at her own feelings. However, such behavior should not be encouraged by great shows of sympathy. Passive tolerance is sufficient.

2. Provide a steady stream of family information.

Many young people say that phone calls and letters pump their heart like a life-support machine. But parents have to know what to say and what to write. Peggy wants to hear the small details of what is going on with her brother, with the roof repairs, with her pets, because this is a way of being assured that she is still embedded in her family. What Kevin takes to be a sign of immaturity

("It's childish, the way she keeps phoning home, asking about every little thing.") is simply an expression of a persistent human need to be part of the daily lives of those we love.

3. Listen.

Parents need to develop new communication skills—to be interested without prying, to listen to the downside of a young person's life without dismissing it with false reassurances. Instead of pushing aside complaints with remarks such as: "Why can't you be more positive?" or "I'm sure things aren't all that bad," they can acknowledge a young person's feelings with: "You sound upset/unhappy/anxious. The changes must be difficult." Sometimes a daughter's or son's unhappiness arouses so much anxiety in the parent that she dismisses it: "Things can't really be that bad. I'm sure you're having a good time anyway." But if a parent cues herself to listen to the downside, a young person feels the power of the parent's focus, confirmation of the parent's validating response, and feels supported. When someone we love listens and understands, our sufferings gain definition and lose weight. "Sharing the load" is more than a figure of speech. It really does describe that sense of burdens being lifted from one's shoulders as problems are spoken and understood.

4. Respond calmly.

Calm parents are better at listening to what a daughter or son is saying and are better at communicating their love. Calm parents are better containers for a daughter's or son's anxiety. They also show thresholders that they are strong enough to take what is thrown at them. When a parent is neither disappointed nor anxious, a thresholder won't be.

5. Key into the positive things.

After acknowledging the downside, a thresholder can be praised for managing the challenges that face her. By being able to see the positive side, parents show that the thresholder's problems are not "the end of the world." By pointing out a son's or daughter's ability to manage some things, parents can reinforce a sense of competence.

HOW THRESHOLDERS CAN ADDRESS PROBLEMS LIKE PEGGY'S

Even the biggest problems are made up of small parts. Overcoming disturbing eating habits or finding a way through those mental blocks may seem like something only a trained analyst can handle, but thresholders can learn to manage themselves.

1. Identify the problem.

Keeping a diary is a simple but effective way of tracking bad habits. Peggy could try to identify when she is likely to overeat—and therefore when she is likely to purge. When is she likely to feel most lonely? What she does now (eat) doesn't help. Think of an alternative—phoning home, going for a walk, knocking on someone's door.

2. Avoid temptation.

Once Peggy has tracked her habits, she can target the other habits that structure her eating problems. For example, she avoids eating in the cafeteria, and she likes eating alone. It is easier to say, "I'm going to eat with other people today" than it is to say, "I'm never going to be bulimic again."

3. Challenge the negative thoughts.

If she catches herself saying, "No one wants to eat with me in the cafeteria," she should warn herself that she must make an effort to find a companion. When she says, "I just can't concentrate," she should do some relaxation exercises (deep breathing, stretching, clearing her mind) and then read a page or paragraph and write down what she did take in. She does not have to focus on the final essay or exam or class discussion—just on the page in front of her. As she grows less anxious about her concentration, she will take in more information.

4. Practice self-calming.

Many of the problems underlying Peggy's poor habits come from anxiety about what she feels. She could find a quiet place where she could sit alone for ten to fifteen minutes each day, focusing on her own thoughts and feelings. If she feels herself buffeted by anxiety, she can take deep and regular breaths and wait for the anxiety surge to pass. She could learn to tense up and then relax the muscles of her hands, shoulders, neck, and face. Practice in weathering these attacks will diminish her anxiety. She will be able to say to herself: "This is an uncomfortable feeling, but I know how to ease it."

Entering a Different World (Carlos)

The move into the wider world has different meanings for each person, and these meanings are shaped by the family that is left behind. Being the first in one's family to go to college, or to live away from home while going to college, both adds excitement to the process and creates a burden of expectation. Such young people are often labeled "the smart one" and carry the weight of others' expectations. On the one hand, they want to live up to their family's pride—but on the other, they may worry about becoming too different.

Some thresholders are gripped by the anxiety that in leaving home, they are leaving their family behind. Growth seems like growing away. Often these young people have had special privileges—such as mentors or scholarships or inborn talents—that their friends or siblings lacked. Their unease at moving on, or moving away, can be compounded by guilt. "Why have I been more lucky than the others?" they ask themselves. They may be strangely relieved by failures, which ease this guilt.

Thresholders often need to be aware of the contradictory emotions success evokes for them—a boon for their family in one sense, but a division from their family in another. When young people feel that, by moving away to college, they are moving into a different world, their new, not-yet-firm sense of adult self fragments—unless it can be glued together with a parent's validating responses. With a parent's assurance that a thresholder's success is a family delight, and that in success or in failure, he is their cherished child, the thresholder can reshape the distorted fears.

VALIDATION: REFLECTING BACK THRESHOLDERS' STRENGTHS

Young people need their parents to focus on them in a way that brings their soul to light. Parents mirror growing children. They express pleasure or anxiety about what they do. A sense of self develops, good or bad, quick or slow, strong or weak, in tandem with a parent's responses. As children grow into teenagers and thresholders, they require a wide range of reflections that acknowledge the strangeness, the unexpectedness, the glamour of their growing self. However important friends and colleagues become, young adults still need from a parent the kind of eye-to-eye contact that says: "I see you, understand and admire you." This is what many young people want when they complain that parents do not "really know" them.[5]

This eye-to-eye contact, sometimes called validation, involves responding to the feelings and thoughts a person is trying to express, whether directly or indirectly; but it also means giving the appropriate response (for example, being excited in just the right way) about something important or offering sympathy when something goes wrong. Validation means responding to who the person really is. But while young people talk about being appreciated for who they are, they also crave a response that reflects them at twice their actual size. For young adults also want their parents to see them as they want to be. They want a parent to endorse their hopes and believe in the future grown-up.

Parents do this naturally when their children are little. They think wonderful things of their very young children. They invest them with giant talents and charm. The child's normal development is, in a parent's eyes, marvelous and miraculous. Very young children need this irrational appreciation to develop the confidence they will need in life. Teenagers' needs, for all their nitpicking honesty, are not all that different. So while the teenager shouts at her mother, "Can't you see who I really am!" she also means, "Can't you see me as I wish I were!" In the threshold years, these battles may become more muted. Thresholders have more self-control and more pride: If parents do not give a thresholder a satisfying response, then a daughter or son is likely to withdraw, angry and hurt, rather than fight it out, as she might during her teenage years. But the need is no less strong.

HOW PARENTS MISINTERPRET A SUCCESSFUL THRESHOLDER'S NEEDS

All Carlos's things, five crates worth, were forwarded to college last week. He is catching a one o'clock bus to a nearby town, and then a train to the college town. He is edgy and fights with his younger sister, who is usually his closest ally in the family. This quarrel casts a pall over his departure. She refuses to come with him to the bus station to say good-bye.

He is the first in his family to go away to college. His oldest brother did not graduate from high school. Another brother is doing a business course at a community college, and his sister, closest to him in age and temperament, is still in junior high.

"My parents don't really know what's involved. They've left it to me. 'You got everything?' my mother keeps asking, but doesn't really get into it. It's like I'm part of a different world now. But I don't know what that world is. All I know is I have to swim. I have to be a good swimmer there, and I have to pass the courses. So, I don't know whether I'll be able to do that. We'll see."

During his last few days at home, Carlos is apprehensive rather than excited. He repeats: "I'll just go and see how it is. I'll do my best, I guess. It's just wait and see."

From Carlos's parents, Bob and Maria, I hear a very different story. Bob describes his son as having so much talent "no one would notice if eighty percent of it went to waste." From their vantage point, Carlos "never really had to try. Things just come easy to him." Maria says she has always been proud of him, as she is proud of all her children, but for all Carlos's achievements, her pride does not always feel "warm, because things come so easy to him." As she says this, she looks at Bob, who nods agreement.

Bob and Maria feel that Carlos is abandoning them. In their view, he is not merely making a temporary move away from home, but a permanent step beyond them, into a different world. "He can't wait to get away," Bob explains. In this context they feel exploited: "We gave him everything we could. But he thinks: 'I did it all myself.' That's what these kids are like today."

Carlos's lost-boy look is still recognizable in the middle of the first semester. He says, "When I came to college, I was glad to get away. From the time I was about fourteen or so I didn't feel I needed my parents—except that it's difficult not to live at home. But it was only for the home base—I mean, I bought my own clothes. I even made my own way to the eye doctor once the school said I needed glasses. I never looked up to my mom as some kind of authority figure. She sets rules about when to come home and where to go, but if I want, I can always nag her and she'll eventually give in. So it's weird how I miss her, and how messed up I am."

It is his swimming, of all things, that is bringing him down. The times he is achieving in training are well below his personal best. While the swimming coach tells me, "It's hard to keep his motivation up," Carlos tells me, "My life here seems pointless." He is now on probation with the swim team, with his scholarship in jeopardy, for going on a drinking binge during training. His coach reports: "One day you think he's doing fine, but the next day he'll let you down." Carlos shrugs as I relay this remark to him. "Sometimes the coach is on my side, and sometimes he just wants to kick butt. Sometimes I really want to do well, and sometimes I just don't give a damn because the people who really matter to me don't care."

A young person's continuing need to connect with his parents takes both thresholder and parent by surprise. Without family backup, many young people feel that, at this stage in their lives, their experiences lack meaning. Carlos explains this to me when I ask him about some of his low points during the past few months: "You know, it's strange, because when I tell you about my lowest point, you're going to be surprised. My lowest point here was when I got an A- on my first philosophy paper. Me. An A-! And you know why it was my lowest point? Because I was so pleased. I rushed to phone home, and my dad answers and I tell him and he says, 'Yeah?' That was it: 'Yeah.' And then it's like he's asking, 'Is that all?' Mom's a little better, but it's not like she takes it in. So why should I care?"

Parents are never forgiven for not giving just the right response at the appropriate moment. Or, rather, there are particular times in a young adult's life when a certain response is badly needed, and when this need is not met, the failure seems to the son or daughter like a crime, forever remembered and never forgiven. Usually parents remain unaware of this because, even if the child tells them, the criticism seems so absurd that they do not understand the extent of the grudge.

Carlos confronts his parents on his next visit home. "There are kids there whose parents are fit to burst when they get good grades. You don't care about anything I do. I ring you up, using my own money, and I tell you about this grade, and it's, 'So what?' So why should I answer your questions now? You're not proud when I do well, why should you care when I fuck up?"

Like many parents who hear their children catalogue their faults, Maria and Bob are outraged. "How can you say we don't care? How can you say we're not proud of you?" Maria demands. "You should hear your father. Day and night he's telling anyone who listens about his Carlitos. 'He's doing this. He's doing that.' You're our son. How can you say we're not proud of you?" Her defense is whole-hearted, and I wonder if she recalls what she once told me—that her pride was not always "warm." For this is exactly Carlos's criticism—that it's not the right kind of pride. "You're not really proud of me," he bites back, "because you don't really know me. You don't even try to know who I really am."

Carlos says something that sounds absurd to his parents, but he is making a plea that makes all too much sense to him. He is fighting for recognition of both his achievements and his failures. He needs his parents to understand and empathize with his problems. Instead, they take his successes for granted. In his view, this is not because they believe in him (and offer idealization), but because they "don't care"—that is, they don't give him enough focus. While he feels he is sinking in college, Maria and Bob feel he is flying away from them. These mismatched views threaten them both.

Bob and Maria fail to read their son's needs, because they make assumptions about what "kids are like these days." Feeling abandoned themselves by a son they see as moving on, they reflect on their experiences of the empty nest and on the adjustments they must make. Maria says, "Maybe because he's my youngest boy. And he was so cute and affectionate as a child. Such a cuddler! But now he has to go his own way."

So firmly does Carlos's father believe that his son wants to be left alone (and should be left alone), that he refuses to give into his own need to see his son. One day in November, his job takes him within two hours' drive of Carlos's college. He makes the journey, parks his car at the edge of the campus, and then in darkness finds his way to the dorm where Carlos lives. Adhering to his principle that a thresholder needs and wants to be on his own, he does not go to see him. Instead, he stands in the cold night for over an hour just to get a glimpse of his son's shadowy form through the window. He waits until the light is switched off, then imagines himself bidding his son goodnight—and returns to his car.

REINTERPRETING THE EMPTY NEST SYNDROME

For many years, it has been supposed that many parents suffer from empty-nest syndrome. Mothers, in particular, are most likely to feel threatened by the loss of their parental role.[6] No longer needed for the day-to-day tasks of parenting, some mothers fear they are losing purpose and value. How can they maintain a sense of purpose once the most urgent routines of parenting are no longer required? How do they cope with the more lonely, more empty household? How can they find reassurance that they can still protect—and perhaps control—their child? Maria and Bob do not read psychological journals, but they have absorbed these expectations. Maria believes she has to adapt to being no longer needed by her youngest son, and so she does not see what he *does* need from her.

Painstaking adjustments are often required to get a parent's life back on an even keel after so many years of having her routines steered by a child's presence. But this readjustment—with both its very modest sadness ("I came home and the house was so quiet!") and its extensive opportunities ("I haven't had so much energy since I was twenty!")—is only part of the empty nest. Parents' unease at this parting stems from a genuine response to the daughter's or son's continuing need for closeness and care. The parents who are most anxious about a daughter's or son's departure are usually the parents of young people whose need for them is greatest. The pain of the empty nest is not the *parent's* own loneliness but her empathy with the *daughter's or son's* loneliness and need.[7] Parents should learn to trust their own anxiety. When they have a bad case of the empty-nest blues, they may be picking up a daughter's or son's signals.

Instead of reading her empty-nest anxiety as a sign of her own needs, Maria could register it as a response to her son's needs. On one level, Maria does this. She has persistent "nightmares, where something awful happens to Carlos, and I hear about it or maybe even I see it, but I'm far away and can't figure out how to get to him. I look at a bus schedule but the numbers keep disappearing, and then I try to phone the station, but no one answers. I keep having these dreams, and the next day I wake up and think, 'It was just a dream,' but I still feel awful. So it's always a relief to hear Carlos's voice when he phones." But Carlos's voice reassures her because he presents a false front. Thinking that his mother is not trying to understand him, he is selective about what he tells her: "I keep saying, 'I'm fine.' They don't want to know the other stuff."

HOW TO BREAK THE SPIRAL OF MISUNDERSTANDINGS AND MEET A THRESHOLDER'S NEEDS

Understanding a daughter's or son's needs is crucial to their well-being. As Pat Allatt tellingly notes in her study of young adults, "Youth transitions are not voyages of the single mariner."[8] In other words, young people don't make it alone. Here are some pointers for parents like Bob and Maria.

1. Change expectations.

There is a widespread and misleading expectation that once our children hit the threshold years, they are hellbent on rejecting us. Parents do themselves and their children a disservice if they fail to see the ways this truth is limited. For though thresholders do want to grow into independence, they continue to need a basic, bonded closeness to parents.

2. Reinterpret behavior.

Often young people appear to reject their parents when they are actually seeking new validation. They complain about and criticize parents not because they want to push them away, but because they want to prod them into a more fine-tuned response.

3. Keep listening.

Thresholders tend to clam up when they feel a parent is not listening. When parents ask how a thresholder is doing, they should show that they are open to a full and honest answer. This means they should avoid leading questions ("Are you having a good time?") or loaded statements ("You must be so pleased"). Be prepared to hear negative information.

4. Make your admiration clear.

Sometimes thresholders seem to have so much going for them that parents do not realize they still need a family endorsement. Young people still need reassurance that what they are achieving and what they are working for arouses a parent's pride.

At the same time, Carlos, like many thresholders, needs to contribute to his own development. He could:

1. Identify his role in the problem.

Many young people complain that their parents do not understand them. By the time they reach the threshold years, they have the power to build up a parent's understanding. Young people would find communication greatly improved if they were to voice their fears and anxieties clearly. If Carlos were to say, "I'm really afraid of what it will be like for me in college" or "I find the going rough," he could cut through his parents' assumption that everything comes easily to him.

2. Find more positive ways to manage his fear.

The habit of drinking in order to unwind is often established by young people who lack self-calming skills. Carlos is used to letting off steam with exercise, but once exercise becomes linked, in his mind, with his swimming performance, he has no outlet other than alcohol. He could practice swimming or work out in the gym, while clearing his mind of all thoughts about his performance. Many young people benefit from mind-blanking techniques while exercising.

3. Reframe his view of success.

When thresholders fail at things they know they are good at, there is likely to be some thought distortion at work. We can catch these distortions out by tracking behavior. When Carlos does not turn up for swim practice, he must ask himself what he is avoiding. If he understands what he fears, he can address it in a positive way. Instead of reassuring himself by failing, he can seek reassurance through communication with his parents.

4. Acknowledge his need for help.

When bad habits persist, when we do not understand why we are failing to meet our potential, when the harmful consequences of our actions are clear, but when we do not change our behavior, then we need to refer ourselves to someone who can take an objective view. The success rate for therapy at the threshold stage is much higher than it is in later adulthood.[9] A counselor or therapist can pinpoint the destructive solutions or distractions Carlos has been using (through binge drinking[10] and partying). Though a therapist cannot offer the relationship a parent can, with all its dimensions of attachment and support, he can become a safe container for negative feelings. A safe container allows expression of awful or confused feelings for which a young person has not yet found a creative outlet. Listening to outrageous or destructive feelings, the therapist can reflect back positive solutions. Ideally, the thresholder will then develop his own do-it-yourself kit for processing fears, self doubts, and anger.

The Urge to Seek and the Desire to Merge (JoAnnabel)

While 9 0 percent of high school graduates plan on going to college, the significant minority of thresholders who do not go this route face serious challenges. They often have drive and ability but simply feel that college is not for them. Some are eager, after years of schooling, to learn more about the world through travel. Some want to roll up their sleeves and get started in what they see as the real life of earning a living. Some want to exercise their creativity, either in an art or in business. Making a go of these less conventional paths requires courage and focus.

Many young people continue to live at home while they make initial forays into their adult worlds. What they can earn in their first jobs is rarely enough to pay for rent and food on their own. And so the entire family has to adjust to a situation in which the son or daughter is a grown-up, occupying the child's room. These thresholders make strong demands on their families for recognition of their new status, and they, too, suffer ambivalence as they fight for acknowledgment. These thresholders are exhilarated— and frightened—about stretching their wings on a solo flight.

JoAnnabel has always felt different from her more conventional brother and sister. She was a rebel at school. Academic work was a struggle, but she was creative and confident. Her mother describes her as "really the most lively of the bunch." She puzzles over what to do after high school. Should she go to college and encounter the same problems—the difficulty in reading, the sense that she is not as smart as the others, combined with the conviction that in her own way she is equal to anyone? She decides to put the question of college to one side, because this next part of her life is something she wants to manage alone. Throughout her teenage years, her mother has been supportive ("too supportive, too involved," JoAnnabel complains). If, as a thresholder, she can leave their care and "interference" behind, she feels she will have "a real chance to grow up."

She shows enterprise in getting a job in sales, and then trains as a bartender. After six months, she has earned enough money to travel. "I want to tend bar on the beach in Australia," she announces. Her route is meticulously planned. Her budget is carefully drawn up. She knows where she will be able to "party" and where she will have to work to earn enough for the next leg of the journey. She has a list of addresses, of friends of friends, and a list of youth hostels. Her parents' doubts and anxieties are brushed aside by the whirlwind details of her plans. She feels smothered at home. She is ready to take flight.

She gets as far as London, where she lands on her feet, getting a job managing a new coffee house. But after three weeks, she finds she cannot manage herself. The practical self-care she performed at age sixteen without thinking, is at nineteen too much for her. She cannot wake up in time to catch a train. "I set the alarm, but it doesn't help me get up. I'm used to my dad knocking on my door, or coming in to pull the covers off my bed if that doesn't get me up. Even if I hear my roommate moving around, I can't be bothered to get up." Nor can she manage the practical details of eating regularly or going to the doctor when she developed a painful rash on her neck. "I feel stupid and helpless," she explains, "but the worst thing is the fear."

During a lull at work, or when the underground train gives a little jolt, JoAnnabel struggles with panic attacks. Suddenly, she starts to sweat. She feels dizzy and disoriented. A noise, or a silence, makes her heart pound, and she feels it is going to leap out of her chest. Then she begins to choke. "I really lose it. I'm sure I'm going to die." During her first attack, a coworker rushed her to the emergency room, where a doctor massaged the carotid artery in her neck to get her heartrate down. The following day, every muscle in her body felt stretched.

Panic attacks, or what JoAnnabel calls "freak outs," are episodes of intense fear. They are thought to stem from the flight mechanism, which prepares the body to take quick action in the face of danger. When we are sufficiently frightened, huge amounts of adrenaline are released, which start the heart pumping. The purpose is to prepare the body for a quick spring away from danger. But JoAnnabel is not being hunted by a hungry lion. She is hunted by the anxiety of being separated from her parents. She says, "I kept thinking about all those miles between me and my family, and worrying what would happen if all the planes and trains broke down. It seemed there would be some calamity which would prevent me ever getting home again."

Perhaps *The Wizard of Oz* is such a popular story because it taps into this common dilemma of the threshold years: the longing for independence and adventure, and the constant search for a way home again. Parents and thresholders can work together to take the sting out of this ambivalence. They can:

1. Be alert to mixed signals.

When a thresholder makes a sudden bid for separation by putting thousands of miles between herself and her family, she may be inwardly uncertain of her independence. While it may seem unreasonable to put a stop to a young person's plans to travel or work abroad, parents can find special ways of keeping in touch. A parent could visit a daughter or son during her or his absence. The prospect of this visit can steady the young person. Emails are a good means of communication worldwide. Some contacts with family friends or shared organizations (church or school) can provide a notional "home base."

2. Acknowledge feelings.

By increasing their awareness of the dilemmas of leave-taking, what once seemed abnormal or shameful to thresholders becomes expected and acceptable.

3. Respond accordingly.

As parents learn what to expect, they can target difficult feelings. They can safely assume their threshold daughter or son needs a steady flow of contact. Too often, they misread a thresholder's declaration that he wants to be on his own.

4. Learn to anticipate and manage anxiety.

Living away from one's family will be scary sometimes. Patterns of anxiety (which sometimes appear as "feeling lonely" or "being homesick") are signals that we need to "refuel" with parental love—through phone calls or letters or visits.

5. Be patient and optimistic.

Knowing that separation anxiety is normal means that one does not have to be anxious *about* it. Take note of all the times you are not feeling lonely or homesick or just anxious about being on your own. These times will gradually increase.

The impulse to grow intellectually and emotionally is immensely strong during the early years of adulthood. But separation anxieties can impede this growth. This anxiety will ease when parents and thresholders alike come to see maturation as a very slow process—a process managed not so much by separation as by sustaining the connections through which one grows.

CHAPTER TWO

FORMING IDENTITIES

EACH new phase of life offers many chances to be—or to try out—who one is. In the threshold years the self-concept—our sense of who we are—comes under great pressure as we get to know ourselves in the so-called adult world. As young people take on new roles, they see themselves as being very different people— in terms not only of being older and more independent, but also of developing a different personality.[1] This new self-introduction, of course, is part of the excitement of these years, but low self-esteem and depression may accompany any rapid change in self-concept. Some young people construct a false self in defense against self-doubt and change. As Erik Erikson remarked: "In no other stage of the life cycle, then, are the promise of finding one-self and the threat of losing oneself so closely allied."[2]

The term "identity crisis" has been largely associated with adolescence, when peers take on new powers, when young people want to fit in and join the world outside the family, when they become increasingly critical of their families. Hair styles, clothes, speech, and ideas are frequently changed as teenagers try out different persona. "What does it feel like to be this sort of person?" they ask themselves and slip on new identities like a game of dressing up. But many find that, compared to the threshold phase, adolescence was a picnic. The inner self that had seemed to be so tough and sure at the age of fifteen and sixteen seems small and frail at nineteen and twenty. Then they fought against parents' outdated images of them and felt strong as they stirred a parent up. Now, perhaps living away from home, they regret the loss of security they had as teenagers. As adolescence ends,[3] young people are apt to suffer more deeply than they ever did before (or ever will again) from questions such as:

"How do I look to others?"

"What am I, compared to others?"

"How can I connect the roles and skills I've developed earlier with what I want to do and what I want to become?"

"Do I want to connect with the roles that I already know?"

"Do I want to be entirely different from the person I've been for the last eighteen years?"

Personal identity—one's sense of who one is—is both abstract, difficult to define, and commonplace. It is used every day with ease, as we announce who we are on the phone, greet someone on the street, introduce ourselves to someone, explain where we live and what we do. It is as public, stable, and straightforward as our name, but it is also a set of ideas that shifts according to where we are, whom we are with, and what we are doing. It is also private, as we feel much of who we are as invisible and unknown. Our personal identity is composed of many different aspects.

1. There are the stories we tell about ourselves, either stories from our pasts—from our childhood passions and sorrows to yesterday's shopping trip or run-in with a boss. What we experience and how we respond and whether we were victims or survivors, make up part of who we think we are.

2. Our sense of self involves assessments of our behavior and skills—what we have achieved, what we are capable of doing, and what we might be in the future.

3. Our sense of who we are is linked to our relationships—the people we are attached to, how we feel about them, what we give and receive from them, and what we feel ourselves capable of in terms of love and loyalty, deceit and betrayal.

4. Our sense of self is bound by our values and beliefs and the traditions or communities from which they derive. How constantly we adhere to these values, and how well we live up to them, play an important part in our sense of who we are.

Holding these different aspects together is vital to a centered self. Being centered involves a good match between who we feel we are and how we are with other people and with society at large.[4] Centering establishes a way of living so that the "I" of the thinking, feeling self and the "eye" of the world[5] comfortably meet.

Three common difficulties beset thresholders' identify formation, throwing them off center.

1. The first difficulty stems from distorted concepts of identity.

As teenagers enter adulthood, they are eager for all aspects of the self to grow. Being an adult, after all, does not merely mean being able to do grown-up things, it means having a grown-up identity. But not only does one's sense of self fail to grow at the rate thresholders expect, it often regresses during this stage.[6] This can be so discouraging to young people that their self-esteem can take a nosedive. Their entire sense of who they are—in terms of their values, skills, and emotional worth—can disintegrate. These thresholders feel angry—often at parents—whom they blame for their self-doubt. This blame is a sign of their continuing need to develop with the help of a parent.

2. Thresholders are commonly plagued by self-consciousness, which may give rise to a sense of diminished personal authenticity.

An "imaginary audience" is the term David Elkind uses to describe the self-consciousness that strikes a teenager as she assumes that everyone else is as concerned with her appearance and personality as she is herself.[7] The pangs of self-doubt usually associated with early adolescence can return with a vengeance in the college years. While the gawky self-conscious teenager is an easily recognized type, it is seldom acknowledged that self-consciousness in early adulthood has a new sting and tenacity. As young people test themselves in new roles, every conversation, every discussion at work or in class, becomes a proving ground for their entire worth. These young people suffer from constant anxiety about others' judgment.

3. As we enter adulthood, a thorough revision of the self-concept is sometimes necessary.

In childhood and adolescence we often develop untested ideas of ourselves—of what we can do, who we will become, and even where we come from. Many of these ideas no longer make sense in the context of early adult experiences. But giving up a previous self-image is hard. Young people who find they have to revise their identity may idealize and envy others who appear to "know who they are."

These crises often go unnoticed. Unfortunately, one area young people excel in is self-presentation. As they move into their late teens and early twenties, they gain greater control over how they appear, even while, inside, they may feel worse and worse about who they are. A thresholder is often mature enough to conceal self-doubt but not to overcome it. As she conceals it from others, she doesn't realize that her peers conceal similar feelings, and her doubts become distorted. Each feels she is the only one suffering a crisis and hence each feels ashamed.

We need to offer these young people what Sherry Hatcher.

calls "a supportive forum in which to discuss each other's personal passages without a sense of secrecy, aloneness or diminished self-esteem."[8] In other words, we can use our understanding to extend thresholders' understanding of their problems as normal, not shameful, and as starting points of conversation.

Trapped by the Imaginary Audience (Alec)

Many thresholders seem to overcome the worst of self-doubt by the time they finish high school. Their acne has cleared up, their bodies have lost the awkward proportions that sometimes plague teenagers. Many who have had a rough time in high school—because they haven't been popular enough, because they haven't fit in—expect that life beyond high school will be totally different. When they fail to meet a brand-new self on the other side of the door marked Adulthood, they may plummet right back into the acute self-consciousness of early adolescence.

In such a state, a thresholder feels he has no privacy, because, in his mind, everyone is always looking at him. He walks around with a radar system that gauges what other people think of him, how they are responding to him, and what they think he is worth. Even in the most casual conversation in the dorm, in the corridor, in the dining hall, he scans others' responses.[9] When he speaks up, he thinks: "How did that look? Did I look stupid? Did I look smart?" When he is silent, he thinks: "Everyone can see that I don't know what to say." Who he is seems to be made up of fragments of other people's judgments. He tries to impress everyone and panics when he doesn't.

Alec walks onto a new campus, among people he doesn't know, and expects a new self to be born. "You can't really be an adult when you live at home. With your mom fussing around—well, you're just fighting for space, and can't tell whether you're really independent. Mom dominates the house. Her moods and her problems—they hit you as soon as you walk in the house. You can't be a man here. In college I can start being myself."

His earnest pronouncement is touching. I feel the presence of models that shape his idea of a new self. His comments speak to myth-shaping stories of how we become an adult by walking away from our familiar pasts and shaping ourselves in a new world. This belief took hold in our culture long before psychologists proclaimed their theories about people becoming individuals by cutting free from childhood attachments or dependencies. The stark and simple image of a young person creating his future on his own terms is branded on the American imagination. In his *Autobiography*, Benjamin Franklin describes how, on the cusp of adulthood, he walks alone into the city of Philadelphia. Unaided and unencumbered by anything he has loved or known before, he creates a brand-new adult self. This is the ideal of self-creation that forms many thresholders' expectations.

But adult identity forms slowly, over time. Some young people seek out others to give them clues about who they are—and then worry over the clues other people give them. One young man describes "a pressure inside me, and I keep hunting around for someone who can make me relaxed, someone who will make me feel good. I hang out in the coffee shop and I get talking, and then I think 'I'm feeling worse not better,' so I end the conversation and just go away and I feel worse and ashamed, but I keep looking, and I look stupid and I think it's a vicious circle."[10] The expectation that one will grow into oneself with the help of an admiring audience usually ends in disappointment.

Alec's expectations are high partly because he feels he has been through the worst phase of self-doubt. He describes a rough patch in junior high when he felt "fat and ugly and hated meeting people because they'd look at me and see I was fat and ugly." This passed as soon as he entered high school—but in his second year in college he finds himself once again "locked up and banging against these disgusting images of myself." Without the supportive and implicit admiration of parents, without the familiar group of friends who know him "in lots of different ways," Alec is acutely aware of himself as being perceived by others and judged by others. Because they are not yet his friends, he does not know what they think and how they see him, so his sense of self splinters into anxious guesses. "Do they think I look weird?" he wonders. "Did what I just say sound stupid? Could they see I was trying to look smart?"

In his anxiety to impress, he pretends to be what he's not, even telling "tall tales" to match the stories of the people around him. Though he would like nothing better, he says, than to be genuine and open, his greatest need is to look good. "Maybe I can impress this student or this teacher," is the hope that shapes each conversation. Rather than ask, "Who can I become?" he asks, "How can I make an impression?" and then, "How can I change from who I was and who I am, to someone who impresses other people?" He begins spinning tales about his life at home, because he wants to be something different. He justifies these fibs on the grounds that "I want to feel different about myself."

At the close of each conversation, his question is, "How did I look?" He assesses the impression he made and worries that, in spite of his best efforts, he ended up looking "dumb" or "foolish." He constantly feels awkward in conversations: "I'll be talking to someone and say something and they'll say they disagree, and they'll go on and on, and I'll think, 'Hey, wait a minute. I didn't really mean that. I just said that to impress you.' It all makes me look even more stupid, because then I say something different, and I just feel trapped in a stupid discussion and want to get away." He muses over the interchanges of the day, and tries to console himself: "Maybe I didn't look like such a fool." But then he pitches into the next wave of anxiety: "Maybe I did." These thoughts plague him at night, and he cannot sleep.

SHAME AND SHOWING OFF

"Don't try to impress me," wrote one of his professors on an art history paper. Alec had made so many references to so many works of art to show off his sensitivity and knowledge. "Sophomore" means, literally, wise fool. It is appropriate as a designation for the second year of college. This is often when young people are impressed by how much they have recently learned, but have not yet learned the limitations of their knowledge. What I have come to realize through these young people is that the "sophomoric" manner comes from terror of what they do and do not know about themselves.

Alec is embarrassed by his own behavior. Anyone who's been through youth knows what he means when he says he is dying of embarrassment. There are those cringe-making moments that make you catch your breath and brace yourself against the flood of shame. "Dying from embarrassment" is a common phrase and registers a common experience. Normally, we think of exposed crimes and hypocrisies as shaming. But in the threshold years, when the self-concept is under great pressure, we can feel destroyed by what will later seem like an insignificant gaffe. The best thing about being older, I often hear, is that older people suffer less from embarrassment. Yet it is often difficult to remember just how deep that embarrassment cuts into our sense of self. What seems funny in later life, and what is often comic when portrayed in a film or book, plunges into us like a knife when we are younger.

Alec speaks of a gulf between who he thinks he should be and who he feels he is. This is the gulf wherein low self-esteem breeds. He speaks of his shame at not being who he thinks he should be: "I can't understand why ideas of who I want to be keep growing, but are locked further and further inside me. I'm ashamed of how big I want to be, and how small I feel I really am. I blame everyone—especially my parents. I feel they've ruined something inside me."

Like most thresholders, Alec needs both to enhance his sense of who he is and to have some "objective" handle on his talents and personality. He is on a seesaw, wanting to be impressive and also wishing he could be authentic. "I'm so concerned about how people see me that whatever I say is just for show. Even when I try to tell people the truth, it seems like I'm lying."

Alec is unsettled by people who seem at ease with themselves. He sees what other people can do—talk and laugh easily, be warm and vulnerable, do work without feeling it is all too much—and he feels their virtues overwhelm him like a flood. "I sometimes can't breathe. It's like these other people take up all the space, and I'm nothing." He focuses first on one person and then on another. He watches his classmates like a hawk, hoping to pick out some essential flaw in their performance or character. He assesses everyone—his roommate, the person who talks up most in class, the person he sits across from in the cafeteria. From the first day of orientation, he tries to talk to people in ways that allow him to rate their intelligence and hopes to find them lacking so that he will, in comparison, seem okay. Maintaining his precarious equilibrium is an exhausting process.

Unhappy at school, he blames his parents: he blames them for wanting him to go to this college, and for having ideas about what he should do and even what fraternity he should join. He rages against his father when he phones and asks questions that make Alec feel that he "is a gross disappointment, but that's just too bad."

IT'S ALL MY PARENTS' FAULT

As young people disappoint themselves, they often blame their parents—they blame them for being too distant, and they blame them for being too involved. They blame them for being rich, they blame them for being poor. They blame them for being "average," or they blame them for being odd. All good and trusted parents suffer blame from their children. Young people have learned to expect much from their parents. When they were children, their parents could "make everything better." When parents can no longer smooth the wrinkles in their lives or their minds, a son or daughter may name a parent's shortcoming as the cause.

Parents are unsettled by these criticisms, even as they discount them as "absurd." "I did my best" and "I did what I thought was best" they protest. Yet as they defend themselves, sure that they are right and their children are unfair, unjust, and wrong, the stabbing query remains: "Am I really that bad?" and "Do I really make things so difficult for him?" "Have I let her down?" "What did I do wrong?" Caught up in a parent-blaming culture, which sees any child's flaw as a mother's or father's fault, they feel both righteously defensive ("I did my best!") and self-accusing ("I must have done something wrong").

The sport of parent-blaming is played as thresholders reassess their childhood. It is common in adolescence, as teenagers take a look at the wider world and are fascinated by unfamiliar lifestyles. "Why can't you be like that?" or "Why won't you let me be like this?" they demand of their parents. During this time, too, quarrels arise over what they can and cannot do, or where they can go, or what they have to do. Teenager/parent quarrels start with questions about freedom and control and lead into issues of distance and difference, awareness and appreciation.

It is expected that these battles will subside at the close of adolescence. But criticism of parents—how they behave, what they believe, and what they expect—continues into adulthood. This criticism is an exercise of new mental powers and a way of selecting which aspects of their family thresholders want to model and which they want to discard. When young people feel stuck, when they feel inferior, parent-blaming becomes an idle routine. They go over and over aspects of their pasts they don't like but cannot grow beyond.

Alec blames his upbringing for making him feel like a misfit. Loving his home and forced to move on, he denigrates both his past and his present. This can relieve him of self-blame, but it prevents him from helping himself develop what he really wants—authenticity. Thresholders, however, can help themselves break through the disguises of this awkward age. They can:

1. Monitor what they say to others.

A diary of conversations or statements that are untrue or misleading can provide an effective focus. When they see those false claims or poses on paper, they will be unlikely to find them impressive or convincing themselves.

2. Learn to manage anxiety.

If a young person looks over this diary and sees when the urge to impress got out of control, then she can begin to identify particularly anxiety-provoking social situations. She can consider the question, "What am I really afraid of?" or "What is the worst that will happen if someone does not find me impressive?" These reflections will probably diminish the fear that lies behind the anxiety—usually the irrational fear that someone will obliterate her with disdain.

3. Confront that imaginary audience.

A self-conscious thresholder should summon up the images of those people he believes are watching him. He could describe what he supposes to be others' impression of him. He can then consider how those impressions might be accurate, how they could be inaccurate, and how they could change. Accepting the vagaries of others' views will make them less frightening.

4. Escape the spotlight.

Spending at least fifteen minutes in a quiet place each day with a clear mind is good practice for getting rid of disturbing mental intruders.

5. Imagine authenticity.

Most thresholders long to be themselves, not someone else. Imagining one's true self is a step toward becoming that person.

6. Make good use of your sensitivity to others' responses.

Self-consciousness can be an asset. Alec could be encouraged to make use of his interest in others' responses. Think what a good actor he would make—or a lawyer, ready to argue someone else's case. His keen awareness of others' responses could serve him well—as long as he also values his own feelings.

Going Away and Finding the Same Old Self (Ellen)

Most young people believe that outside their family environment, they will have a chance to bloom. During the adolescent years, their family and perhaps their friends have irritated them with their stodgy views of who they are. Some, at this stage, feel they are not well matched to their families and expect to find a sense of homecoming elsewhere.

They then find that the distance they so looked forward to is a fiction. They escape to a job or a college a thousand miles from home, but their parents are still "inside" them, still entwined with their thoughts, plans, fears. They want to remake themselves, and they resist the realization that their childhood will always shape their identity. Stuck with the myth that maturity means independence, separation, and severing family bonds, they feel they have failed some maturity test as they acknowledge the persistence of previous emotions and habits. At the same time, their parents may seem all too distant. Under the sway of the assumption that it is time to let go, parents often stand back, keep silent, and let their sons and daughters work things out for themselves. So while thresholders step out into the world, expecting to lay claim to their true selves, they open their arms to embrace emptiness. They then have to engage in painstaking revisions of who they thought they were.

These thresholders respond to a normal identity crisis—to the proliferation of questions such as "Who am I?"—with the answer, "No one." People who appear to be centered—trusting their own thoughts and experiences, able to speak their minds in public and in private situations—arouse a deep envy. The term "poisonous" is an apt description for envy—not because it infects the person envied, but because it feels like poison to the one who envies. This violent emotion can rage even in the most gentle thresholder.

Ellen was delighted to be going to college. Having grown up in a farming community in the Midwest, she had always felt there was a world beyond the one she knew—not the world of bright lights and big cities, but a dimension she felt was lacking among her family and neighbors. She wanted to leave her midwestern home, get away from her family, do her own thing, and meet different people: "I love the people I grew up with, and my parents have always been kind and as generous as they could be. There have been lots of ups and downs, moneywise, in their lives, but they've always trusted to hard work. Things were really bad when I applied to college, even the application fees were hard to rustle up, but they did it—my uncle helped out, and now things are a little better, and I have bits and pieces of funding from all over. We got federal financial aid and a university grant, and I'm still walking on a cloud because it's all turned out."

When Ellen discovered, at the age of twelve, that she had been adopted, she felt that some prior knowledge had been confirmed. "I know this is ungrateful, because my mom and dad have been so kind, and they didn't tell me until I was older because they wanted to make sure I felt I really belonged to them, but I was also pleased because I was genetically different from these people, and that made me understand more about why I kept wanting to know what was beyond all this."

Many children hold similar beliefs even of their biological parents. A young child's excited self-discoveries seem special and unknown to others. Alongside her everyday life is a world of imagination and secret knowledge. Her everyday parents do not come up to the standards of her very private sense of self, so she forms fantasies of other parents. These common fantasies (which Freud called a "family romance") are reflected in the many fairy-tales involving a child of royal descent living for a time with an ordinary family, mistaken for an ordinary child.[11] In Ellen's case, hard facts justified her sense that she "was different, fundamentally, from these very kind people."

When she discovered she was adopted, she felt immense hope for a future she had previously not thought possible. "The night they told me—it was winter and real cold, but I climbed onto the flat roof just outside my window. Everyone else thought I was asleep, but here I was, wide awake. I watched all the neighbors—who was out, who was coming home late. There they were going about their routine lives and I had just been given this precious secret. I thought if they knew what I was feeling that moment they would envy me. I thought everyone should envy me because I now knew that I was really special."

Ellen believed that when she left home for the wider world of college, she would flower into her real self. Her actual experience made her feel she did not belong anywhere. "I came here and I met all these different people. Some of the kids here are really smart, and have read loads, and my head swims when I hear them talk. I like hearing them talk, but I clam up when they try to talk to me because I know that anything I say will be hopeless." She is quick to dismiss my reminder of how much she has had to work to get here—her after-school job at a supermarket, her grant-winning application. "There are lots of kids here who haven't had any money all their lives, but they've really worked and made something of themselves. They're working now to help pay for college, and they still have time to do their work and their job, and they walk into their classes better prepared than I could ever be. It's confusing to meet so many different people in so short a time. Yeah—it's confusing."

There is often a thin line between a thresholder's admiration for other people in her new world and an envy of them that swamps her. These young people vacillate between enthusiasm for a stimulating environment and depression, bred of the belief that everyone is better—smarter, more streetwise, more directed, prettier—than oneself. But the next time I see Ellen, six weeks later, she is in an up mood. She laughs when it takes me a minute to recognize her. She, too, is aware of how different she looks now, from when we first met six months before. Her hair is short, well cut, with red streaks in the natural brown. Her casual clothes seem carefully chosen. Appearance-wise, she fits in well.

It is a fine day in early November, and she wants to show me the campus as we talk. She tells me how she loves the library and the natural history museum close by. "They have a kind of silence you don't get anywhere else on campus." She seems proud to have her special places, but when I ask about friends she grows silent and stares at the ground as we walk.

"It's great how I'm now with people who have a much broader perspective," Ellen speaks with care. "I wanted to be shaken up, mentally, and discuss all sorts of things I never would have dreamed of talking about with my friends in high school." Yet the exposure to new ideas also makes her feel inadequate. "How did these other guys grow up so fast? How do they know so much? And they're so self-assured. I look at them and think, 'Maybe I can learn to act like them.' But I never think I'll ever really be like them. They can look at a book and start discussing it, with real ideas of their own. When someone turns to me and starts talking, I think that all they're doing is showing how that compared to them I'm nothing."

It is painful to hear young people speak like this, again and again. When I begin to protest on her behalf, reminding her of her achievements and value, she takes my cue: "I know I have something to contribute. I know I have good ideas." Yet soon her resistance runs out of steam: "When I say something," she adds, "the words seem all flat and empty, and I end up feeling like a jerk."

HOW THRESHOLDERS' SELF-DOUBT CAN DISTORT THEIR SENSE OF SELF

Our sense of identity encompasses beliefs that are personal and passionate and necessary—not only to our happiness, but also to our sense of being alive. So much does our sense of well-being depend on positive feedback from others, that we are geared to protect it by picking up more positive messages about ourselves than negative ones. So, when we're in a healthy frame of mind, we focus on the good news. Normally, we look at the world in ways that bolster our sense of self. When we think about ourselves we focus on our honest acts, not our less honest ones. We prefer to be near people who like us and avoid people who don't. We trust the judgment of people who think well of us, and we criticize people who find fault with us. In this way we maintain our balance in the interpersonal whirlwind of everyday life.

But self-doubt can dismantle this device and leave us defenseless. Instead of finding supporting evidence for the good in us, we look around and see confirmation that we're no good. In a healthy frame of mind, if someone refuses to talk to us, we think "What a rude person he is." But when Ellen makes an unsuccessful attempt to start a conversation, she thinks she is at fault. "I'm not worth talking to," she concludes. Normally, when we get a disappointing grade we remind ourselves of past successes and future opportunities, and shrug off the disappointment ("You can't win them all"). When Ellen sees other students getting better grades, she immediately discounts her past successes and concludes that she is worthless: "It just goes to show how stupid I am." Every experience leads Ellen to the same conclusion: "There's no point in trying anymore."

The distorted thought patterns associated with depression can be especially destructive during the threshold years. A strong developmental urge during this phase is to develop a sense of competence,[12] and when this is thwarted, young people despair. I hear perfectly healthy and intelligent twenty-year-olds say, "I'm a loser."

For Ellen, day-to-day interactions grow increasingly uncomfortable. Each greeting, each conversation confirms, through the distorted lens of depression, her lack of value. When someone who sat beside her in the previous class, sits elsewhere today, she is convinced the person wants to get away from her. When the professor calls on her and nods when she speaks, Ellen thinks what she said was too stupid to comment on. Increasingly isolated,[12] she blocks herself off from experiences that might bring her out of her depression. Her identity regresses at a time she knows it should grow. Her interpersonal skills regress, too. Under constant pressure from her own self-denigration ("I always look stupid," "There's no point in my saying anything") she becomes irritable and depressed. As is common, depression distances the people who love her, rather than stimulates in them the support she needs.[14]

The long summer at home, between her freshman and sophomore years, offers little reprieve. Her parents note she is moody and irritable. They accuse her of acting "high and mighty." They accuse her of ingratitude, an accusation, she says, that "really shuts me up." Already struggling with both wanting to be different from her family and wanting to be loyal to them, their words lodge themselves permanently in her mind. "It's been such an awful summer. I work in town, and I come home and I do the chores my Dad expects me to do, but then all I want to do is lie in bed and cry. I don't want them to know how unhappy I am, but then again it would be good to have their sympathy. It really gets to me that they judge me like this. Every time I think about maybe trying to talk to them, I remember what they said earlier, about being ungrateful. I'd like to talk to them, but I can't."

Unlike a teenager, Ellen does not want to dump her unhappiness on her family and draw them into it. Like the young adult she is, she wants to protect them from knowing how unhappy she is. Like any teenager, she hates being "judged," but as a thresholder, she also sees their point of view, understands what it is they are complaining about. She feels too cut off from them to explain herself and too hurt by their accusations to bother defending herself. Unlike a teenager, she is careful to avoid quarrels.[15] But this means she does not express her need for the comfort and support she wants. Her greater maturity allows her to control the displays of feeling, but it does not allow her to manage her problems. Paradoxically, her maturity prevents her from getting the help she needs to grow further.

When I meet her again in her sophomore year, she speaks of her growing anxiety about what she is capable of learning. "I'm supposed to write a paper criticizing this chapter my professor wrote. He wants us to outline a 'counterargument.' How can I criticize someone's work, in an essay I've spent one term on, when I'm reading stuff that people have worked on for ten years?" She tries to keep up with the other students by preparing for each class and doing all the required reading; but she feels she is still behind, because she cannot process what she reads. Her fellow students think she is a nerd—totally absorbed in her studies—and her underperformance in class makes her seem, according to her, doubly ridiculous. "I spend all this time working and achieve zilch. You do one essay and one exam a term. You're judged just on that—you're not the well-known person, the all-around person you were in high school. You have no personality, no brain other than that mark on your transcript."

She compares herself unfavorably to her relaxed and outspoken roommate. "Kate is everything I'm not, and everything my parents didn't want me to be. But here she is, doing okay on who she is. When I watch her I feel frightened—the way she goes off with guys and lets her work pile up, and then gets As when she races through it. Maybe I'm not so different from my folks—you know? I mean, maybe I'll always be stuck with being unable to look beyond what I already know."

She is tearful and irritable as she describes herself moving further and further away from who she thought she would be. The language spoken by the professors—particularly one in sociology—is like a foreign language: "Suddenly there are all these words I know, but don't make sense. There's 'deficit of democratization' and the 'structure/agency debate,' and a whole bunch of far worse stuff. Every time I look at the class handout or open a book for this course I think, 'This proves it. I'm the most stupid person here.'"

She is so distressed after a sociology seminar that she bursts into tears. The professor asks her to see him during his office hours, but this personal attention terrifies her. "I still cringe when I think of that meeting. He starts off all cheerful and asks me how I'm enjoying the course. I couldn't believe what he was saying. I couldn't believe he didn't know how much trouble I was in. I sit in his class and I'm sure it's obvious to everyone that I can't get the gist of what's going on. I feel everyone is looking right into my head and can see there's nothing there."

MANAGING IDENTITY FRUSTRATION

Ellen displays classic symptoms of the thresholder self-doubt we also saw in Alec: inferiority (everyone else has read a lot and understands it), embarrassment ("I still cringe when I think of that meeting"), and self-consciousness (she is sure everyone in the class is aware that she is the stupid one). As with Alec, her appreciation of others' abilities is self-defeating ("When someone turns to me and starts talking I think that all they're doing is showing how that compared to them I'm nothing").

There are many possible routes to managing her sense of having no self.

1. Isolate the various problems.

Since young people have to manage various things at the same time, they often feel problems come in big packages. Ellen could practice unwrapping those packages and picking out each item. She is having trouble with one course. This is one problem. Some of the other people in her class do not seem to be having the same problem. But is that really a problem for her, too? She could push that one aside, and think how to solve the first problem.

2. Describe the problems.

Ellen needs someone to work with her to assess her strengths in detail. She doesn't know why she gets a B in one thing and a C in another. Sometimes she doesn't even get her marked essays back. When she does, she finds the comments too general and too distant to be helpful. If she could ask for more detailed criticisms, she could see a clearer path to improvement.

2. Solving problems gives power.

The root of envy is helplessness: she cannot do anything, she feels, to be the person she wants to be, so all she can do is envy someone else. But if she can identify a specific problem and begin to solve it, then she will gain control over her life. She can make some things better—and when she feels effective, she has less need for envy.

3. Confront anxiety.

Anxiety is destructive during these years not only because it's uncomfortable but also because it interferes badly with learning. Learning is as much about confidence and curiosity as it is about understanding and memory. Learning, especially in higher education, involves exploration, reflection, and a mental playfulness that we lose when we are anxious. While working or studying, practice relaxation.

Imagine a place, either real or imaginary, where you can relax and feel cared for. Imagine yourself unwinding and setting aside all your worries. Then, think of something that is bothering you—but try, at the same time, to remain physically relaxed. If you are able to do this, you are likely to experience less anxiety when confronted with stressful situations—such as examinations or class discussion. Monitor self-talk (for any sign of that judge that keeps saying "stupid").

4. Respect yourself.

Spend some time each day to reflect, "What do I feel about this?" or "What do I think about this?" All too often, thresholders are working so hard to learn what other people think and know that they forget to value their own thoughts. All too often, they conclude: "What I know isn't worth knowing; what I think isn't worth speaking." Reminders that their own experience and knowledge is central to who they are can bring back confidence.

Alec and Ellen will eventually find their way through these lows: Eighteen months later, Alec is taking a break from college, hoping that hard outdoor work will boost his confidence. Ellen is still in school, but is cautious, still wounded by self-doubt. Like so many others, these young people may put these years behind them, but general confusions about growing up make the road far rockier than it need be.

Parents can reeducate themselves about young people's development today and revise their expectations about parenting. Too often they brace themselves for the teenage years and then expect the intensive parenting to be at an end. The signals sent out during the threshold years confuse them. As Alec's mother says, "I thought he'd come through adolescence. Now I see him so low and somehow, you know, both restless and idle. Here he is—

twenty-one—but so unsettled. I'd love to see him sorted out, but I've run out of ways of helping him."

Here are some learning points for parents to become more sensitive to a thresholder's masks.

1. A new surge of arrogance at this time often signals self doubt.

The need to think that he is better than others, or that all other people his age or in his environment are stupid, is a sign that he does not fit in. The thresholder constructs a superior mask to explain his failure to fit in. If we show affection to an arrogant child (rather than "put her in her place" or "get him off his high horse"), we will be responding more effectively to the self-doubt that lies behind the arrogance.

2. The need to tell stories that highlight superiority is a sure sign of wearing a mask.

When this occurs we can curb our own excitement. Parents love to hear stories in which a son or daughter shines. But when a thresholder is encouraged to relate tales in which he gave a brilliant punch line or stood up to a boss or was singled out in class for special praise, we should tread carefully. Though we do not want to diminish a thresholder's genuine excitement in signs of success, we don't want to encourage storytelling.

3. Envy of others, or constant focusing on others' abilities, signals self-doubt.

Parents see a thresholder's potential. Despair, to them, seems so inappropriate that they find it difficult to take seriously. If a thresholder sees most people as smarter than she is, or more employable or personable, she needs help focusing on what she herself can do to improve her life. Instead of saying, "You're every bit as smart/successful/attractive as he is," ask, "How do you want to make things better?" and "What can you do?" Envy blurs our focus on the real problem and its possible solutions.

4. Parents can encourage their children to name their desires, their likes, and their hopes.

They can suggest that children engage in some nostalgia, to bring up their pasts and recall the personal experiences that make them special. These young people need help in refocusing on themselves and finding new confirmation in their memories and goals.

When young people expect to embrace a well-defined identity as part of their legal coming of age, then they feel inadequate and ashamed if this doesn't immediately happen. When our daughters and sons stand between adolescence and adulthood, sometimes part of both and sometimes part of neither, they need a parent to reflect fondly on their past and hopefully on their future. As people who love them show faith in who they are, however ill-defined they are, their changing identities will find a center.

CHAPTER THREE

MAKING CHOICES

FORMER president Harry Truman is reported to have said: "I have found the best way to give advice to your children is to find out what they want and advise them to do it." Wise though this remark is, it overlooks one of the most difficult problems young people face as they become adults: All too often they simply do not yet know what they want to do. As young people feel pressured to make decisions about future courses and careers, they feel as though they are standing on a precipice and being commanded to fly. For many thresholders, and their parents, the greatest challenge is to answer the question, "Where do I head for when I get going?"

In a society that provides so much freedom, so many opportunities—and so few charts and anchors—choosing a path (and therefore closing off other options) can be confusing. Those who are struck dumb by the prospect of making decisions need help managing the stress and risks of choice.

Those crucial decisions of the threshold years—what to study, where to live, which jobs to seek—are both necessary and tiresome. Growing up means being responsible for the choices we make, and this can be daunting. "Maybe I won't like what I choose," "What if I mess up?" "What if it's too hard?" they ask. The process of making choices can trigger high anxiety and low self-esteem as a thresholder assumes everyone around her has a better-planned future than she does. It can lead to an unsettling series of decisions, which are rapidly reformulated, as none seems to be the right one. Some young people describe being caught up in a useless spin of self-questioning where "What do I want to do?' constantly echoes in their brain. They know that, in theory, opportunities are *out there*, but they do not know how to meet up with them.

Many thresholders feel paralyzed as they confront their options. Some worry they will make the wrong choice and end up doing what they do not enjoy or what they are not able to do well. They worry they will miss out on something by choosing one thing rather than another. "Potentialitis" is the term used to describe the paralysis that strikes young people when they feel they must keep their options open at all costs lest they lose the glow of endless possibilities ahead of them. With new opportunities come anxieties: Am I making the right choices? Do I like this course, this major, this club? Will I succeed in what I'm planning to do? What am I giving up, by choosing this rather than something else?

Some young people feel in conflict with what their parents want for them. Even though they say to themselves, "The decision is up to me" or "I don't care what my parents say," deep down they do care and feel trapped by what they know their parents would prefer. They may worry that a parent's hopes do not match theirs or that they have been so used to thinking along a parent's lines that they cannot yet formulate what they want.

Far more than a passing phase, an inability to make choices can put the brakes on development. Unable to identify their interests, unable to form goals or commit themselves to plans, many thresholders disengage from the entire process. They may become apathetic: "I don't care what I do." They may opt for simplistic optimism: "Things will turn out okay." Parents are stunned to see a once forward-planning daughter or son shy away from the task of shaping her or his own life. Just at the point at which they are expected to be independently motivated, they suffer a loss of all desire and direction. Puzzled and impatient, parents diagnose stubbornness, laziness, lack of backbone, or "immaturity." "Why can't you make up your mind?" young people often report being asked. "Isn't it time you settled on something? You have to make plans. You can't just drift. You have to have some direction in life." These responses compound their problems: the people who might offer them guidance, instead "badger" or "judge" them.

The following conditions play a role in the special problems today's thresholders have in making choices:

1. Normal self-doubt and indecisiveness can be aggravated when thresholders are offered too much choice and too little guidance.

2. Parents' disappointment at a daughter's or son's indecisiveness leads to further anxiety and conflict.

3. High expectations of personal fulfilment make the limitations of any particular choice difficult to tolerate.

Parents need to educate themselves about the new worlds their sons and daughters move in. Modern trends and expectations are making choices much more difficult for this generation of thresholders.

CHOICE IN A COLLEGE CONTEXT

Many colleges make choices difficult for young people by offering too much choice. Young people approach college courses as they would a cafeteria, with multiple offerings, attractively displayed, fully prepared, ready for consumption. As colleges package discrete units of learning, young people are tempted to indulge their love of variety and to satisfy every curiosity—while parents often look for courses that will prepare a child for an employable and profitable life. The scene is then set for a clash between thresholder and parent—a clash that further diminishes confidence and optimism. The challenge is to identify one's wants and needs. Such feats are possible, but they demand an enormous amount of time and energy for a young adult trying to find out about future prospects and current interests. And often they have to please not only themselves but also a parent (who is paying for the education).

Expectations for college have risen in some respects and fallen in others. More people expect to complete college, and people expect it to do more for them. The current cultural obsession with perfection, with total fulfilment, affects young people choosing courses.

Over the past decade, colleges have extended options for students. A growing trend in liberal arts colleges is to allow students to form their own curriculum. Even math and science majors have enormous freedom in the arrangement of courses.[1] The active role a college student is now expected to take in constructing (not merely choosing) a major increases the decision exponentially. It is somewhat like asking an employee of a new firm to write her or his own job description for a job that will be the starting point of a career. High expectations for interesting courses stall young people as they search for the perfect academic package. They then battle with the anxiety of making the perfect choice. Their logic is: "Given I can do anything, what would be the best possible thing to do? I can't waste my time with anything less."

At the same time, young people expect less from college than did their parents and grandparents. In the past, higher education was a passport to a secure, well-paid job. Times have changed since the days that a college or a course or a degree was a ticket, either a meal ticket ("At least I'll be able to earn a living") or a fast-track ticket ("A law school graduate from this place will enter the best firms"). Now a college degree is just one of many qualifications an employer will consider. Even graduates from the best universities have to stand up to stiff competition in the job market. Even the most highly trained professionals can be unemployed or stuck in unrewarding positions. The job market, even with educational qualifications, is competitive and changeable. To a parent this means: "You should study something useful." To a thresholder this means: "Nothing's a sure meal ticket, so I might as well please myself."

CHOICES ABOUT ENTERING A CAREER

The model of a useful education may be outdated. The number of jobs have proliferated in the past ten years, and many of these have no defined structure. The model of planning a career in terms of naming a distant goal, and then taking reasonable steps toward it, no longer fits the realities of a working life. In all probability, our daughters and sons will, at thirty-five, be in a very different career from the one they start in their early twenties. They may be in jobs we cannot yet name, because they do not yet exist. Yet repeatedly thresholders report being asked about their "plans." When they can give no answer to the question, "What do you want to do?" they are often made to feel inadequate, irresponsible, and immature.

But with the rapidly changing structure of employment, it is more difficult to see far ahead. Few young adults can reasonably say: "I am going to enter such and such a business, and then reach one level in two years, and another in five and another in ten."

Young people are pressured to draw a straight path, but they need guidance to see how each path has many diverging ones ahead. They are pressured to commit themselves to one goal, but they require skills in flexibility and adaptation.

If parents acknowledge young people's uncertainties, and revise their expectations of a thresholder's decisions, they can begin to offer appropriate support.

1. A model of decision making should be both grounded in the present and flexible about the future. An important set of starting questions is: "What do you want to do now or in the immediate future?" and "What is possible now or in the immediate future?"

When some matches are made between desire and reality (what one wants to do and what one can do), the next step is to envisage a variety of possibilities from these matches. "A job in sales" may not lead to a specific career, but a job in a music sales department will provide experience in sales, knowledge of new equipment, and information about how a business is run. From this, the young person could follow a variety of other choices. A job filing papers in a law office will not lead up through the ranks to partner, but it provides work experience and information about life as a lawyer. Each choice should be seen as an opening into others that may not be visible at present.

2. Imagination is as important as structure and logic.

Young people can be encouraged to visualize their futures at different times. See which they are more at ease with—futures close to them (three years from now) or more distant futures (ten and twenty years from now). Try to think how their present choices might eventually match up to those imagined futures. Envisioning a variety of outcomes will ease the anxiety of making one choice.

3. Parents and teachers can work with thresholders to help them get in touch with their preferences and wishes.

Set aside questions about career and future (temporarily) from the conversation, and ask the thresholder what she likes and what she dislikes about what she is studying or working at now. Encourage her to consider what she admires about the lives of people she knows. These reflections will highlight interests and preferences that can then be linked to present choices and subsequent paths.

4. Parents can ask themselves how genuinely open they are to what a daughter or son wants to do.

How tolerant, after all, are we of different career and study patterns? We may need to track our own comments for negative signals. Do we remind our daughter about the downside of a career she mentions? Or do we offer emotional and practical support by finding out what she could be doing now that could lead to that career?

5. Good communication encourages decisions based on preferences and abilities.

It includes discussions of options, risks, implications, and consequences. It then encourages young people to identify what they can't control and what they can. They can remind themselves that they have the power to change some things in their lives, and that they will keep this power even after they have made important choices.

Making choices and shaping one's future is a part of defining the self. Decisions have to be made slowly and carefully. Parents and teachers can help with these decisions, while letting the thresholder make up his mind. We can do this by asking questions that encourage our children to think clearly for themselves.

Choosing a College Major (Marsha)

Many decisions made during the threshold years have immense symbolic meaning for both thresholder and parent. While choosing a major in college seems a minor matter compared to other life-shaping decisions, it looms as a crucial task of the junior year.[2] On one level the issues are: "What subjects interest me?" and "What classes do I enjoy and value?" but on a deeper level, the question is, "What do I want to do with my life?" Since few twentysomethings can answer this question, they tend to go through three or four tentative choices[3] before making a final one.

Young people are expected to lay the path to their futures just at the time their self-concept is rapidly changing. While psychologists have long recognized the impact of sexual frustration on one's general well-being, they are slow to recognize the impact of thresholders' developmental frustration—the humiliation and chagrin at being unable to feel focused and directed and on track. The anxiety of not knowing where one wants to go and what one wants to do gives rise to an unease that parents and teachers often characterize as "foolish," "irresponsible," or, of course, "immature." "Why can't you settle down?" they demand accusingly, when what a thresholder needs is help tolerating and containing uncertainty.

Marsha comes face to face with these contradictions as she approaches her twenty-first birthday. She describes herself as "cornered, and really angry, now, with my dad." She tells me she does not know what she wants to do and no longer wants to think about it. Her conversation keeps coming back to questions about the decisions she has to make and the impossibility of making them. She is stuck in a familiar thresholder pattern where anxiety about a decision overwhelms her ability to make any decision.

This "mental loop that isn't going anywhere" surprises her and everyone who knows her. Marsha always impressed her high-school teachers with her strong sense of purpose. "She's full of energy, very positive," her high-school English teacher tells me. "She's all go."

When I meet her for the first time we are in her father's home in Washington, D.C. It is a hot and muggy July, and she has just graduated from high school. I need a long drink of iced-tea before I can do much more than go through the routine of greeting her, but Marsha seems happy in the heat. She wears a bright smile and bright colored clothes to match. She has something of a cheerleader's confidence, and as she speaks it is clear that she expects adults to be charmed by her. "I'm going to be a journalist," she tells me as she prepares to leave for college in Seattle. "When I graduate I'll start working for a good local paper. I'll stay there a few years to learn the ropes. That's what I've always wanted to do. Ever since I was thirteen, I read papers and noticed certain articles by these various writers, and thought: 'That's what I want to do.'" She has her course schedule pretty much planned—an English major, with courses in journalism and creative writing. Her parents enjoy her buoyant self-confidence and often reward school achievements with material things ("I got a Polo backpack when I made the honor role"). But they also shower her with smiles and praise for being, as they say, "one great kid." While she speaks, her eyes wander from my face and focus on the distance, and I feel she is putting forth an effort— not so much to please me as to impress me.

When I see her next she has started her sophomore year. Her appearance is much the same—she is still tan, still wears her hair tied back and fiddles with a bobbypin that keeps the bangs out of her eyes—but her manner is very different. She seems on edge, no longer eager to impress me, but keen to defend herself: "I don't need to be reminded about what I said last summer, and I don't want to hear about it. I was just a stupid kid." Fourteen months later, she seems wiser, but certainly not happier. "My freshman year was nothing like I thought it would be. I mean I walked into the college newspaper office and I thought I'd be welcomed with open arms. I know it seems stupid *now*, but that's what I thought *then*. What in fact happened was that the editor shrugged when I told her I wanted to work on the paper. She asks for a portfolio of stuff I've published—I was eighteen and she wants published articles! So I started to spew out all these ideas and she looks right through me for about five minutes but then says if I want I can write something on spec. You know, they'd look, but wouldn't make any promise to take it on. I wrote some things, but each time there was something either wrong with my style or my subject. Eventually I was just cold-shouldered out. I've accepted it, I guess, but I still get this awful jab in my stomach when I meet someone who works on the paper. And every time I read it, I feel so bad, because so much of the stuff in it is real good, and maybe I just can't do what I thought I could do. This has really thrown me, made me rethink everything. Even English classes are a struggle. I'm doing okay, but nothing special. Here, I'm just one person in a whole class. Back home, my English and French teachers loved me. Really. In my senior year in high school I was the apple of their eye."

Thresholders who believe, in leaving high school, that they have a clear sense of where they are going, can have a real problem tolerating uncertainty. Since Marsha is someone who has a clear-cut plan for her future, change proves more difficult and disheartening. It is not simply that she is now "just one person in a whole class" rather than the apple of her teachers' eyes: she has lost the purpose that both anchored and directed her. Having been given the cold shoulder by the university's press room, she decides to switch her major to chemistry. "I want something that stretches my mind and makes use of my memory, which is pretty good. I can see myself making a good career out of this.

I'd like to work in industry, but probably in a small up-and-coming company. I'd like to plan and direct projects."

Sometimes thresholders feel better as soon as they form a plan. As Marsha speaks, some of last year's pertness returns. She sees her way forward and has a good sense, already, of the shape of a very different career from the one she had settled upon in her early teenage years. But by the middle of her junior year, her plan for being a chemist has evaporated. "I don't really know if the choices I'm making are the best, or if they're going to have the best outcome later on. That's kind of scary, because you just never know what's the right thing."

"POTENTIALITIS": IN SEARCH OF THE PERFECT CHOICE

Many thresholders are obsessed with putting together a unique and marvelous major. This is part of their battle both to feel special as a student and to look good to future employers. But so many young people are now studying all sorts of things that it is very difficult to find something that stands out.

I accompany Marsha to a session with a course counselor, scheduled routinely when a student announces a last-minute change in her major. The adviser takes her through the multiple options that are now open to college students, also reminding her that certain majors are no longer possible at this late stage in her junior year. Marsha is edgy and responds to the counselor's probing questions without interest, without emotion. Questions seem to disturb her and, as they continue, she grows tearful. "I just haven't decided yet," she announces. Fearing that she can lose everything by choosing the wrong thing, she cannot choose anything.

This is a common response to a wealth of choice and to that healthy (but sometimes confusing) urge to have a very special life. Unfortunately, when thresholders feel edged into a corner by their own uncertainty, their parents often lose patience with them. "Why can't you just get on with things?" a thresholder's parent often demands. "Just decide!" But in this state, they cannot think constructively.

Marsha is engaged in a fantasy world. She spends hours spinning out scenarios of what she'll become, what her life will be, if she studies philosophy or if she studies Chinese. "I keep imagining these situations where I'll look good and know what I'm doing. I like thinking about my apartment and what it'll be like when I finally get a job in the real world and what I'll wear, and what it'll be like, knowing what I'm doing in life. But I don't see how I'm ever going to get there." The possibilities ahead catch her imagination but do not motivate her.

While thresholders feel comforted by imagining future plans but lack a supporting structure for pursuing them, they can lapse into a manic phase of decision making. Marsha makes and remakes the same decision over and over again and loses credibility in others' eyes. Coming from a family with three generations of college graduates behind him, her father Colin believes he knows what college is all about. "When I took a course I wasn't expected to like it, or to find everything interesting every minute. I was expected to be learning something."

There are common disagreements between thresholder and parent about the purpose of education: Is it a ticket to a future career, or is it an enrichment experience? Marsha's father feels he is wasting money on his daughter's tuition. He is afraid that his daughter will leave college without learning anything of value. "These days you can get a degree without taking one real course," he says. The clash blocks her father off as an available resource for discussion. Though she once enjoyed talking to him as "someone who maybe knows more than me about the world but still values what I have to say," their discussions now are humiliating: "My dad now wants these conversations with me. And conversations turn into arguments, because conversations are him telling me what I should be studying and what my attitude toward my courses should be. He can't see that my life matters to me now, that I can't keep thinking long term. I thought long term in high school. Why am I still thinking only long term? And then he gets impatient with me: 'You're not going to make anything of your life. You're just goofing around.' We have these awful fights, and I just don't want to talk to him for days after, because I feel he's totally against me and thinks I'm not looking at life in the right way."

But Marsha's battle against her father is a false defense. In the culture driven by the myth of maturity, she believes that her father is right. Believing she has lost his respect, her spirits dive.

DISTORTED VIEWS: "I WISH I KNEW WHAT I WANTED, LIKE SHE DOES."

Decision paralysis has a domino effect. Thresholders who are under pressure to make what others call "sensible decisions," tend to lose confidence in their ability to decide anything. Instead of focusing on themselves, they suffer thought distortions that make them envy others.

Undecided, and finding indecision intolerable, Marsha sees the people around her—her new classmates, her friends from high school, her cousins—as more certain and better directed. She thinks that Leah, who has always wanted to study biology, and Pam, who knows she wants to be a poet, and Neil, who plans go into a family business, not only are doing better but are somehow better people. She receives a card from a friend who is doing volunteer work, teaching English in Thailand. The postcard, filled with tiny writing, tells how hard but exciting teaching is, how hospitable the people, and how beautiful the countryside. She tells Marsha of her eagerness to learn more about this culture. Marsha then tells me, "There are people here who really know what they want to do, and who know what they're capable of doing. I envy them so much it hurts." Her envy leads to constant regret for what she did not do. It leads to more grand plans, to which her father responds with anger.

"I should have taken a year out," she reflects. "I should have done something different. If only I had those experiences my father wouldn't be able to humiliate me like he does now. Then I'd have some experience different from his, and he couldn't be so critical of me. I'm determined to do volunteer work somewhere really wild this summer, maybe help preserve forests in the Philippines, which he turns up his nose at. But at least I'll have a different slant on myself."

Regret about what one has missed, musings about what would have happened if one had done something different, get in the way of productive thoughts. She broods angrily over her controlling father: "I knew better than to broach the subject of a year off. Maybe Mom would agree, but only if I was going to do something real noble, life charity work in Mozambique. My Dad wouldn't agree, though, even then. He wants me to get on with life."

Marsha is at the point where she dare not try, dare not see what she can and cannot do. She has lost the ability to work toward something, because she has lost the belief that she can do anything. "I thought my last semester's grades were bad, and I know my parents were disappointed, but last year's grades were brilliant compared to what I'll get this semester." She loses concentration easily. She begins to read, and her mind wanders, caught by the spiraling daydreams of her future. She tries to decide what to do now by evaluating images of her future, seeing herself as a hotshot journalist, a groundbreaking chemist, a star history professor. "I keep going around in circles. I just can't decide. Dad says if I can't make what he calls a sensible decision by May, I'm going to have to quit school and get a job. It's like I'm failing because I just can't decide. And it doesn't help when he starts on about how classes aren't supposed to be all fun and I'm going about my decisions in the wrong way. It's like: not only can't I make a good decision, but I don't even know what a good decision is."

LEARNING TO ASK THE RIGHT QUESTIONS

We can modify our way of approaching thresholders who suffer from choice paralysis. Injunctions to "make a commitment" or "just decide" or even "decide what's best for you" may not work when a young person is too confused to know what she wants to do. Instead, we may have to work with her to ask new questions that can then lead to discoveries of what she wants to do.

1. A young person like Marsha needs practice getting in touch with what she herself wants. Centering exercises, in which she focuses on her own preferences, would clarify her goals. She could ask herself:

When do I feel most interested?

How do I see myself ten years from now—or twenty? What goals do I have for myself?

Who are the people I respect? What do I respect them for?

How am I similar to my father and different from my father?

How am I similar to my mother and different from my mother?

If a parent poses these questions, and stays calm while a daughter or son struggles to formulate the answers, together they would get a better sense of where the young person might want to go. But thresholders like Marsha can also engage in these reflections themselves.

2. Thresholders in the grip of choice paralysis need to feel a parent's support.

A parent's approval can give a swift injection of confidence even to thresholders who appear indifferent to a parent's view. When a parent is at odds with a daughter or son, he often feels his child "doesn't care what I think" or "won't listen to a word I say." In fact, thresholders remain highly sensitive to a parent's view of them. They need to feel that a parent has faith in whomever they will become. Marsha is hurt and angered by her father's apparent lack of faith in her. The tension between them makes her feel worse about herself and, therefore, makes her state of indecision even more disheartening.

3. Choices have to be manageable.

When young people have difficulty making a decision, the importance of that decision can be magnified. They speak of making decisions in college that will affect their entire lives. Though this is possibly true of each and every decision we make, focusing on the very long-term can make us dizzy: We simply cannot see that far ahead. Therefore, if thresholders focus on their current interests and hopes, the process will arouse less anxiety.

4. A large reference list of possible paths and outcomes makes any decision easier.

It is difficult to keep up with the proliferation of possible career and developmental paths. All too often parents look back to their own youth for reference of what is a useful or sensible program. An educational and career counselor, with up-to-date knowledge of training and employment, can help both parent and thresholder see new routes and therefore make sense of a variety of choices.

5. Emphasize opportunities ahead.

When choice-paralysis sets in, thresholders need reassurance that they will still have options, even as they make definite decisions. It can be calming to present their decisions like the branch of a tree and show how many further branches can grow from it.

Reluctant to Face Choices in the Outside World (Tim)

Part of growing up is taking control of our lives and making the day-to-day choices such control requires. But taking control can be frightening, and many thresholders are highly ambivalent about being real adults. When they confront a situation in which they have to make a choice, they freeze. They stare at their futures like a deer dazed by oncoming headlights.

As young people undertake serious job searches, they feel real life closing in on them. They may find that the majority of entry-level jobs are humdrum and poorly paid. Being grown up can suddenly lose all its glamour. "I don't want to think about being grown up in that way," they may insist. Or, "I didn't study and get these grades just so I could earn a few dollars." Some consider further training—perhaps as an accountant, lawyer, bartender, computer programmer, or teacher. Once a young person slumps into a state of apathy, no choice has any special appeal. Each decision depends on some other decision: They do not want to compete for one job, unless they are sure they do not want to train for another career. Unable to decide about training, they claim they cannot decide about the job. Or, they contemplate different enterprises—starting a business, for example, or doing volunteer work abroad—and get excited about each, yet lose interest in taking the initial necessary steps.

Beneath their lethargy lies panic. If we help soothe their fears, focus on a series of short-term goals, and track their strategies, we will be able to shift their gaze from those terrifying questions ("What am I going to do with the whole of my life?") to the practical maneuvers that will ease them across the threshold.

Tim is among the growing group of thresholders who put off thinking about his future. When I first met him he was still in college and winced when I asked about career choices: "It's frightening, thinking that what I decide to do now will affect my entire life. I guess I've known this for years. I'd think about being grown up and I'd wonder how I'd ever be able to decide on a career, and stuff like that. This was when I'd take ages just choosing from a restaurant menu! It's the kind of thing that everyone laughs at and tells you it'll be okay when the time comes. But it's not okay. I'm really stuck. I don't even know what I have to know about either myself or the world to make decisions."

I see him again, eight months after graduation, and he is bemused by the fact that he never thought beyond college. "When I graduated people made these suggestions—I could try marketing, I could go to law school, I could take a business course. But I don't want to mimic my sister or my brother. I want to do my own thing. But I don't have any idea what I want to do."

While it is common for young people to feel they do not know what to do, indecision is dangerous when it leads to an inability to make any choice. Tim cannot decide whether he wants to take a job, go to graduate school, or travel. He says he has to sort this out before he does anything. He does not want to take a job, only to quit in order to travel or go back to school. He does not want to go back to school unless it's the right thing for him. He would like to travel and broaden his experiences, but he cannot plan that far ahead.

Tim is the youngest of three children. His sister, the oldest, is now floor manager of a large department store, married, with a young baby. At twenty-nine, she has passed all the significant markers of being a real adult. She has her own apartment, a child, and a career. His brother is in law school. Though he does "not want to spend my whole life feeling I'm not as good as my sister and my brother," he does not want to compete with them, either.

Initially, he is pleased to be officially grown up: "Once I graduate I won't be the little kid anymore. I'll still be the youngest, but I'll have adult status." Yet Tim, tall and lanky, gives the impression of being still unused to his adult size. He sits with one leg crossed over the other, jerking intermittently as though in a reaction to a doctor's hammer against his knee. In his nervous, angry reflections, he combines an adolescent's pent-up energy with a young man's stress under pressure. There is also something boyish in the way he searches my face as he speaks, hoping to find some solution to the problems he describes. We talk about his father, who irritates and sometimes frightens him, his interest in folk music, and his niece whom he adores, but he keeps coming back to his difficulty in making choices: "It's like someone's pushed me into an empty cell and ordered me to weave a whole bunch of plans out of nothing."

He describes his unexpected disorientation and lethargy. "I can't understand why I'm so unhappy and why I have this inertia." He avoids his mother, unable to tolerate her disappointment alongside his own depression. He avoids his father, who will pester him about being a man.

He had looked forward to life beyond school. He looked forward to freedom, but the freedom was envisioned primarily in negative terms: "Before, I thought it would be great to make your own choices—no one telling you what's the best thing for you. No one telling you how to think or what you had to learn. Just lots of opportunities. That's why I thought I'd be having such a good time. Instead, I'm in a kind of daze all the time. I just can't get it together."

His initial "first thing on the list of things to do after graduating" was to get a place of his own. His spent his teenager years in two homes—that of his father and that of his mother and stepfather. He liked college because he had all his things in one room. Now he has moved from the suburbs where his parents live, in their different homes, into the city. Living off the allowance his mother still gives him, he has a room in an apartment with a couple who need a tenant to cover their mortgage. He is glad to have his own room, glad to live with people who "aren't my family and don't really care about me, so they don't interfere." From time to time he meets up with old friends, but feels he now has little in common with them. "I'm always relieved when it's time to go. They're full of what they're going to do after work, or where they're going to spend their weekend. I don't really want to do anything."

He talks about his future as though it were a magic lantern, presenting different images for entertainment only: "Maybe I'll go back to my hometown and set up a health food store. Maybe I'll do volunteer work in Kosovo. It would be so easy if I were a sculptor or writer or something. Or if I had some sure-fire idea for a business or something. Then I could say, 'This is my mission in life. I know where I'm going.' But I don't know. I don't know what to do." He feels he has to make a good strong start. He doesn't want to take a menial job. He would find it boring and he is afraid of being stuck in one forever. He describes himself at the point at which "planning doesn't make sense, because I know I won't follow it through."

Parents respond with anger and disappointment when their nearly adult children seem to "lack backbone." They accuse them of being "spoiled" and expecting too much. They argue that a job is not always satisfying but is nonetheless necessary. Conversations become lectures about "real life" and thresholders switch off.

Tim's mother, Karen, says her son is wasting himself. "He has no plans. I can't understand why he isn't more inspired. I remember how excited I was, that year I graduated. I'd walk around downtown at night, and the street lights had a kind of magic, everything was magical because it seemed to represent my brilliant, seductive future." When he tries to talk to his father about his sense of "going nowhere," his father protests: "What do you mean? You go to college, and the world's your oyster. What's your problem?"

Today's thresholders repeatedly say that they feel they live in the shadow of their parents' energy, an energy that was born during the cult of youth and hope for change, an energy that was replenished with rewards for hard and honest work.

Like many of today's thresholders, Tim also feels himself in the shadow of the generation now approaching thirty, who were exhilarated by the proliferation of career opportunities. He sees his sister's generation of young black women as "buzzing with the need to succeed. I went into work with her one day, because she was trying to give me a jump start when she saw how bummed out I was in Boston, and I felt I'd been dropped into another planet. These guys were willing to work any number of hours. And the couple I live with are the same. They're never home. They never see each other. They want to make a name for themselves and they want the high pay that goes with a high profile name. And if that's what being grown up is, I don't want to join the grown-ups. It's as though growing up means everything I was certain about becomes full of doubt."

Avoidance is a common strategy for persistent indecisiveness. Tim explains: "I look at my watch and say, 'You can have five more minutes, and then you really have to write an application letter.' But five minutes go by and I'm still on the net or watching the tube, and then—presto!—the whole afternoon is gone."

Day after day, Tim puts off doing anything toward actually getting a job or making any decision about a job. He says to himself, "Tomorrow I'll go to a career office" or "Tomorrow I'll work on my resume," but the following day or the day after, these tasks remain undone. "I really kept things together in college, and was aware I was doing okay. But this—this is a bust."

He stops speaking to light a cigarette. The habit is so new that he looks awkward as he smokes. Hunched over, wearing a T-shirt that shows his recent weight loss, I wonder whether he is on drugs. I ask and he shrugs.

"I'm getting to the point where what I do just doesn't matter. At first I kept thinking, 'This is going to lead somewhere.' Now, I don't. Even the littlest things set me off. Like I'm afraid I won't be able to fill out a form. I'm afraid I won't find my way to an interview. I'm afraid of what will happen in the interview. It's all like going back to square one, as though you haven't achieved anything."

As people hear him, they hear a temporary discontent, a young person's blues. They expect him to get used to things and then get on with things. But he taps into a deeply unsettling truth about his situation: that the first steps are very difficult, that highly qualified people tend to expect more job offers than they get, that applying for jobs and being refused jobs is humiliating.

For each thresholder, making the choices that are necessary steps through these years poses different risks. Young people often have a sense that in taking their first full-time job, they are being catapulted into adulthood. They may fear what will be left behind. They may fear their own inadequacy. The slower they are to act in spite of these fears, the larger the fear grows. The following strategies can be used by parents, counselors, or thresholders themselves to jump start on active, persistent, and positive job searches:

1. Acknowledge the real problem.

There are so many possible jobs and careers and training programs that it is difficult to make decisions about what to do. But if parents believe that this problem is not real, the thresholder feels the problem is his alone. Only if a parent is aware of the maze a thresholder faces will conversation be comforting and constructive.

2. Assess what can be within your control and what cannot.

Consider what can and what cannot be controlled. These could form different lists. In the "controllable" list would be putting in a job application. In the list of things outside one's control would be the actual job offer. But on the first list would be one's response to a job refusal: It could be defined as a failure or as a to-be-expected experience. Putting something off versus doing it today is in the "controllable" list.

3. Formulate strategies.

Any newcomer is better off with a map. Though thresholders cannot have a map with their lives drawn on it, short-term markers can be useful. They can map a plan for investigating possible jobs or careers, then making a decision by a given date. Waiting to be absolutely certain about something before embarking on it is a "strategy" to avoid.

4. Track resolutions.

Passive thresholders can be encouraged to keep track of their resolutions and then their actions—preferably by keeping a diary. They can then see what they have failed to do after resolving to do it. Once they start taking steps toward a goal, they will see that they are not helpless and that making decisions is possible.

5. Focus on a range of options.

Often the inability to make a decision is overcome when we realize that the future will always hold new possibilities and that our options can be reviewed at any time.

6. Be realistic.

Keep in mind that these are just the first steps in a long adulthood. They do not have to be perfect. Making a start and feeling your way are good enough goals at present.

7. Address the fear.

Procrastinators are often stalled by fears they cannot name. Sometimes they fear the commitment that a good job requires. Sometimes they fear that a decision will trap them into a dull adulthood.

How can parents contain a son's or daughter's fears? In infancy, they do this by soothing their anxiety with cuddles and words. So profound an effect does this early holding have that parents retain a long-term influence on a child's panic button. In childhood, parents contain a son's or daughter's fears by putting them in perspective. "It's only a dream," we say of a nightmare. "It can't hurt you," we tell a child terrified of a spider. "It's not real," we say of a horror film. Also, we help them deal with more realistic fears. We tell them how to be careful—on the street, in the kitchen, in the yard—so they can avoid scary situations. But in a broader and deeper way, we offer our own care, so that they can get on with their lives, in spite of frightening things.

During adolescence, parents often feel that it is their duty to increase a daughter's or son's fears. Teenagers are so bad at assessing risk that adults have to remind them that many things—cars, sex, drugs—can be dangerous. At the threshold phase, however, awareness of risks can be once again overpowering. No longer do young people fancy themselves as immortal—as they did during the mid-teen years. Instead, they feel vulnerable. But they are now more ashamed of their fears than they were as children. Parents, having learned the importance of stirring up the fears of their fearless adolescents, need to be attuned to new fears that can paralyze their thresholders.

A parent can contain a thresholder's fears by showing patience when she or he trips on the first few steps of adult life. A parent can contain a thresholder's fears by acknowledging them. Adult life is scary. Making choices and finding direction is difficult. A thresholder can tolerate this frustrating process when the parents tolerate it. And parents can hold on to them as they explore their world, allowing them back to refuel on reassurance, involvement, and care.

Thresholders make decisions about their futures in a rapidly changing world. There are fewer well-defined paths. The personal and professional terrain will have to be constantly negotiated and renegotiated. Each young person's successful transition will depend on her ability to tolerate these uncertainties.

CHAPTER FOUR

EMOTIONAL EDUCATIONS

Ask young people and their parents what they expect of the threshold years, and they are likely to talk about independence and learning. This is the time when they expect to develop minds of their own. But one of the most important tasks of early adulthood is forming close connections to people outside one's family, in one's own adult skin.

The new attachments thresholders form are powerful influences on their education. Through these, they learn about bonds outside their families and explore new forms of attachment and dependence. They learn about their capacities to support others, to join groups or communities, to exercise care and integrity as adults. At the same time, they take tough courses in betrayal and fickleness, from both friends and lovers. They learn that they themselves sometimes lack judgment, that their ordinary common sense can desert them after a drink or two, and that they can do the stupid things they thought only stupid people did. They learn about their own unexpected vulnerabilities: What it feels like to be dumped by a boyfriend when your mom is not around to give you a hug; what it feels like to fall in love without your high-school friends following every detail of the relationship; what it feels like to have your high-school girlfriend write to you from her college five hundred miles away to tell you she has fallen for someone else. Anxious and confused, thresholders recount situations—at parties, in an office, in the dorm—which make them shiver and burn with shame. "Why on earth did I do that?" or "Why didn't I know better?" and "How could I make such a fool of myself?" are some questions that burst from young people as they talk about personal interchanges in emotionally charged relationships. These experiences contribute to the often-ignored *emotional* education as thresholders learn how to manage themselves within a range of relationships.

Emotional education does not begin suddenly during the threshold phase. It begins at birth, the beginning of our interpersonal world, when we experience the essential role played by others in our bid for contact, comfort, and life itself. From early childhood, we learn about attachments to people outside our families. Friends, teachers, and neighbors present opportunities to exercise skills in relating to and understanding others. But what we learn as thresholders can be described as higher education.

The significant themes in this education involve:

1. Sexuality

Sexual desire can become a source of personal knowledge and personal power. Thresholders explore their sexuality in new ways. We hope that young people emerge as adults with the ability to place desire in the context of significant relationships. We hope they are able to recognize their own desires and differentiate, for example, situational stimulation (from a party atmosphere or the mellow effect of alcohol) from a personal attraction. We want them to be able to identify their own sexual orientation and distinguish what they really feel from what is expected of them. They also learn about the limits and extent of their own sexual pleasure.

2. Romance

Romances have a new intensity as they are shaped and reshaped by changing gender roles and by new variations in the war between the sexes. Young people pose serious questions about love, loyalty, and compatibility. With this depth comes a greater vulnerability. Teenagers may weep copiously over a romantic breakup but recover far more quickly than thresholders are likely to.

3. Friendships

Friendships lose the ready-made patterns of high-school groups and become the basis of enduring social networks. Thresholders forge alliances and explore similarities and differences among their peers. Friends provide much-needed protection as they replace a family's day-to-day company and comfort, but they also present new perils. Thresholders can sometimes regress to earlier stages of dependence on friends and create strangling alliances.

4. Groups

Joining groups and forming networks provide a sense of social belonging. We expect, through group participation, to improve our ability to understand and communicate. We hope thresholders will learn to belong and fit in—without losing their ability to stand up for their ideas and their own interests.

5. Mentors

At a time of rapid growth and learning, teachers, employers, and coworkers become guides into adulthood. While teachers were taken for granted in the high-school years, they often come to have for thresholders a mystique and become objects of worship. Mentoring relationships can arouse deep, unexpected attachments.

The challenges of an emotional education are:

To extend awareness of oneself in relation to others.

To manage the inevitable suffering within relationships, so that thresholders can put boundaries around it and prevent it from taking over their lives.

To take a stand and protect one's own interests in a close relationship.

To forgive oneself for making mistakes—as well as to face up to the consequences of mistakes and find solutions to the problems that may arise.

Pondering the Shapes of Desire (Vera)

Learning about sex through one's own experience, learning what the fuss is all about, is a crucial step in growing up.[1] It is often assumed that, as adolescence ends, young people will already have some sexual experience. In my sample the majority had—but a significant forty percent had not.[2] As I was to learn, however, the question of whether or not one had engaged in sexual intercourse played a minor role in the plethora of half-formed questions surrounding the emotional aspects of sex education. Thresholders are eager to talk about the ambiguity of desire, the shape of vulnerability, and the limits of self-control.

The myth that children grow up fast is nowhere more entrenched than in ideas about what they know and do not know about sex. Adults frequently remark that young people are all too familiar with sex, that it is a taken-for-granted part of their daily lives, and that by the time they are in college, sex is nothing special. At first glance, Vera exemplifies a young person's know-all-about-it boredom. A closer look, however, shows surprisingly little understanding for her age.

Now twenty and in the middle of her sophomore year, she describes the sex she has as "okay." "In high school I always worried about it," she explains. "I worried about what would happen to our relationship if I did, and what would happen if I didn't. And I'd go wild if I heard it got around—you know, whether I did or didn't. Here it's just a matter of a guy being turned on and wanting it and you wondering whether this is a definite 'no.' As long as you're careful, it's no big deal."

Is this evidence of a been-there-done-that attitude? As Vera continues, it is clear she is expressing neither acceptance nor boredom but a numbness bred of ambivalence. Vera does not know when she is attracted to someone or whether she simply likes him as a friend. She describes a weekend with a group of friends, all of whom she liked. When one young man said he wanted to have sex with her, she was initially confused. In her view, there was nothing special between them; he was simply one of a group of friends. But since she "sort of liked him," she thought there was no reason to decline. At first she focused with pleasure on the fact that he had chosen her. Then, she said, she felt "stupid, because he just wanted sex that night."

Many young women are unable to mark the difference between their own desire, on the one hand, and a response to someone's desire for them, on the other. Their sexual education, thus far, tends to be about safety and resistance—rather than naming and assessing their own feelings. They know that condoms are necessary, and they know they have a right to refuse. But beyond that, there is often very little help we give them in interpreting their experiences and using those interpretations to gain better control over their interactions.

Vera is flattered to be desired, but she has very little to say about her own sexual curiosity, exploration, and pleasure. Technically, she is sexually active, but neither active nor sexual in her own feelings. She knows the young men she hangs out with will want to sleep with her and sees that as part of the deal.

This attitude sends chills down the spine. Why doesn't she

know better, any parent or teacher would demand? Is there anything that can be done to drive this lesson home? Researchers are now finding that this attitude is common. It seems to be a result of common sex-education messages.[3] She has been taught to take responsibility for her health and to avoid pregnancy. She knows not to get so drunk that she does not bother to insist her partner wears a condom—as some of her friends do. What she does not know is the importance of pleasure or of a satisfying mutuality.

Sexual pleasure is one aspect of self-knowledge and personal power. While parents and teachers emphasize restraint in the teen years, the threshold years surely offer opportunity for a broader discussion of feelings. This is a time when young people want to process their experience and put it in a wider human context: "Which of my experiences are shared by others and which are unique to me?" they ask. "How do I handle my sexual feelings when they seem at odds with my emotional bond to someone?" they wonder.

In engaging in new discussions with our young adult sons and daughters, we should stand back to assess how we usually engage in sex talk with them. Teenage and thresholder sex is usually presented as full of impulse and passion, recklessly driven by hormones. The assumption that young people are in danger of being swept away by passion leads to a bias in what they are taught. They are warned to be safe and careful and restrained. They are told of their right to say no but not how to identify the desire to say yes.[4]

Thresholders with a typical sexual education are often unable to interpret their feelings.[5] As a result, their problems seem either enormous or trivial. Even when they are trying to reflect on their experiences, they speak in the negative terms they are accustomed to hearing when thinking about sexuality. Vera knows she has a lot to learn but does not have anyone to help her learn. "Sure, I'm more mature about sex. I don't giggle about it with my girlfriends like I used to. All those conversations we used to have now seem silly. But I can't say I feel happy with it or how it works out most of the time."

We talk about how sexual feelings are often confusing. I tell her that adults are confused, too, about what they feel and for whom. She seems relieved and is silent while she takes in this news. It is easier for her to reflect on her own feelings when she is not brow-beaten by the expectation that mature adults glide easily through their own sexuality. When I ask what are some of her feelings associated with sex, the first thing she says is, "It makes me feel sick." We are both shocked and listen to the silence. After a moment, she adds: "I mean, I sometimes feel sick. Sometimes I look at this guy I'm seeing and think: How could I ever make love with him? I feel him in me, and I want to puke. But at the time I think it's no big deal, so it seems silly to make a fuss."

SEXUAL CONTRADICTIONS

As we engage with thresholders in new conversations, it is helpful to remember that young people's sexual stories are tales of regret and disappointment as often as they are tales of pleasure. The sorrows of young love are part of a neverending story, but today's thresholders experience them within a culture that is itself confused. Their environments are awash with contradictory messages about sex.

Within the past thirty years, sex has become an expected part of young people's lives. A college that set down dorm rules governing visits by members of the opposite sex would now seem out-of-date and out of touch. At the same time, however, sex is portrayed as fraught with danger. Rape, AIDS, and pregnancy advisory centers are advertised in every library and restroom, where machines dispensing multi-colored condoms are constantly filled. Toilet stalls in women's restrooms carry graffiti naming two-timing guys or jocks who trick you into bed.

Sexual messages are wrapped with both sophistication and caution. Sex is accepted as no big thing, yet thresholders need constant warnings that it exposes them to attack and disease. Young women are encouraged to feel powerful but also are warned that rape is common. They are expected to be sexual, but warned to say "no." They see films portraying sexual ecstasies, yet they exchange stories in which sex is "no big deal."

Young men are expected to have strong sexual desires, yet are condemned for them. Their social culture is more informal than ever, yet their behavior is policed by accusations of harassment and assault. Young men and women expect to be equal, yet they often feel hostile and wary toward one another. Thresholders' first adult experiences of desire and need occur in a climate that is both political and personal and highly confused on each front. It is not surprising, then, that their sexual feelings are charged with ambivalence.

SEXUAL AMBIVALENCE IN CONTEXT

The ambivalence Vera feels is shared by many young people. Until they know whom they really want as a lover, how often they want to make love, how to achieve and offer pleasure, young people will vacillate between desire and revulsion.

This ambivalence also occurs within close romantic relationships. Love does not, after all, solve all problems. At twenty-one, with a long-term boyfriend she deeply loves, Fran says, "Spending the night with my boyfriend can put me in a foul mood. He's all relaxed and loving, but there's something inside me wanting to kick and spit. I hate—you know, it's so hard to talk about this, because people think: 'Oh, yeah, she's frigid. That's her problem,' but that's not it. Even when there's pleasure, part of me can hate it. What can be pleasant one moment, can scratch me up the next. And this messes up everything with my boyfriend. I want to get away from him, just be on my own. Being on my own is bliss."

For Fran's roommate, Lara, however, there is a strong link between love and desire. "My mom was great and really helped me through adolescence. She used to say that sexual feelings are your body's way of saying: I love you." This positive message can also lead to confusion. What does it mean when her boyfriend does not respond to her desire to make love? "He sometimes isn't interested. He wants to go out, or talk to his friends, and then we fight because I want to make love, and I feel worthless because he doesn't."

Young people have no measure of normal desire. On the one hand, it is all around them, in the films and TV shows they see and the magazines they read. On the other hand, they are taught that desire should be controlled. They are at an age when it is normal for them to have strong sexual desires. But at the same time they are at an age when they are persuaded to play down the importance of sexuality. Lara fears her desire might become uncontrollable: She might turn into someone who wants sex all the time. Sometimes she can think of nothing else. "I get into this weird mind set where I think sex is the most important thing and I worry I'm not doing it enough. Then there are times when I make myself sick, and feel like a blob, because I just want to fuck and fuck."

These young women are trying to read the mysterious meanings written in their desires. They are working to get the measure of their needs and are worried, in their very different ways, about issues of sexual closeness and personal boundaries. Vera asks: "If I sometimes feel sexually repelled by a man, does it mean I don't like him?" and "How attracted do I have to be to someone to want to sleep with him?" Fran wonders: "How can I love someone and want a continuing relationship with him, but so easily have enough of him sexually and so often find solitude so pleasurable?" Lara asks: "If someone doesn't want to make love with me, does that mean he doesn't love me? Do I want sex too much?" Other young people face even more complex questions. Annie, at twenty-two, reframes her sexuality as she identifies herself as a lesbian. While on the one hand she is exhilarated by naming the feelings she has experienced as both immutable and unthinkable, she now faces a host of new questions: "Does my new recognition of my sexuality change my identity?" and "How does it affect my friendships with girls I like but don't desire?"

Even when young people have the courage to speak these difficult questions, discussion is problematic. When Fran tries to discuss her concern with her boyfriend, he is too hurt to talk. "I thought that if I was honest we would be okay. So I tried to tell him how I feel. It was scary. His face froze, and his skin went clammy. I could feel his heart beating hard. He didn't want to talk about this." When Lara broaches the subject with her mother, she looks worried and suggests therapy. Vera snorts when I ask whether she has tried to talk about this with anyone else: "I can't say these things to my mom, and my friends just shrug it off. It's like: what else is new?" Annie opens a conversation with her mother, who is calm, but dismissive: "It's probably just a phase."

I see Vera again during her senior year. We speak about a number of things—her plans for the coming year, her assessment of what she has learned in college, and the travels she wants to take before she has "to work forever in a job." When I ask about her love life, she shrugs. "Guys come and go. You have to be tough, and not give them more than you want, and get rid of them when you want. That's how I handle things, anyway. I'd love to know how other people do. It's not that I don't talk about it to other girls—it's just that, even with my close friends, you're either dealing with all these stupid judgments about what sex should be or you just talk about how we expect too much." She continues to think of sex in terms of "not being put off by the guys I have sex with"—not in terms of pleasure and connection.

One year on, Fran is not sure about her future with her boyfriend, though they are still deeply attached. "Sex has been a real problem. He takes it personally that I'm not crazy about making love, and the whole thing gets so tiresome. I feel guilty, so then we make love when he wants to, and then I get irritable because it's real tacky having sex when you don't want it." I ask what she thinks would make this problem easier. She thinks for a moment, "I'd really love to know how many other people felt like I did. It would be great to hear how other people have handled this. It can't be all that uncommon—I mean, is it?"

Over time, these young women may integrate their own desires into their lives. A quicker route from experience to education would involve parents' awareness of what their children might be feeling and what problems these feelings might pose.

Modern generations of parents pride themselves on being open with their daughters and sons, but sex talk is still difficult. With sex, facts are not enough. We can encourage them to talk about feelings and confusion. We can emphasize diversity rather than consensus, so that individual differences are expected and explored. Here are starting points for posing conversations and reflection:

1. Observe the sexual imagery and information so widely avail-

able from television, advertising, music, and movies. Consider the differences between your expectations and your reality. Ask yourself what you value most in your own experiences, and what disappoints you.

2. Can you distinguish between your own and others' needs? Can you reflect on the selfish-selfless divide—whereby someone is considered selfish if she focuses on her own needs. Remember, if other people's needs matter, then so do yours. But only you can voice your needs.

3. Do you need distance and space even in a close relationship? If you know this, then it is easier to negotiate your needs.

4. Practice saying what you want and don't want. Above all, notice what you want and don't want.

Thresholders' Broken Hearts (Ric)

When people speak about losing their first love and reflect on its unforgettable pain, they are in all probability not really talking about the first emotion they called love, but their first love that occurred in the threshold years. For it is at this phase that they are able to love in ways that promise lifelong commitment. It is at this phase they are able to see themselves as the adults they will become and envision their futures as shaped by adult attachments. Hence, romantic breakups during this phase of life can deliver a harsh blow.

The stereotype of young love is of casual coupling and uncoupling; but listen to thresholders talk about relationships, and you know they think it is a serious subject. Often this generation of young people is cynical about marriage: "These days, marriage doesn't mean a thing. Why bother with it?" they ask.[6] At the same time, they have high ideals for personal relationships—for trust and openness, for support and affection. Aware that divorce is common and that separations are likely to be acrimonious, young people nonetheless have high hopes for their own romantic attachments. Uneasy about being either a man or a woman in a culture in which battlelines between the sexes are constantly drawn and redrawn, each thresholder hopes that she and he together will work it out. But ideals that survive contradiction are ideals that are both most fragile and most highly valued. Romantic upsets, therefore, can shatter optimism about the entire future.

Ric is twenty-one when I first speak with him. When he speaks about his future, there are few certainties. He does not know what career he wants to pursue or where he wants to live, but he knows he wants to marry Anita, whom he started going out with in high school. Many thresholders, seeing their own romantic bonds take shape, reinterpret their parents' relationships. Critical and reflective, they use their parents' experience to distinguish and define their own. As Ric speaks about his future with Anita, he begins criticizing his mother's past: "If I think about my childhood I think about a bunch of weddings. Her first was when I was three. I don't remember much about it but there's this picture of me holding her hand, and she's all in white, and for some reason I'm dressed all in blue, and I'm squinting into the sun and holding flowers. Then that fell apart and she married Jeri, and that wedding was in Tahoe in the spring on top of a mountain. I really liked Jeri, but one day it was all over and I never saw him again. When I heard about her next marriage I couldn't be bothered and we had a big fight, and I ended up not going, and she took it really hard. I felt bad, and tried to make things up, but I was glad to be away at college when this stepfather left."

Young men and women often criticize their parents: how they treated their partners, what they failed to do, how they made unsuitable choices and took foolish risks. Ric tells me how utterly different his own life will be, how he will avoid every pitfall. He will be faithful, because nothing threatens a marriage more than infidelity. He will not get bored, because boredom threatens a partnership. He likes the daily domestic routines that his mother found stifling. "I like complaining about my feet being cold and her telling me to wear layers of socks. And I like doing stuff for her, little things, like getting the books she needs here because the bookstores here are so much better than at home."

He is proud of his ability to keep the relationship going. Anita attends a local community college and lives with her mother. Ric's college is three hundred and fifty miles away. Anita comes up when she can. Ric goes home one weekend a month. His money goes on travel and phone calls.

As he speaks about his commitment to Anita, his self-respect is visible. He sees himself as the mature one and his mother as "silly." He describes her optimism about each marriage and her determination to swear off all men when a marriage ends. His mother, Zara, is more objective about Ric's chances. She says: "I don't think Anita is right for him, but I'd bite my tongue out before I said anything to him. He'll just come back with a ton of reminders about my own mistakes."

It is ironic that so many parents think a son's or daughter's romantic partnership signals a move away from the parent. Instead, this is when our children are aware of a special psychological intimacy. They see a parent's relational history as their own private map and ponder over what they want to replicate in a parent's emotional world and what they want to avoid.

The breakup that occurs at the end of the following summer is, for Ric, a setback on all fronts. When a young person is dealt such a blow, it fills every corner of his mind. In later adulthood, he will begin to have some control in setting pain to one side. He will be able to get on with at least some of the rest of his life. At this stage, however, all his mental energy goes into processing the pain—understanding what happened and why. "I knew something was going on last time I was home. We went to see a film with some other guys and she just talked to her girlfriends the whole time and ignored me and I felt I was tagging along, and when I said something she looked at me like: 'Are you still here? Why are you bothering me?'"

Breakups are most likely to occur at key turning points of the school year—at the beginning of the school year or during winter and summer holidays. This was no exception. "I thought we'd sorted things out during the summer. We were both working, but it was so much easier seeing her, and I thought things were going to be okay. Then she comes in when I'm packing to go back and tells me it's over."

Ric is in a state of shock. He packs, kisses his mother goodbye, and catches a train. All the while he goes through these practical motions, he thinks, "I can't believe this is happening." His chest hurts when he breathes. As soon as he enters the dorm he has to run outside to get fresh air. But the sense of being trapped and breathless follows him. He cannot find anything or anyone to comfort him: "I felt so lonely these past few months I thought I'd die. No one here understands. I try to talk to my roommate, but he doesn't understand. He thinks the college girls are dangerous. He treats them like shit because he knows they'll make hamburger meat of him. He'll bring a girl up here and sleep with her and then tell her to get out, he's ready for a shower. I wouldn't be like that—not in a million years. There's no point talking to him. Even Connie, who's one of my best friends here, doesn't understand. She talks about it being for the best and says I'll get over it, and it's only because Anita's my first love that I'm so upset. I can't think straight anymore. I can't believe this's happened—but I feel it every minute."

NEW ATTACHMENTS AND NEW GRIEFS

The grief young people experience when a relationship ends is very much like the grief a person feels when someone close to him dies.[7] Without adequate support, the end of romantic attachments can spell danger, especially for young men. As one counselor remarked: "The boys fall apart when they break up with a girlfriend. They can't study. They start to drink. If they come to me with problems about their work or their parents, I can help them. But when they come saying they've just broken up with a girlfriend, I see a red flag."

As young men become genuinely romantically attached, new vulnerabilities are exposed. Though women are often said to have a tendency toward overdependence in love, men's dependence is seldom addressed. The vulnerability that young men in love experience stems, paradoxically, from the firm self-boundaries they developed in early childhood. As infants, they are bonded to the mother, and feel almost blended with her.[8] In early childhood, as they become aware of how different are boys and girls, men and women, they see how distinct they are from their mother. This means that at a time when their gender identity is forming, and when they are still very dependent on their mother, they face a terrible dilemma: in keeping that close identification with their mother, they put their gender identity at risk; in preserving their very separate identity, their sense of being one with the mother is at risk. It is common for these issues to remain with them well into adulthood: Intimacy can feel dangerous because it can threaten their sense of self.

Boys' and men's tendency to preserve emotional independence is tied not simply to cultural norms but to their psychological development. In merging with another person—especially with a woman—their sense of self changes and often feels threatened. When they accept this change, they literally give part of the self over to the person they love. This is likely to occur at the time they make their first adult commitment (not necessarily their first sexual attachment). Hence, young men rather than teenage boys are most at risk from heartbreak. Ric describes this terrifying vulnerability when he tells me how he felt when Anita broke up with him:

> She was going on and on about how we didn't have fun anymore, and how I took her for granted. She was saying things that didn't make any sense at all. I couldn't say anything. I watched her, and every time she moved it was like something inside me was moving and hurting, and I just stared at her and she said, 'See, you don't even care.' And then she started crying, and I felt dead inside. I think I said something and tried to get through to her, but I was only thinking about what someone's supposed to do in this situation. I didn't feel anything except fear and I couldn't explain it to her, so I just sat there and let her go.

Ric continues to feel "dead inside" but, like many young men, does not seek help. "This is just something I have to get through," he tells me. "I can't go crying to mother, you know. I'm twenty-two. A man. You swim, or you sink."

Over and over again I hear this from young men: They have to be able to handle things themselves. I let him make his point but try to argue that we all need comfort and understanding, and that this need is not a weakness. He listens and reflects for a moment, then shakes his head. "This is something I have to get through myself." His mother takes a similar line: "My heart goes out to him, but he doesn't want my help." Four weeks later, she phones to tell me Ric has left school, and neither his roommate nor his friend Connie knows where he is. His teachers say that he is behind in his work, that deadlines for papers have been missed, and that he failed one midterm exam and did not show up for another. He escaped by "drinking to dark" and was hospitalized for several days with alcohol poisoning. "This is the worst of any of his insults," Zara says. "He was this unhappy, and he didn't come to me."

Ric later reflects: "I couldn't concentrate in class. I couldn't study. Sometimes I thought people could see what a mess I was in. Sometimes I thought it was so weird that no one did see it. When I tried to tell my mom I had to go out of the dorm to find another telephone because I didn't want anyone to hear me. But I also thought they already knew."

Young men trying to manage their pain face a double jeopardy. As one college counselor said, "They heartily believe they have to manage things themselves. They still have these macho ideals. The more they hurt, the more stubborn they are about toughing it out alone. Losing a girlfriend is humiliating, and going to the counseling service just seems to make it worse, in their eyes. I wish there were some way to get through to them, before it's too late."[9]

Common beliefs about the importance of being independent are particularly harmful to thresholders as they try (all too often unsuccessfully) to manage the inevitable ups and downs of their changing relational worlds. The usually sensible Ric prefers to blot his pain with (nearly) lethal amounts of alcohol than admit his need for help. His mother, Zara, says that when he refuses to turn to her for help, he is giving her the worst insult ever—yet she believes that "he doesn't want her help," and so she leaves him alone.

When thresholders are unable to manage pain, they often panic. They become impulsive, doing anything to relieve their pain. Ric needs to develop skills in managing pain. Thresholders can develop these skills by practicing the following:

1. Keep the loss in perspective.

This involves being able to reflect on the loss and see it shift in importance over the course of his life. He could imagine himself as an old man. What would he like to have done by then? He could imagine himself in midlife. What daily routines would give him pleasure?

The point of these exercises is to extend his focus away from the here and now.

2. Name the pain.

Thresholders who are overwhelmed by their feelings often lack self-awareness. It is the inability to confront those feelings that gives them their larger-than-life size. Ric should be able to accept what's happening. He should be able to say to himself, "Yes, I've lost this precious thing, and this is very hard for me." He could write about his feelings or talk to a friend. Confronting his feelings will not make them go away, but it will lower their magnification.

3. Seek positive distractions.

Thresholders are often unable to manage their feelings positively. Instead, they use alcohol or drugs. Exercise is a good way of working off tension and releasing hormones that make one feel better. Joining a group activity can also ease that acute unhappiness at breaking up with someone. The important thing is to identify some things that still provide pleasure.

4. Maintain motivation.

Strong negative feelings often decrease motivation. Thresholders commonly complain of being unable to concentrate when they are unhappy. Ric needs to be able to work and play in spite of it. This would keep him in the flow of life, and also distract from the intensity of the disappointment. On the work side, he could break down each task into various parts, and tackle one part at a time. He will probably find that he can do them as well as when he was not so unhappy. He should then allow himself to feel pleasure at whatever he has achieved.

On the fun side, he could rigorously set aside "non-work time" in which he does something he normally enjoys doing (even if it does not appeal to him at the moment).

5. Finally, thresholders gripped by bereavement need a forgiving environment—one that accepts there will be tripping points along the way to adulthood.

Six months later, Ric is back at school, planning to use the summer to make up the time lost. He will get some credits at a local college, which will be accepted toward a degree. "I won't be graduating with the rest of my class and that's a real downer, but on the whole things are much better." He does not want to talk in any detail about his depression. "It's so spooky, when I think back on how I was thinking. Anita didn't want me, so I was shit, and everything that happened, every little thing, was just further proof of what a shit I was." When I asked him what has helped him through, he says, "I guess it was Connie, at first, but then Mom was just so great about it. But the school was great, too, because they could've kicked me out. But they're letting me transfer these credits, so I can graduate—and here I am."

With a network of concerned friends, parents, and college policies, even those thresholders who hit rock bottom will come through.

Friendship as a Lifeline during the Threshold Years (Tanya)
Teenagers undergo tough lessons in friendships. They learn what it feels like to be in the inner circle of a group and what it feels like to be cast out. They practice speaking their minds, and they find that sincerity sometimes binds them to a friend and sometimes rips a friendship to shreds. Emerging from high school, young people enter the threshold years with the

assumption that, in terms of friendships, things can only get easier.

And they often do get easier. Friends formed at the entrance to adulthood can provide irreplaceable channels of creative communication and self-awareness. Friends can help with the self-questioning, self-doubt, and self-discovery that are essential to further development. Friends inspire one another, providing a wealth of future possibilities.

But in the threshold years, friendship also presents new dangers. The rosy glow so many people have of their last year in high school may occur because of the rough times that come immediately after. Studies of friendships in the college years[10] show a common regression back to a time when we cannot distinguish ourselves from others—and do not want to. The signs of these regressive attachments are:

1. Clinging
Some thresholders fear that they will be lost if they lose a friend. They feel they lack the skills to make friends and must cling to the one they have.

2. Placation
Rather than stand up for themselves or say what they think, some thresholders will do anything at all to preserve a friendship and avoid an argument. "I'll do whatever you want" or "Whatever you say," is the operating principle here.

3. Blending
All too often, instead of honing their identities in friendships, young people blend with a friend who seems more sure of what she or he is doing. Thresholders speak of "becoming like" their friends and needing a confident friend in order to make sure they are doing the right thing.

Many thresholders see themselves as grown up, but the transition to college awakens old fears and vulnerabilities. As Tanya begins her college life, she wonders whether she can really, as an independent person, attract friends. Combined with new academic pressures, Tanya feels "unwanted and out of place and I really wonder whether I'm going to make the grade." She spends the evening in her room, and as her roommate studies, she makes lists of people she'd like to invite to a party. There is a mix of fantasy names (film stars, novelists) and real people (students and teachers). She imagines how everyone will come and greet her when they arrive. She imagines what she'll wear and how people will compliment her. She hates her own childishness and resents being ambushed by pain at things that should have been long forgotten: "I might as well be fourteen again, and hearing about a party I'm not invited to."

In this state of regression, thresholders cling to the first person who offers friendship. Dependencies that would have been spurned in high school now seem inevitable. When Tanya meets Viv and "they hit it off, like I've known her all my life," she forgets all she learned in high school about standing up for herself. Terrified of returning to her former friendless state, Tanya hangs on for dear life. She tries to "keep things sweet" between them. "We agree about everything," she explains. When I visit her again, six months later, she is now Viv's roommate. Two desks are set side by side against the wall. Dividing them is a row of candy—jelly beans, licorice sticks, and Gummi bears. The pens and paper on each side of the desk are mirror images of one another. Even the books are piled the same way on each desk.

I ask Tanya about her friends. "But you remember Viv?" she asks, shocked by my lack of understanding. She says they are still best friends and they always agree. "I never like to argue," she tells me. "If I say something and she disagrees, I panic. She can get real nasty sometimes, and I don't want that. I don't know what I'd do if she decided she didn't like me. I'd hate being alone again."

But friendship is not only about agreement—thinking the same and being the same. It is also about passionate difference and clashing moods, and so becomes a laboratory for practicing being in relationships. In this arena, skills are tested that will be used later with partners and other friends. One of the hardest things in any relationship is learning how to disagree, and how to feel securely liked, when we are aware of being "not like"—that is, being different.

This constructive conflict can be learned in young people's friendships—through the intense discussions and late night musings. Friendships during these years allow us to explore our differences, to discover ideas and attitudes and talents very different from those of our friends. "I don't agree!" can be a wonderful revelation, the conclusion drawn through a vital exchange of ideas. When thresholders are so afraid of being alone that they dare not disagree, they lose out on these mental exercises and explorations—and lose out on authenticity. How can Tanya develop her own ways of thinking when thinking on her own threatens her with loss? How can Viv develop her own ways of thinking when she speaks to such a compliant and frightened audience? Together the girls form an *isolation à deux*, protecting one another from loneliness but preventing each other from further developing.

Tanya insists that her friend and roommate Viv is now her "surrogate family. I look after her, and do stuff for her. You have to give more to your friends than you did in high school." "Doing stuff" for friends can indeed give thresholders a sense of competence and play a part in growing up. For Tanya, however, care involves servicing Viv to keep her in a good mood, but Viv wants more "space." She suggests that she and Tanya not go to breakfast together every day. Tanya shrugs: "Whatever." Inwardly she is crushed.

Tanya's fear of losing her friend dominates her thoughts. Even during final exams, when I next see her, she speaks of Viv and leaving Viv rather than of the term paper she has already had to get an extension on, or the English exam she's taking tomorrow. Instead, she tells me she is worried about leaving: "I'm afraid that everything I've built up here—socially—will fizzle out during the summer. I can't stand the thought of coming back in the fall and being just where I was last fall—no friends, really out of it. She said something about finding a new roommate, like maybe we should have a change, and I just panicked. It's okay. We're all settled to be roommates next year. But that idea . . . I can't tell you how I felt. Just *stung*. If we grow apart this summer, I won't be able to face the year."

In the emotional hothouse of the dorm, these problems are rampant. Her words remind me of a terrible tragedy at Harvard in 1996, when the threat of losing a friend proved too great for sanity to bear. During the tense summer exam session, Sinedu Tadesse, a third-year student from Addis Abbaba, woke up, as usual, at 8 A.M., then took a hunting knife and repeatedly stabbed her roommate, Trang Phuong Ho. Thao, an overnight guest who was Trang's true "best friend," tried to stop Sinedu, but was also attacked. After she murdered the friend who, in her eyes, was abandoning her, Sinedu hanged herself. Sinedu wrote in her high-school yearbook that "friendship is one of life's most precious treasures." She thought she had a kindred spirit and exclusive other in Trang. When Trang decided not to room with her the following year, Sinedu felt bereft of the one person who had once liked her and been willing to be with her. Without the protection of this close friendship, her world became an impossible place.

No longer whole, no longer a good, acceptable self, she enacted the final despair by committing murder, and then suicide."

Early adulthood can be a time during which strong, good friendships are formed, but dependencies may warp these connections. Two lonely people may cling to one another, each testing the other for signs of greater need. Two depressed people can cling together and confirm their bleak visions. As the closeness becomes claustrophobic, one becomes "mean," taunting the other with her or his dependence, wanting to wriggle away from it and yet caught by the fear, "Who else will be my friend?" And the one who appears most needy, whose fear of loneliness is closest to the surface of consciousness, panics at any sign of distance.

It takes years of seeing oneself fall into these patterns to identify them. At the start of adulthood, we do not have the advantage of looking-back time. To promote awareness, thresholders can refer to (and parents can put to them) the following questions:

1. Do you want to be just like a friend?

Do you feel anxious when your friend expresses an opinion different from yours? Do you continue to have your say or argue your case—or are you driven by anxiety until you reach some consensus? Remember, in a friendship your own opinions should be welcomed, even when they differ from those of a friend.

2. Are you as important as your friend?

When you are planning where to go or what to do, are you able to have an equal say? In a real friendship each person is equally important. Are you able to ask for help, as well as offer it? Are you able to borrow clothes, as well as lend them? Can you suggest an "agenda" for an outing? If you are unsure, count the number of times you say, "I don't mind" or "It's up to you."

3. Can you complain effectively?

All friendships have their ups and downs. If a friend offends you, you should be able to discuss this.

4. Can you refuse a friend's requests?

If you feel unable to decline to do something your friend suggests or if you feel anxious when you want to decline a request, then there is no equality. Try sticking up for yourself and see what happens.

The other side to establishing respect within a friendship is having some confidence that you can make other friends. Thresholders already have basic skills in greeting and talking to people, but here are some reminders:

1. Don't be afraid to try to make a friend.

It is very unlikely that an invitation to chat will be totally rejected. But if it is, this is just one person, with her or his own concerns. Try again, and be patient. Most thresholders want more friends.

2. Approach individuals rather than a group.

It is much easier to start up a conversation with one other person than with a pair or a group, whose dynamics you may be interrupting.

3. Don't be too eager.

It is unsettling for someone to see that a casual conversation is becoming intense. Being desperate for company puts people off. Avoid being too insistent on setting up another meeting, and cue into signs that the other person wants to end the conversation. He or she should not have to say more than once, "Well, I have to go now" or look at a watch.

4. Track your ability to listen and to speak.

A good listener keeps the conversation going and makes someone want to return for more. When you speak your mind you will be far more interesting than if you parrot another's thoughts.

5. Monitor yourself.

When a friendship gets going, reflect on the questions listed above. Clinging to a friend can become a pattern—but self-awareness, particularly during the threshold phase, can break these patterns before they become ingrained habits.

Thresholders in Groups (Deborah)

Friendships formed during the threshold years are often those that last for life. Certainly they make a lifelong mark on the people who form them. They become substitute families. Friends drop in on one another, casual and unannounced, to talk, to hang out, to air their problems with work or lovers or families. They are companions and caretakers. They easily take on the role of the nagging parent and careless child: "You can't go out like that. It's cold. Where's your coat?" or "Don't be late. Remember we have to review after supper." In their banter two young men echo the parent/child relationship but are just friends looking out for one another. But sometimes thresholders go overboard in their efforts for peers to replace their families.

At twenty, Deborah felt she was saved, socially and spiritually. Sitting alone one evening in the cafeteria, a young woman took a seat across from her. "You look like the saddest person in the room." Deborah felt this young woman looked into her soul, and understood. She went to a meeting with her and, while at first repelled by the blandness of the people there, gradually found the social side of the group so satisfying that she felt bonded to them. "They would always hug me when we met, and tell me I looked great, and they made me believe I was enormously valuable. I finally felt at home. Here were people who were my brothers and sisters, who accepted me and thought I was special."

The retreat to a cult is an extreme form of a common pattern in the threshold years. Young people anticipate meeting a wide variety of people. Lonely and needy, however, they rush to form cosy groups. Sororities and fraternities are just traditional forms of what thresholders seek—a friendship system that is like a family. But since it is not a family, there are cruel rituals and rites for belonging that are supposed to forge a "blood bond." Young men accept life-threatening challenges as they are rushed by fraternities. Young women become clones of other girls in order to be liked by them.

Thresholders can, with apparent spontaneity, form remarkably homogenous cultures. When Deborah walks into her business management class, she thinks with surprise, "I didn't know there was a uniform." She mistakes the fitted tops and jeans for a dictated dress code. "I sat down in my blouse and slacks and felt awful. Everything my mom told me about this being a great opportunity to meet people struck me as the stupidest thing anyone ever said. I spent the entire class fuming at my mom for not knowing anything."

Deborah says that everyone she knows belongs to some kind of group. "The segregation here is unbelievable. We never would get away with this in high school—tables for black kids, tables for white kids. You can talk civilly to different people, but no way will they be your friend. And then there are the jocks and the rich frat guys. This is like some unfriendly suburban community. My group is the most democratic around."

But once inside the group, the cult leader casts a shadow over Deborah's happiness. "At first I had all these fantasies about him, how he would single me out and love me and have sex with me. At first, even when he was abrupt and angry, I thought he was terrific. But then I saw how cruel he really was, that made everything seem different. How could what these other guys offered me be real, if he wasn't for real? I realized he was just using me, like he was using everyone else. I was so depressed I couldn't do anything. I couldn't get up in the morning. I couldn't go to classes. I felt trapped, but I was also afraid to leave."

Parents should cue into a son's or daughter's declaration that she has found "another family." What she is saying is that she still needs a family and needs constant reminders of her closeness to that family. Instinctively, this is how Deborah's parents responded. Her mother, Rennie, refuses to abide by a hands-off-she's-now-grown-up policy. She phones, writes, comes to see her—all against the community's rules, which decree that visits have to be cleared through a committee and phone calls can be taken only twice a week, at specified hours. Rennie also resists her daughter's argument to leave her alone, since she is now an adult. The hostility mounts between them ("She makes me want to scream," Deborah tells me. "I tear her letters to shreds.") but the connection between them is not broken.

A year later Deborah is now at a different college, closer to home, but she lives on campus. "My parents have taken everything so well. It hasn't been easy. Leaving my group was a hard hit for them, financially, because they had to pay the whole year's tuition. But without them, I couldn't have survived. Leaving my group was like losing a hundred boyfriends all at once." When I ask whether she suffers from loneliness now, she laughs. "I met this student from Thailand. He was in the kitchen, and it was so cute—he didn't know how to open a can or wash a plate. The other guys were moaning about it, and I just told them: 'Don't worry. I'll be his friend.' It's things like that keep me going. I guess I'll never be Miss Independent. It helps to know that."

Deborah remains someone who views attachment very much in family terms—in terms of routine care and day-to-day belonging. But as she becomes aware of this need, and her pattern for fulfilling this need, she can moderate it. She can also use her awareness to appreciate the potential strengths in the emotional patterns that once made her weak: now she can be a good and useful friend.

A New Phase of Crushes (Anna)

The threshold years are defined as the entry to adulthood. Young people are now often living, learning, and working among other adults, some of whom act as mentors to guide them. Mentors have an insider's knowledge and reveal that knowledge to specially selected novice adults. A mentor may be an employer or manager who sees that a new recruit has promise and is worthy of careful grooming for the next rung on the ladder. Sometimes a professor mentors a student who seems unusually eager and able. The mentor feels enabling and protective, and the person mentored feels grateful for being favored with attention.

Though these relationships have a professional basis, they also have deep emotional roots. These friendships, so distinctive of the threshold years, can spur young people forward, but they can also confuse and confound them. Instead of guiding them forward, thresholders who bond with a mentor figure can lose self-esteem. Some thresholders simply parrot or mimic the mentor. Or, if cast off by a mentor, they can become convinced that they are worthless. Some thresholders need help in breaking free from people who are (to them) larger-than-life figures.

These enabling friendships often have the flavor of a school-child's crush. A crush on a rock or movie star can steady someone who is beginning to look outside her family for models and idols. Crushes on mentors act as crutches on the long route to becoming "a real adult"—but often with mixed results. These crushes provide a temporary impetus toward knowledge, but they also skew reality—both for the student and teacher. Crushes are dangerous but also supportive and exciting. Anna explains why she focuses on her history professor: "When I get to talk to him, one on one, I have this direct line to knowledge. And when he smiles at me—'cause I think he does think I'm cute—I feel like I'm okay, even though there's so much I don't know. He can teach me so much, make me into a real thinker."

Anna has always been an extremely motivated student. She is used to shining intellectually for her parents and her high-school teachers. She wants to recreate a surrogate family, complete with figures of authority who both judge and love her.

"Her" professor is described by her friends as "distant" and "judgmental" and "scary." Anna, however, feels he has a "soft spot" for her. She rises to the challenge to tame him, to get his attention and approval, and exercise her own sexual power over his intellectual power. In spite of the clear and present dangers of such a liaison, the professor responds.

"He was the first professor to make me feel special. And then something just flipped inside. It was like God looking down and stroking my head. This school is so big. I was always on the edge of things. Suddenly there was someone who was really 'in' and who was singling me out. I was in seventh heaven. Finally someone was giving me the seal of approval." When he loses interest in her sexually, she feels she has "flunked out as both a woman and a student."

In psychoanalytic theory, "transference" is the tendency to put people in the position our parents once held for us. It is a response to people whose opinions of us have great authority—in particular therapists and teachers. Since our feelings about our parents include an especially powerful form of love, transference involves a potent mix of dependence and attachment. This is a common and complex part of any relationship we have to a teacher who really makes a difference.[12]

Thresholders who are most passionate about ideas are often those who are most keenly aware of their need for good teachers. For young people who value learning, but who are also unsure of their own ability to learn, a close relationship with a professor offers special access to an educated mind. Sexual attraction and education are easily mixed. For Anna, her crush is a way of fusing the hunger for learning with the need for guidance. During these years, young people learn quickly, and as they learn they become increasingly aware of their ignorance.

Unfortunately, mentoring can become entangled with sex and power. A young person's adoration can be so flattering that the mentor's judgment is clouded. Whereas we are familiar with the story of one White House intern and her powerful mentor, we are less well-acquainted with the thousands of young adults who confuse sexual intimacy with a mentor's real care.

Crushes on a teacher tend to be most common and most passionate at the peak rate of learning. Wanting sex with a mentor is a way of seeking his approval, feeling his desire for her, and also feeling her power over him. It is a pattern that can break the generations apart with accusations (of "sleeping one's way to the top") and counteraccusations (of sexual harassment). In any mentoring relationship, there is a precarious balance of power. A mentor, by definition, is in a stronger professional position. But mutual respect is important, so the basic health check for friendship also applies to mentoring relationships. Are your needs and wishes as important as those of your mentor? Can you complain effectively? Can you refuse your mentor's requests? A final question is: Is the relationship comfortable—or simply flattering?

GETTING THROUGH

No one can be protected from all sorrows. Everyone must make her or his own mistakes. Difficult, different, and lonely situations provide the background for adaptation and learning. What we can avoid, or correct, are patterns of false adaptation—patterns that emerge in situations that are too difficult to adapt to positively.

When we try to guide young people into adulthood, we can coach them to learn from their experiences. When it comes to their emotional educations, we can show them that learning is lifelong, that the notion of a stable emotional map as a mark of maturity is another myth to abolish. Being an adult means that we keep learning, and keep identifying new confusions, which we see our way through, one step at a time.

The emotional education of these years should involve a better self-understanding. Sometimes parents can help their daughters and sons along this route by becoming their emotional coach, which means helping them talk about their feelings and finding ways to manage those feelings. During the threshold years, young people tend to be highly reflective, far more so than they were as teenagers, and they can develop good skills in observing themselves and building a vocabulary for their feelings—which means far more than naming them. They need to understand when they are prone to feel the panic that springs from dependence, the adoration that stems both from a passion to learn more about the adult world, and a desire to have someone hold one's hand, just like a child's, as they step into it. While thresholders may be reluctant to talk about their private and developing emotions with parents, parents can guide them into self-reflection and self-management.

1. Insight

This involves the ability to identify patterns in our emotional life, learning how to make the best of those patterns—or avoid them.

2. Pain management

This involves dealing with pain—through exercise or relaxation or positive distraction—and avoiding self-medication, with alcohol, drugs, or shopping binges.

3. Monitor dependence

Managing one's vulnerability during this phase is extremely difficult, but the basic friendship health check list will help track one's ability to act on one's own behalf in a relationship.

4. Self-acceptance

Self-forgiveness and a sense of humor (being able to laugh at yourself) and seeing interpersonal needs as potential strengths will help thresholders through the rough patches in their emotional education.

THE PRESSURE OF GREAT EXPECTATIONS

MODERN youth is anything but carefree. Many of today's thresh-olders have been on the fast track since the age of three. Parents groom them for nursery school, then primary school, then high school. Throughout childhood and adolescence, they are put through their paces in dance, art, drama, gymnastics, sports. "We want her to be a well-rounded person." "We want him to develop a whole range of talents," parents say of four- and five-year-old children. They then eagerly assess a child's abilities, personality, and appearance. As adolescents, children are expected to rebel against parental pressure, but in fact teenagers tend to share their parents' educational ambitions for them.¹ Among their high-achieving peers, they discuss colleges, courses, careers.

I hear a familiar mantra when young people talk about pressure in high school: "This is when you're under the most pressure," they tell me. "These are the years that affect your entire future." "It's a really rough time. Going to work every day or being at col-lege will be a lot easier." Teenagers grit their teeth and get on with things—under the false assumption that in a few years they will be mature, independent people. When, instead, they experience new doubts or difficulties, they feel trapped: "This is my life forever," Christa reflects, "one hurdle after another." However casual they may seem to grown-ups, who are often taken in by their liveliness and bravado, thresholders worry constantly. They worry about "getting bad grades and letting down my parents, because they've put so much into my education." They worry about "messing up in this job, which I was really lucky to get." They worry about "losing all my friends and being alone." They worry about "being stuck with a really boring job and not doing anything with my life." They worry about being exposed as what they most fear they are: inadequate and inept. Some thresholders are then driven to prove their competence. As they shore up their successful persona and disguise their self-doubts, they fall prey to the impostor syndrome.[2] Here the operating principle is: "I can be so easily exposed as a fake, therefore I cannot afford to let any flaw show." Every failure to make the best grade, every career setback, every disappointment takes on an importance far out of proportion to its real significance.

Thresholders suffering from the pressure of high expectations seem to have the least cause for self-doubt. They are the ones voted by their high-school class "most likely to succeed." They gain top places, win essay prizes or internships with prestigious companies, and serve on student council. They are the daughters and sons every parent is proud to have. They are the students of whom their teachers have high expectations—of whom teachers say, "Oh, I'm not worried about *her*. She'll always do well."

We see such people among our colleagues, neighbors, friends—maybe even we see this syndrome in ourselves. It occurs as young people shift into overdrive to meet others' expectations. They avoid doing anything in which they don't shine. They forget the crucial skill of failing gracefully—which means admitting failure and trying again. Instead, they create smokescreens of anxious excuses for the most minor mistake: "I didn't bother trying.

It was all too stupid," they insist, while thinking, "I can't do this. *I'm* stupid."

This syndrome can carry on well into mature adulthood—but it takes hold at the cusp of adulthood and is a response to the terrifying self-doubts experienced in the threshold years. It is also a pattern that can be corrected more easily in the threshold years than at any other time. But correcting it requires a conscious reframing of self-expectations:

1. It involves developing realistic expectations about oneself.

2. It involves being able to measure one's abilities in a non-comparative way. This means taking a positive look at what one has achieved, even when one sees other people achieve "more."

3. It means reducing anxiety about standing out in a crowd. This involves reframing how one sees things and questioning what one values—but it also involves managing stress in competitive situations.

For thresholders and their parents, this reframing is most effective when together they revise their expectations.

In this chapter, two young people undergo a revision of their self-expectations, which is in no way shameful, but which fills them with shame: "I'm not who I thought I was" moves to "I'm a fraud" and then to "I'm worthless." We also see how self-awareness, self-acceptance, and good communication can transform these apparent setbacks into a growth spurt.

When Thresholders No Longer Feel Special (Christa)
The threshold years offer the opportunity for young people to discover and develop a working map of their particular abilities. This always involves some revision of previous views and, in some cases, the revision, which may seem minor to an outsider, feels brutal to the thresholder.

By the time Christa was ten years old, her mother Faye knew she was a star. "I had Christa when I was thirty-eight, and she was well worth waiting for. She was always one step ahead of what I expected in her development. Everything an especially talented kid was supposed to do, she did, but earlier." In school Christa "brought home nothing but As." She was popular, pretty, and the first to be chosen for a team by any captain—until she became captain herself. In high school she represented the school in important tennis tournaments and took the lead female role in the senior class play. No one was surprised when she got perfect SAT scores. "She's more like a friend than a teenage daughter," Faye explains. "She's never any trouble. She is just one good surprise after another. I saw her off to college without a care in the world. This kid is a pro."

At the end of her first semester in college, Christa barely passes in two courses and fails a third. She is put on academic warning. When she comes home during the break, she stays in the den, with the curtains closed, and sleeps on the couch or watches television. She is reserved, sullen, and irritable. She tells her mother that the professors are "stupid" and "don't care about the students." She finds the other students "unfriendly and snobbish."

The first year in college is sometimes burnout time. Having put so much effort into doing well, graduating at the top of the class, and doing all the things successful high-school seniors do—in sports, in drama, and in the social hierarchies of friendships—many young people come to college already out of breath.

It is common, furthermore, for thresholders not to perform at the rate and level of their high-school years. Adolescence is a time of rapid intellectual growth. This is a time during which knowledge is absorbed quickly and intellectual curiosity is easily awakened. But a different type of learning occurs at the transition to adulthood. Young people often need more time for reflection, more time to absorb their experiences and realize the growing and multiple aspects of themselves. As they reach this stage of slower, deeper development, they feel they are losing direction and losing confidence.

GOOD STUDENTS, LATE LEARNERS

Star performers in high school are in many ways to be envied. They gain their teachers' respect and affection. They bask in their parents' admiration. Their day-to-day lives, both at home and school, are easier. Parents tend to give more freedom to adolescent daughters and sons who are good students than to those who struggle with their grades. Parents have fewer quarrels with teenagers who make the honor roll. The A-student has a far better chance of negotiating curfews or an increase in allowance. Parents also tend to buy high flyers more things: Designer jackets and flat-screened computers and new cars are sometimes rewards for good grades. Doing well in school creates a halo effect, as though the ability to get As were proof of overall worth.

The rewards of being a good high-school student are high, but a strong track record also pumps up the pressure. Looking as though they are sailing through without effort, these star performers are under strain. Christa is seen by her mother, her high-school classmates, and her teachers as "blessed with talent and charm." Christa sees herself as "sometimes lucky, but mostly a fraud." During the years of earning grades and taking exams, she faced the same pressure her friends faced, but while Christa came through with the trophies, her friends learned to accept a mix of successes and failures. They learned to mess up and move on.

Christa knows perfection is fragile. "Things just clicked for me in high school, especially during the last two years. My SAT scores—they were a fluke—but they set up everything else. My senior year was an act I don't think I'll ever be able to repeat. Those weeks around graduation, I kept thinking, 'Life will never be as good as this again.' And I kept getting these waves of panic because time wasn't going to stand still. It didn't matter how much I wanted it to."

Young people who feel dissatisfied in some way with their high-school years and their teenage persona will be looking out for opportunities to grow and change, but the "perfect girl" is on the lookout to re-create her high-school world. She does not want to change, she wants to make sure things stay the same. When this cannot be done, she feels exposed as a failure.

In her freshman year at a prestigious East Coast college, Christa finds herself among a clutch of bright people and believes she has slipped in by mistake, that her entire run of success had been a mistake. She remarks ruefully: "Being accepted by this place is probably the worst thing that could have happened to me." Here, she does not rank among the best tennis players. Her old study habits leave her far behind many others. Studying for college courses seems totally different from her learning process in high school. It comes as a shock that she cannot complete the preparation for her classes, that her language teachers expect so much vocabulary mastered each week she does not see how anyone else manages it.

"I never though of myself as someone who got bad grades. But when I got my first C, I just thought—that's it, that's who I am, and I couldn't do anything about it. I felt that this C was the truth, and everything else was a sham. My mother wouldn't recognize her precious smart daughter if she saw her at school."

Maintaining one's spirit in the face of disappointment is an important skill. It is crucial at this stage of higher learning to tolerate failure and frustration. If a young person can respond to a poor grade with, "This is harder than I thought. Maybe I need help, and maybe I need to work at it," then the setback is likely to be temporary. When the response to a disappointing grade is, "I guess this is all I'm really worth," then she is not motivated to do better; she simply despairs.

THE DANGER OF SUCCESS-ONLY EXPERIENCES

A continuous roll of success in the adolescent years can leave the thresholder without some important skills: thresholders need to tolerate being less than the best, and often they need to tolerate being lower in the pecking order than they ever were before.

All too often parents and teachers believe that the best way to motivate a child is to expose her to a string of successes. The assumption behind this is that if a young person experiences success, then she or he will gain confidence and be further motivated. What is often ignored is that success-only experiences leave a question mark hovering over failure: What is it like to fail? How will people treat me if I fail? How do I pick myself up when I'm down? How do I live with myself if I'm not a star?

Christa's response to the discovery, "I'm not a whiz at this" is "This is shameful." She avoids situations in which she may be threatened with "looking bad," and starts missing classes and seminars when she is afraid she won't shine. As she hides her sense of inadequacy, she falls further and further behind. If she has to work hard to pull in Cs, and if a C grade is perceived as a failure, then she sees no point in trying.

She is angry with her parents and teachers for "making me think too much of myself. I look like I'm just lying here," she says, patting the couch in the den where she is now sitting, "but in my mind I'm kicking and pushing my complacent mother, and smashing her face in. She just doesn't understand. The idea that things aren't going to work out really wallops you. Some people say you find out who you really are at this age. I think I always knew I didn't want to find out. Now I just pretend to be someone, and I don't think I can keep it up."

A few weeks later, when I phone to check in with her, Christa has stopped pretending—and she has also stopped everything else. She failed to turn up for her chemistry final and declines to retake it. She declares that she wants to go home.

The girl who won prizes in high school becomes a first-year college dropout. While her mother sees her as "no longer herself," Christa believes that she has simply peeled away the facade to reveal her true self. She begins to reassess her "untroubled" adolescence: "I was the good girl by default. I did everything that was expected of me. I did things to get others' approval. I chose my college because of its prestige and not for any real reason. Even before I came here I knew, somehow I just knew, that I wouldn't belong and that somewhere along the line I'd made a huge mistake, and that here I would be found out. I tried to talk to my mom and got nowhere. Her eyes went wide and silly and she laughed."

In her journal, Sylvia Plath described just such a response and explains why successes can be so threatening. She catches sight of an internal critic, a "murderous self" whose "biggest weapon is and has been the image of myself as a perfect success: in writing, teaching and living. As soon as I sniff nonsuccess in the form of rejections, puzzled faces in class when I'm blurring a point, or a cold horror in personal relationships, I accuse myself of being a hypocrite, passing as better than I am, and being, at bottom, lousy."[3] The young woman who is thought to be "a perfect success" becomes, in her own eyes, an impostor when she makes the slightest slip.

Many thresholders share this double vision. They see themselves as others do—perhaps as "the perfect daughter" or "the girl who wins prizes." They also see themselves as someone very different—as stupid, awkward, talentless people hiding behind a perfect image. When any inadequacy is exposed, they fear that all their achievements will be stripped of meaning and they will be exposed as valueless. As Christa comes face to face with her hidden fears of inadequacy, her motivation crumbles:[4] "I keep going through these old photo albums. There I am, smiling away after a tennis match. And here I am after rehearsing the senior play. I really look the part of the happy kid, don't I? But I remember that match. I was so worried because I had a biology test the next day and I hadn't studied for it. And I'd just seen my best friend walk off the court with Alicia, who I really hate and who's always hated me, and it blew me away, thinking what they might be saying about me. And these pictures of the rehearsal? I noticed the flash of the camera and thought, 'Oh my God, my stomach is sticking out.' I wanted that part so badly. I knew I'd go berserk if it went to someone else. But it was agony being on stage—all those people looking at your hips and legs. Whatever they said afterward, I kept on wanting to ask, 'Was I really okay?' I also wanted to ask, 'Did I look fat?'"

Christa now believes that it was a false self that crumbled during her first year in college. In high school she had looked the part of a confident young woman but always felt anxious about her looks, her future, and her friends. When she got to college, the insecurities became unbearable. She suffered the shock of being ordinary. In her view, she now has "no personality, and there's nothing special about me at all." She watches her class-mates blossom, and every time they succeed, they prove to her that she is a failure. These are people who have what it takes, she thinks, and they are "nothing like me. I had no idea how to cope as an ordinary person," she tells me. "And no one let me see how ordinary I always was."

At twenty, Christa looks back on the transformations of the last year and a half. "I have a hundred different versions of what happened and why. Sometimes I think life was perfect then, and I should never have left that time in my life. Sometimes I think I knew even then that underneath everything was awful." She imag-ines scenes from what she calls her "old life," when she told her mother about the outcome of drama auditions, her placement in the graduating class, the results of her college applications. She imagines her mother's voice as she speaks on the phone, telling a friend about her daughter's latest triumph. " 'You can be anything you want to be,' " my mom always told me, and I believed her. I was so excited about leaving home, going to this snazzy college. When I got there, I was completely thrown. Everyone back home thinks I got here because I'm smart and that I was going to do well because I'm smart. They don't realize that people just thought I was smart because somehow I got that reputation. What hit me as soon as I got here is that I'm dumb. I don't belong here. I don't know how I got here. If I could just do okay, that would be fine—something to aim for. But everyone expects me to do more than okay, and I won't be able to swing that."

PARENTING PERFECTION

There is a growing difficulty among thresholders in dealing with the discovery that they are sometimes "just average." This diffi-

culty emerges from new trends in parenting and teaching practices. Many parents, aware of the importance self-esteem has on
a child's well-being, try everything to sustain a daughter's or son's
sense of being "good" and "valuable" and "wonderful." In the
name of protecting a child's self-esteem, some parents and teachers try to create an environment in which criticism is not allowed,
in which children are fed a steady diet of praise.

If a child is told that every picture she draws, every essay she
writes, every prank she plays is wonderful, she is discouraged from
developing standards of performance. She grows confused about
what doing well means. This makes her uneasy with reality testing,[5]
which means taking on board fair and objective assessments of her
work or talent. To thresholders who have been overprotected with
praise, criticism implies falling short, and falling short implies failure. The messages parents give their children, "You can do anything,"
and "Everything you do is wonderful" are well meant; but these messages deny children experience in dealing with critical appraisal.

Thresholders are like apprentices to adulthood. Quite simply,
they need to learn the ropes. This involves assessing their abilities
realistically. "What are my strengths and my weaknesses?" they ask.
"Why did I get a D on this paper and a B on another?" "Why did
my coworker get promoted before I did?" "Did I manage this problem well, or was I just lucky?" Answering these questions is crucial
to negotiating one's way in the adult world. An environment that
protects from all criticism stunts judgment and sends the message
that anything less than "wonderful" is unacceptable. While parents
and educators mean to encourage children by prohibiting criticism,
they may actually be diminishing their motivation.

Many parents have trouble themselves admitting that their
children have limitations.[6] This stems from a medley of good and
genuine feelings: the love that makes our sons and daughters
appear unique and splendid, the fear that any limitations stem

from our failings, the belief that we must never discourage a child from following a dream. But parent-love is double edged. It is supportive, but it is also demanding. A parent's idealization ("You are wonderful") creates expectations ("You should be wonderful"). Daughters and sons need a parent's idealization to be balanced by validation and focus. Thresholders need their parents to see what they are capable of doing and not doing. They need parents to admire them for who they are.

Children work hard to make adults understand their need for a realistic view of them. Even a seven-year-old will quarrel with an adult who overpraises her. So frustrating can constant praise be that a child will ridicule the loving adult who offers it. Hearing excessive praise for a routine drawing, a child will crumple it up rather than accept inappropriate praise. Adolescents have their own ploys for avoiding excessive praise. They respond to admiration with groans: "There go those stupid grown-ups again. They really don't know anything." Teenagers are as likely to seek acknowledgment for their worst qualities as their best ones. They hate being criticized or "judged," but they also hate being found adorable and wonderful. They fight for their right to have rough edges. They shake off a grown-up's simplistic idealization. Adolescence is often a time when parents are given tough lessons in accepting their imperfect children. Christa, however, is the model child. As a teenager, she was "more like a friend than a daughter." She did not rattle her mother's idealization. Now, both she and her mother have some hard work to do.

QUARRELING LESSONS

A smooth passage through adolescence often leaves parent and thresholder knowing one another less well than is good for either.

Faye's assumptions about who Christa is and what she wants have not been challenged. In her eyes, Christa is "the ideal kid." Christa's attempts to open a conversation about how far from ideal she feels are stalled. When she tries to articulate her fears that "everyone's going to be disappointed with me in college," her mother responds with amused disbelief. Instead of picking up her cue to start a discussion, Faye ends it.

Quarrels between teenager and parent are often attempts to shake a parent into new awareness of what the daughter or son thinks or feels. Usually these take place in the free-for-all of adolescent anger, when teenagers rage with unfettered self-righteousness: "You don't understand me. You don't know who I am," and then proceed to enlighten a parent about who they are. Typically, teenagers work hard to shape a parent's recognition and acknowledgment of their newly forming self. They offer a hundred reminders each day that the habitual ways of viewing them are not quite right: "I can go by myself." "I know how to do that." "You don't have to keep telling me, I know!"

When these unsettling intimacies do not occur in adolescence, the threshold stage is particularly stormy. Thresholders, unlike adolescents, are too proud to rage openly against their parents. And their parents, expecting that the more intense phase of parenting has drawn to a close, are often unprepared to offer the focus and support young adults need. When Christa protests, "I'm not who you think I am. I'm not your perfect girl and believe me, I don't always shine," Faye is at a loss to understand what her daughter needs. Like many parents who feel frustrated by a child's unhappiness, Faye, in a heated moment, cries accusingly: "After all I've done for you, after all the opportunities we've given you—you just throw it all away." And Christa strikes back with her accusation: "I hated that college. I spent twelve miserable months there and messed up my life, all because of you and your stupid dreams."

A stalemate between thresholder and parent freezes the chances of recovery. And the problem with a stalemate is that no one in the situation sees how to end it. "I can't see what she wants from me. Nothing I say is right," Faye tells me. "I start to talk, and she tells me I don't understand. She says I don't see her for what she is. She's so cranky when I'm around. I'm better off steering clear of her."

Yet it isn't distance Christa wants; it is a new response from her mother. Frustrated by her mother's apparent refusal to listen, Christa criticizes Faye for not hearing what she is trying to say. She criticizes Faye for not being aware of how she feels she has changed. Christa criticizes and complains to correct her mother's view.

Parents often respond to constant criticism of what they do and what they say as a form of rejection. But young people want to feel their parent's involvement. Quarrels are a way of soliciting a parent's help in being centered. They involve a plea for acknowledgment of feelings and goals. Complaint and criticism are forms of influence and correction. It would be an enormous help for parents to look on these quarrels in a new light, to take new pride in their battles, to feel more positive about the contributions they are making to a young person's development at this time. When Christa tells Faye, "I'm not who you think I am. You don't know me. You've never known me," Faye should not feel rejected by her daughter. Instead, Faye could extend her hand, sit beside her, and say, "Tell me who you are. I want to know who you are. I love you, whoever you are."

GROWING UP AMONG THE STARS

Questions such as "Who am I?" "Who can I be?" and "What can I do?" are synonymous with youth, but more and more young people are terrorized by them. Why is destructive self-doubt increasing?

We live in a culture that fosters particular brands of self-doubt and insecurity. One of the crucial questions we ask as we measure self-satisfaction is, "How am I doing relative to other people?" Our expectations are linked to the possibilities and probabilities we learn from watching other people. In the generations reaching adulthood before 1950, the family and the neighborhood provided the primary comparisons. How am I doing compared to my father or uncle when they were my age? How am I doing compared to my older sister? Am I managing to hold my own with my friends?

Today's generations continue to ask these questions. We still model our plans and goals on others, and we have a natural competitive streak that makes us want to (at least) keep up with others. But as we look around our immediate surroundings, we not only see "people like us" in our family and neighborhood and schools. We see a galaxy of celebrities, some known for their talent or brains, some for their beauty, some for their guts or stamina, some simply for their notoriety. To "be someone" in contemporary culture carries the implication of being known or widely recognized. Being someone has changed from being a respected member of a community to being a world celebrity.

A celebrity culture is one in which celebrities participate in our daily lives, right alongside the people with whom we work and play. The familiarity we feel with these strangers and our focus on people with whom we do not interact are sometimes attributed to the manipulation and greed of the media.[7] But we, too, bolster this culture each day, as we plaster their photographs on walls and lockers, as we avidly read gossip features, as we think about our own lives in relation to the scattered and distorted information we have about celebrities' lives.

The importance and impact of the celebrity culture vary for each person, and vary at different phases of a person's life. In late childhood and early adolescence, celebrities can be a common focus among friends. During the threshold phase, they create an uneasy frame of reference. The lives young people compare theirs to are not the lives of people they sit next to in church, on the train, or in the office, but those they read about and watch on television. For many young people, this notional association with intimate strangers is fun and comforting. But for others, awareness of these distant and idealized figures sets up comparisons that leave them feeling unimportant and left out of the first rank of human beings.

Young people who are centered can use their own thoughts and feelings and judgments to shape their lives and to make decisions about career and family. They live and learn among people whose responses are rewarding. The feedback they have in their everyday surroundings is satisfying and motivating. But the celebrity culture can throw people off-center as they believe that the significant world exists somewhere else. When they are thrown off-center, the thinking, feeling self is hedged with disguises and defenses.

Recognition and appreciation are basic human needs. Through them we get resonance—a social and personal feedback that confirms our value. In a celebrity culture, what counts as valuable recognition and acknowledgment becomes skewed. As Christa says, "If I don't stand out, I might as well be nothing." She buys into the culture that proclaims that people who are unknown do not matter, and that being ordinary means being worthless.

It is the competent and apparently confident young people who are most likely to be sideswiped by this terror. For it is the competent and apparently confident children who are most likely to believe that a parent's, teacher's, or friend's approval is based on their achievements. It is these young people whose parents and teachers are most likely to have great expectations. It is these young people who are least likely to have developed, over the years, positive defenses against comparisons to those celebrities known for being "the best."

In a mistaken bid to motivate our children, parents and educators often tell them that they should reach for the stars. The urge to see our children realize their potential is normal and healthy, but this encouragement can sometimes give the confusing message that only if one touches stardom is one successful. Combined with the cultural value placed on highly visible and marketable success, young people often feel inadequate.

Parents can help center a thresholder with some simple strategies.

1. Focus on a daughter's or son's own views.

Ask how they are doing. Don't *assume* they are doing really well. Don't *tell* them they are doing very well. Key into their perspective. Ask whether they enjoyed doing something. Avoid saying, "You must have enjoyed that!"

2. Listen.

Break away from the assumption that you already know your daughter or son. You don't—because he or she is changing rapidly. Be prepared to hear new things. Note whether you are uneasy with what you hear. If you are, your child has probably picked up on this.

3. Discuss alternative plans.

When thresholders realize previous expectations are unrealistic, they may be dazed by what they see as their "failure." If a parent accepts alternative options, then the thresholder will be more comfortable with them. Many young people feel cornered simply because they imagine that their parents would disapprove of their changing plans or shifting self-assessments.

4. Reshape expectations.

As we deal with young people, we have to open up our expectations. Achievement and development will not be linear. There are many detours during this phase.

Thresholders themselves have their work cut out to end the stalemate:

1. Put disappointment through a reality check.

Many young people identify themselves as "failures" when they are simply not as successful as they expected they would be. Ask yourself whether getting lower grades in college than you did in high school is really a personal failure. Ask yourself whether it is really shameful to work alongside people who seem better at something than you. Ask yourself whether not being the first to be promoted at work is really a failure.

2. Learn to tolerate self-assessment.

Focus criticism on the actual project and not on yourself. Look at a classmate's work or coworker's performance and ask, "What is good about that?" and "What can I learn from it?" rather than, "Why is he better than I am?"

3. Recognize achievements.

Young people who are anxious about objective assessment tend to magnify their shortcomings and minimize their successes. Think back on the past day or week and identify what you have achieved. Also, think of something you would like to achieve, and haven't. Then think up ways this could be done. Remember, planning and trying are themselves achievements.

4. Put doubts to creative use.

Many thresholders who say, "I'm not who I thought I was," view this discovery as a sign of failure. Instead, this should be used as a springboard for asking, "Well, who am I?"

5. Speak up.

Tell people who care about you that your plans have changed. Explore alternatives with either a parent or adviser. Remember, changing expectations are part of growing up, and good communication will help a parent's expectations change along with yours.

Positive Reframing of Expectations (Rusha)

It is encouraging to see how some thresholders reframe their self-expectations and refocus their aims as a normal process of development. It involves the courage to speak to parents who may have huge emotional and financial investments in one's future. This is never easy.

Rusha remembers, at age eleven, announcing her determination to be a surgeon. Her aunt had just died from breast cancer. She remembers the hug her mother gave in response to this announcement—an embrace filled with gratitude (for trying to comfort her mother after the loss of her sister) and pride. For Rusha, this goal became as much a part of her as her wideset eyes and easy smile. Every form, every c.v. she ever filled out was marked with the assurance of her future path. Yet at the age of twenty-two, and three months into the pre-med course, she knew in her heart that she had made the wrong decision: "I kept feeling worse and worse about it. I'm not sure that I even noticed this right away. I kept trying to look the part of a dedicated pre-med. And I kept feeling I wasn't doing a good job."

The rapid growth of intellect that occurs during the teenage years often heightens expectations. Both young people and their teachers expect the development to remain at this pace in college. After all, life should be upward and onward, shouldn't it? This is what Rusha expects and she is then disheartened by her performance. She begins to disguise what she believes are shameful failures.

Throughout adolescence she had been "straightforward and truthful." As she phones and writes to her parents, however, she spins scenarios of her life in the classroom and in the dorm that are more wishful than real. "We've always been close, especially me and mom, and I pretty much tell her everything, just as it is. Now I make up things, sometimes stupid little things, and I don't even know why. If I stay in all weekend, I tell them I went to a party or to see a movie. If I make myself a sandwich for dinner I tell them I just came back from the cafeteria. I lie about my grades, though eventually they'll learn the truth. And I certainly lie about how I'm feeling. But I'm not sure I really care about the truth anymore."

Rusha feels comfortable with her family when she is doing well but uncomfortable when she is not. She describes their standards as "rigid," and fears how they will respond, once they learn of her problems. "I started talking about maybe taking time out and maybe switching my major, but my mom says, 'You want to do this. Of course it's going to be tough sometimes. But it's what you've always wanted.' So I say, 'Yeah, mom. Sure,' because anything else is too much trouble, and I don't really know if I do want it or not. It's better just to toe the line and keep smiling."

She feels a new aloneness and accuses her mother of hypocrisy. "What grown-ups say about making your own decisions is one big con. What they're banking on is that your 'decisions' will be theirs. My mom just likes telling people her daughter's going to be a doctor." She also accuses her mother of favoring materialist values. "She doesn't put money high up on the list of things that would make her happy, but she goes on at me about financial security." Rusha's accusations are targeted toward her mother's failure to listen. "I can't get her to see how things really are for

me. She won't listen to me when I tell her pre-med isn't right."
Rusha then gives up trying to make herself heard. Instead, she
paints false pictures of how things are. While mother and daughter speak, they no longer actually talk.

Rusha explains, "I can't talk to my mom. I feel how disappointed she'd be, and I can't go on to tell her how messed up I
feel, and she doesn't want to hear that anyway because her line is,
she's done her stint as a mom and it's time I managed myself.
What does she think? Does she think I'll just stop being her
kid?"

Rusha feels threatened with exposure every time she fails to
come out at the top of the class. "I pulled out all the stops for
my presentation. After everyone in the class did theirs, the professor comes in and says some of us are going to be disappointed
because we're marked on the curve and we have a fellow student
who's a real 'wow' at things. And I thought of what I'd written
and was sure he was talking about me. I thought it would be a
replay of high school when my teachers would post my write-ups
of experiments because they were such good models. But it wasn't
me at all. It was some guy, and the teacher read some of his out,
and talked about presentation and everything he said made me
see that what I'd done was crap. I was lucky to get a B minus."

Caught in the impostor syndrome, her self-image does constant U-turns. One minute she expects the professor to praise her
to the skies—the next she is sure he is criticizing her. For a young
person who fears exposure and seeks perfection, the B minus is
not a mark on one piece of work but a judgment on her soul.

The professor helps her address her problem of writing what
he calls "high-class bullshit" and holds a workshop on reliable
case presentations. He asks the students to focus on what they mean
to say and to think about how they can support what they
believe. He holds exercises in listening, and he finds individual

voices interesting. "It's helped me to feel I have something to say, even though I'm not the best in the class," Rusha explains. "A lot of the other professors tell us we have to learn things by ourselves."

This break from prejudice about learning by oneself, however, boosts her confidence enough to speak to her academic adviser, who says, "If you feel this way, why are you still in pre-med?" This simple question shocks Rusha. "I stared at her. I didn't have an answer. It didn't occur to me that it mattered how I felt."

Still under pressure from her mother's expectations, Rusha sticks with the pre-med course. She feels increasingly guilty as she discovers she is very different from what her parents wanted or expected her to be. I see her several times during the next ten months, and it is like picking up an ongoing conversation. She muses about coping with a subject that does not suit her.

She sometimes lapses into a pose in which she suddenly looks like a wax model of her more animated self. "I can't understand why I'm so unhappy, and why I have this inertia." She hides this from her mother, unable to tolerate her mother's disappointment alongside her own depression. "She thinks I've got it together. Inside I feel like shit."

Finally she has the necessary conversation with her mother. "I was dreading it. I mean, this is one stupid and one very expensive mistake. It meant telling her I'm not what she thinks I am. It means paying for another year, at the very least, of college. But I'm not going to survive here if I don't change track. I started telling Mom how much trouble I was having here. It's real hard to say, 'What I said before was a pack of lies. I'm not really coping with the pre-med courses.' There was this silence and my heart was pounding. I know you're supposed to be grown up, but if your parents give you a hard time about this sort of thing, it makes everything worse. I felt I was falling into a hole. And then my mom said, 'Okay. What do you want to do?' And I started crying because I was so relieved."

Thresholders often have an epiphany about a parent that forever changes their perspective. Suddenly the complaints and recriminations that formed the repertoire of teenage conversation ("She always wanted me to be something I'm not" or "She never listened when I said what I wanted") dissolve into thin air, and a young adult is left staring at the simple, dazzling love a parent has always had. Rusha sees this at a time of acute self-doubt and panic at the prospect of disappointing her mother.

Once Rusha's mother, Hannah, does listen, the problems evaporate. There are practical matters to sort out—more financial planning, more course advice—but nothing like the dead end Rusha feared. Hannah explains: "When Rusha said she wanted to talk to me and came home during the middle of the quarter, I thought she was going to tell me about real trouble—you know, like AIDS or drugs. Hell, I thought she was about to go to prison. When she started talking about changing her career I thought to myself: 'Is that all?' It's absurd to say I'm disappointed. How can a daughter like that be a disappointment? I was just surprised and then so glad she spoke up, because now I understand."

Thresholders are still closely guided by a parent's dream. Parents' voices remain part of our mental machinery throughout life, but as we make our way into the threshold phase, we catch them out. If they remain loud and unlistening, we feel battered and undermined by them. If we engage them in conversation, they can take up a more accommodating position among our mental hardware.

Parents encourage their children throughout their lives. "Maybe you'll be the one to design a really comfortable typing chair/discover a cure for the flu/invent an easily-programed video recorder/start up a chain of bakeries for your wonderful cookies." Parents encourage their children with their own dreams, but at the same time, they must learn how to ground their sons and daughters in their own realities.

We can all learn from Rusha, who summons the courage to speak her mind, and from her mother, who has the courage to listen. As she comes through her rough patch, she reflects: "No matter how old you are, you still need help from someone. Everybody always needs someone, even if it's just someone to talk to. If you're going to be independent, you need someone's help. I suppose at some stage of my life I'll be really grown up and won't have my parents to go back to, but now I can't imagine being independent without their help."

CHAPTER SIX

FOOTHOLD IN THE
ADULT WORLD

THE grandparents of today's thresholders often describe to me their entry into adulthood. This occurred at sixteen, when they left school and took their first job. There they felt the power of being a responsible adult and the personal boost of being valued and shown respect. The parents of today's thresholders talk about their first foothold in the adult world, often after graduating either from high school or college, when they were inspired by dreams of a better future, in a society eager for their contributions.

A select few of today's thresholders have similar experiences. They enter the world of work, stimulated and gratified by the ways their talents and training can be put to use. But at least one-third of today's thresholders, however well qualified, find only menial jobs that neither challenge nor interest them. Four years after leaving college, 13 percent of graduates are still in this twilight world of employment.[1] The general problems are threefold:

1. Expectations do not match experience.

Many young people think that good character and education should lead to a great job. When they find this isn't the case, they feel discouraged and betrayed.

Thresholders have to put these problems into a social context. Both education and employment have undergone revolutions that have overturned traditional career patterns. Once, a diploma from a good college ensured a good job. Now, as the number of people in higher education increases rapidly, it is only the baseline for entry into employment.

Both parents and thresholders need to adopt realistic expectations of their first footholds and reeducate themselves about realistic job prospects.

2. Outmoded time frames make common patterns seem wrong.

Many thresholders feel trapped in pre-adult roles. Often they live at home and have to negotiate being a kid at home, but a grown-up at work. While this feels abnormal, more than half of the young men aged between twenty and twenty-four still live with a parent.[2]

This practice provides protection against young people's poverty or even homelessness. For many young people, it is a life-saving opportunity. But in our culture, in which individualism and independence are so highly valued, this can be experienced by both thresholder and parent as a failure. It is then difficult for a thresholder to sustain motivation and self-esteem.

3. Excessive responsibility is seen as normal.

Many young people want to test themselves by traveling and working. While many thresholders and their parents see any new challenge as character-building, too much responsibility can be character-destroying.

Parents should therefore be alert to possible overload of responsibility. Never assume that because someone is twenty she is old enough to take on adult burdens. Responsibility should be given gradually. There should be frequent "check ups" on a young person's self-management.

4. Emphasis on independence can diminish long-term goals.

Young people who work hard to establish financial independence often downsize their future goals. They concentrate on short-term gains (such as earning money or finding their own place to live) and lack the confidence that a parent's support would provide. Going it alone, they tend not to go as far.

Parents and employers should be forgiving. Mistakes at this time of one's life are not signs of fixed character flaws. Mistakes are part and parcel of this transition period—which stretches longer and longer the more complex our society becomes.

Boom-Time Drifters (Pete)

They are called the "boom-time drifters."[3] Unable to find a satisfactory job, even in a strong economy, many young people drift in and out of menial jobs, each one "temporary," but none leads to anything better. While some thresholders simply need a short-term hibernation phase before they focus on the careers ahead of them, for many this phase becomes long-term.

Pete always had the support of his parents to make the best of his abilities. His family was quick to value what he was good at and to minimize the value of skills he did not master. They encouraged him but were relaxed about his grades. They were tolerant, too, when Pete decided to leave college after his second year. "Dad said it didn't matter if I wanted to drop out, as long as I got a job and could pay my own way." As Pete speaks, he looks past me, focusing on a distant idyll. "He's a lot less tolerant now," he concludes briefly.

Many parents believe that leaving college signals the end of the need for the type of emotional and financial help they would previously give to a child. Once Pete is out of college, they believe he is on his own. "He's not a kid anymore," his father, Barry, says. "I can't keep holding his hand."

To make ends meet, Pete took temporary work, then found a couple of jobs in sales until he decided that they were not for him. He was offered a room in a friend's apartment and took a job as a catering assistant (setting tables, washing dishes, cleaning) in a self-service restaurant. When his friend moved out of town, Pete went back home. He continued to work in a series of jobs and more or less settled into working in a storage company, packing boxes. He is dismayed by what the world of work offers and what it expects. He cannot not see why he has to endure this drudgery. "I left school because I was sick of all the assignments and grades and classes, and I got a job, but that was even worse, and I knew I was the one who got myself into this awful fix. It's not really living, is it, being cooped up doing the same thing all day, and being with people you don't really like, and at someone's beck and call?"

As much as he dislikes his job, he is afraid of being fired. He sees financial doom as just a paycheck around the corner. He lives at home because he cannot afford to live elsewhere. "Every time I walk through the door it's like another failure. I'm reminded I haven't gone anywhere in the last three years." At home, he is a kid again, being told to pick up after himself and clean his room. He does not feel real as either an adult or a child and drifts through each context, detached and bored. "Sometimes I look at other people and hate them because of what they have. I don't think I was a grumpy teenager, but I've become a grumpy adult."

Many young people have their egos shattered by the minor downs of young adulthood—the first few dud jobs, the first batch of mistakes, the rustle of panic as they realize they are in charge of their own life. As they see themselves disappointing others and failing to meet their own expectations, thresholders feel utterly bruised and overplay the negative aspects of their lives. They downsize their own ambitions and seek very modest comfort. Pete enjoys having some money in his pocket—he does not care how little. He likes coming home, going to a movie or watching television, changing into sweats and thick cotton socks and "vegging." He loves the feeling of being so "mellow" that he can barely lift his head. He describes pleasure in negative terms: not stressed, not anxious, and not thinking about his future.

A year later Pete is still working in the same storage firm. He goes through the necessary motions but puts forth as little effort as possible at work. He feels as though he is moving in a fog. "It's hard enough to get there and do my shift. Planning my life is something far beyond me." He drifts further and further from the life he once hoped for. His reality is so different from his expectations that he cannot make sense of his experience: "When I used to imagine my grown-up life, I saw myself managing things, real stylish and smart. I can describe the suit I'd wear, and how I'd take phone calls and deal with people. I don't know at what point in my life I stopped having control. I hate it here, but I can't move on."

Pete earns his keep. He offers his parents part of his paycheck for his room and board, which they take, Barry says, "as a token, to remind him nothing's for free." But planning and focusing seem beyond him—partly because he now sees himself "basically on my own. I mean, I sill live at home, but if I needed them for other stuff, too, it would be a real put down."

Many thresholders need emotional refuelling before coming to grips with the challenging world of employment. When their need for their families humiliates them, and when their families do not take on board the current realities of young people's employment, they then battle with a vision of themselves as "wasted" or "past it."

Pete describes himself as "old." Standing at the threshold, both he and his parents position him as an adult who has some-

how missed his chance: "Sometimes I sit up and think of everything I've done. There's all the bad things I've done and all the
good things. But I can't think of what I'm going to do next,
because I just don't know." When I ask him whether he thinks he
just needs some more time, he says, "Nothing happens. Time
won't change anything. There are just these dead hours. I look at
the clock at work and I think I'm not going to last another hour.
Time just seems dead."

TIME ANXIETY

We live in a culture obsessed with time. We worry about being
"on time" or "on track." Are we on time with our life plan? Who
is ahead of us? We worry whether we will make our mark or
prove ourselves by the time we are twenty-five. We also live with
the implicit assumption that a worthwhile life is fast paced.
Whatever lip service is paid to the problems of the time-famine
in contemporary life, where working hours seep into early morning checks on websites and late emails, there is a caché attached
to being busy. Today, long working hours and squeezed leisure are
part of what we think of as a good life. The question, "How are
you?" is now often answered with "busy" and "too busy." This is
a complaint that thinly disguises a boast about leading a full life.

Thresholders have another, special problem when they worry
about time. They grapple with a prolonged process of growing
up in a culture that values independence and self-reliance. As they
take longer to reach these desired states, they feel they are never
what they should be. Neither adolescent nor adult, they do not
know where they stand on any timeline. Time shifts meaning.
One moment, their futures seem to extend infinitely, and the
next, their future seems terrifyingly foreshortened. We laugh at a

twenty-two-year-old who talks of feeling old. We shake our heads when we hear a thresholder speaking about "ending up" as he is now. We watch with amused amazement as they scan their reflections for signs of aging. But for thresholders at an impasse, the anxiety about time is real.

When Erik Erikson studied the development of young people, he noticed this strange disturbance in their sense of time. "It consists," Erikson explained, "of a sense of great urgency and yet also of a loss of consideration for time as a dimension of living. The young person may feel simultaneously very young, and in fact baby-like, and old beyond rejuvenation. Protests of missed greatness and of a premature and fatal loss of useful potential are common . . . ; the implied malignancy, however, consists of a decided disbelief that time may bring change, and yet also of a violent fear that it might."[4]

In this frame of mind, it is impossible for Pete to deal with even the small negotiations of time in day-to-day life. It is hard to go to bed, and it is equally hard to wake up and face the demands of the day. It is difficult to plan ahead because he is in a state of not knowing what he wants or who he wants to be. He is afraid that things will never change. He is also afraid that things will change—but for the worse. He is deemed immature by his father, his employer—and by himself. He therefore has no positive forum, either at home or at work, to focus his goals and assess his potential.

Time passes in a cycle of useless questions: "What did I do wrong?" and "How can I find my way to real adulthood?"

PARENTS' PASTS AND CHILDREN'S PRESENTS

When parents have unrealistic assumptions about maturity, they cannot give necessary support. Barry's angry incomprehension at his son's moody lethargy leads to a stalemate. The discomfort Pete feels at home—a kid who is too old to be a kid, whose presence at home is a sign of failure—is bred in the context of his father's expectations. "It gets worse and worse just being around my dad. There are these constant jibes about me and my life. I feel bad enough. I don't need his help making me feel bad."

Barry came of age in the 1960s. At twenty, his favorite novel was Philip Roth's *Letting Go*. It gave him a good slant, he said, on why he felt claustrophobic within his own family. "My folks were into all my business—girls, school, body functions, everything. I always said I wasn't going to pry into my kid's minds and watch over them. By the time Pete was thirteen I let him think for himself and judge things himself. If college isn't for him I'm not going to make a tragedy of it. He can do something else. There are lots of ways to go some place."

He falls silent, musing on his own words, defending the position he has taken, even now as he feels it has gone wrong. He looks around the room, the den, scattered with family photos. "That's me," he explains, pointing to a wedding photograph, "that's me and Sue when we were his age. That's how young we started our life. We were his age when we built our first house."

In the photo Sue stands with a ring of wild flowers in her hair. She is wearing silver hoop earrings and a white cotton dress embroidered at the neck. Barry is long-haired and bearded in the photo. They look almost impossibly young, younger even than their twenty-two-year-old son looks now. But, as Barry says, at that age he was well launched as an adult. He had begun his own business, importing and selling the first wave of pocket calculators and digital watches. At Pete's age, Barry could afford a half-acre plot of land, and he and Sue designed their own home and helped build it. Breaking away from his parents and starting his own family did not seem so daunting.

While some parents, looking back on their own threshold experiences, feel protective of their sons and daughters, Barry's easy glide into adulthood leads him to assess Pete as "immature, somehow real slow in taking hold." But given his son's age, Barry feels it inappropriate to help him along: "I've done what I can do." But without that help, Pete continues to drift. His sense of being a disappointment mounts:

> Everyone's supposed to be some kind of a success in my family. It's strange, you know, I never would have described my parents as pushy. I never felt pressured in school. If I did okay, then that was okay. I know my dad thought I was really bright, so I never questioned it. I never thought that not being a great student meant I didn't have a good mind. I did things with my dad around the house. We sanded these doors together—they're nice wood but they were covered with some hideous green paint—and we got them all nice like they are now. We fixed up our bikes together, and we did a lot of biking. It was cool. Now there's nothing. I walk into the room and there are these waves of disapproval.

Pete describes an ideal upbringing and ideal support from parents who admire what he can do, pick up on his good qualities, and put other measures (grades, place in his class, position on a team) in perspective. But this family sanity is eclipsed in the threshold years by an outmoded model of maturity. According to this model, Pete should be leaving home and making his own way in the grown-up world. Barry fears that meeting his son's apparent needs would do him harm in the end. It would "make him think we're always going to be there for him." Expecting him to be "mature, with a good grip on his life now," Barry believes he has to be cruel to be kind. This theory, formed in a father's kind heart, is cruel indeed.

HELPING A DRIFTER FOCUS

Sons and daughters of any age are bruised by a parent's disappointment. A parent's understanding energizes them. They want to hear a parent say, "You're not a disappointment. I know this is a difficult phase. I don't need you to be a shining 'success.' I just need you to find your feet in life. It might take a while."

Structured conversations about possible alternatives can bring new goals to light. Discussions of plans, both short term and long term, can clarify what's possible.

When a few distant goals eventually light up their horizons, young people then have to plan possible strategies to reach them. Thresholders in a drifting pattern may regress to the point at which they agree where they want to go but reject any reasonable means of going there. Parents may have to do some research themselves to suggest possible plans for attaining goals.

These discussions are unlikely to flow effortlessly. Parent/thresholder discussions about the future are often tense. When parents express their frustration, they put the thresholder on the defensive. "What's wrong with you?" a parent demands. "Why can't you get a grip?" At these unanswerable questions the thresholder turns away. Why bother to talk with a mother or father who "doesn't understand," "can't see," and "has no idea" about how life really is.

Instead, parents could see how "life really is" at least from the thresholder's point of view and then assure him that this reality can be tolerated. A parent can say: "Yes, there is uncertainty. Yes, there may be disappointments. Yes, there will be difficulties. But these can be managed, one at a time."

How Thresholders Can Suffer from
Premature Responsibilities (Carri)

There is no simple measure of maturity. It is difficult to predict how much a young person can manage on her own. New research shows that the brain itself often keeps its adolescent characteristics until the age of twenty-six.[5] This means that some young people are not prepared, physiologically, to take on adult responsibilities involving self-control and self-management. Some young people can therefore be hopelessly out of their depth in adult situations.

When things go well enough for thresholders, they learn from their experiences. As they take on adult roles, they learn what kind of behavior works and what kind doesn't. They learn how to organize their work during the day, remembering what has to be done—usually by catching themselves out when they forget something. They learn to gauge their own limits—usually after tiring themselves out and noticing how easily they mess up when they are fatigued.

Making mistakes is part of this learning process, but making too many mistakes tends to be overwhelming. Instead of being able to see what went wrong and correct it for the future, they cover up or offer excuses. They are constantly late. They forget to do the jobs they've promised to do. They do not complete jobs. And they promptly forget their day's troubles by enjoying the nightlife. These apprentice adults are charged with being "irresponsible" and "immature" and "spoiled." But in fact they are suffering from a kind of culture shock, in which ordinary information cannot be processed. Given too much responsibility at too early a stage in their development, they are quite simply out of their depth.

Carri's mother, Fran, works on the commonsense principle that young people learn to be responsible by being given responsibility. At nineteen, Carri wants a break from the structures of school and home. "I may want to go to college, but not just yet. I want to go out in the world and be a grown-up. In fact," Carri laughs, and looks impishly at her mother, "I want to get as far away as I can from my parents."

Her mother acknowledges this with good humor. The press release they give me of Carri's past is that she has been boisterous, and they have quarreled over her social life, but she is responsible and mature. As a teenager, Carri held down jobs from the age of fourteen, when she started to babysit. For the past three years she has worked three evenings a week in the junior department of a chain store.[6] Like many thresholders, she has had a great deal of experience looking after herself. Her parents divorced when she was five. When Carri was eleven, her mother trained as an accountant, and by the time Carri was fifteen, Fran was working long hours in a firm whose offices were an hour's commute from their home. Carri was expected to help with shopping, cooking, cleaning. She also managed a household allowance, along with her own earnings. She barely had time to be immature and irresponsible.[7] "She's so grown up now," Fran explains. "She doesn't want to just slip into college. She wants to live abroad and be an adult."

The theory is: being given responsibility will make you responsible. But if a thresholder is thrown in at the deep end, we should remain on parental alert to be certain they don't sink.

EMBRYONIC JUDGMENT

How much responsibility do you give in order to teach responsibility, and how much responsibility will be overwhelming? This is the most difficult question posed during the threshold years. Young people often surprise their parents and teachers with their maturity and enterprise and initiative. An apparently timid teenager can show courage and confidence as she joins the grown-ups. Just as easily, a gutsy and sensible teenager can stumble on the first step. Maturity is an uneven process. It is virtually impossible to grow up, in all respects, at the same pace. Being able to manage adolescent responsibilities is very different from managing responsibilities in an adult environment, with different rules and distractions. If we accept that a thresholder's judgment is often in embryonic form, we can protect her. If we ignore it, our optimism exposes our children to moral risk.

Imagine a young woman taking a year in another country, keen to grow in independence and experience before starting college. Imagine the pull between nightlife and a day job. Imagine a pleasant nineteen-year-old, called Louise Woodward, whose future is threatened because she was not able to manage her energy and her time.[8] At no time in development does a person's goodness seem more fragile—not because young people are bad, but because during this delicate and difficult phase of development, luck plays a disturbing role in the outcome of life's trials and errors. In a protected environment, a young woman is mature and responsible and gentle. Outside that protection, she is stretched beyond her limits. Tempted by the pleasures of new independence, she enjoys a young person's hectic nightlife. Bound by the responsibilities of independence, she is left in charge of two demanding children. The far-too-high expectations adults have of a nineteen-year-old put her goodness in jeopardy.

I think of this dangerous balance between maturity and immaturity when I next speak to Carri. She has been in her job as *au pair* for eleven weeks. We sit in the kitchen of her employer's home, a long narrow room that looks out onto an enclosed backyard. She tells me how she loves London. Though we are looking out on a suburban yard, we are less than half an hour by underground from the lively West End. This is a luxury for Carri. In high school, travel into a city was difficult. She rarely had access to a car, and there were so many rules bound up with using the car that driving into town for a night out involved a long series of negotiations with both her parents and her friends' parents. Here, when her employer comes home from work, some days at six o'clock and some days at seven, Carri can use her time as she wishes. She meets up with other students and nannies she has met through some invisible network. They go clubbing, pub crawling, or just hang out. Most mornings, like this one, she is drained and pale. In this border crossing, the urge to have fun like a teenager clashes with the need to behave like a grown-up.

She and her employer, Eleanor, are barely civil as they share the morning tasks of feeding the children, wiping their faces, performing the rites of cleaning in the galley kitchen. Eleanor lists the highlights of the day's schedule and pauses after each item, looking at Carri to make sure the information has been processed. She knows Carri has been out until two A.M. and, at this time of the morning, is not fully awake. Does she understand that the three-year-old girl has to be at a birthday party in Finchley Park at eleven, and that the five-year-old boy needs to be taken to the dentist after school? Will this schedule remain clear in Carri's head? Carri nods as she wipes the table. "No problem."

But there have been problems before. Eleanor is sometimes unable to wake Carri in the mornings. Carri takes an afternoon nap when the baby has hers, and sometimes sleeps past the two-thirty pick-up for the boy's school. She has been so stressed that Eleanor has had to take time off work to look after her, com-

forting her over a breakup with a boyfriend, and paying for extensive long-distance comfort calls to parents and friends. Eleanor
has seen this all before. "I've had five nannies in the past four and
a half years, and I know not to expect too much. These girls need
as much coddling as my own kids. They have to be watched, and
they need to be constantly reminded what they're supposed to do.
I'll have to phone Carri during my lunch break to make sure she
remembers the dentist appointment and hasn't lost the address of
the dentist. Frankly, she's a pain in the ass. But then they all are.
These are young adults—twenty- or twenty-one-year-olds—but
with no life plan. I can't get over how dependent they still are on
their mothers. They get off the plane and burst into tears. They
want to call their mothers. They are at their boyfriends' beck and
call. They cry when they are ill. They spend hours on the phone.
They need to be watched like a hawk. They are manipulative and
sly."

It is chilling to witness this conflict between generations and
to hear a woman I know to be normally fair and generous con-
demn young people for needing their mothers. But I also see how
frustrating it must be to hire a young adult and then find she
needs as much "coddling" as the children she is hired to care for.

Eleanor's strategy is to cater to some of their immaturities.
Then, she hopes, Carri will be responsible when it counts. But
Carri slips further and further into her role of the teenage rebel.
As Eleanor tries to save her responsible side by bolstering her
irresponsible side, Carri simply conforms to the pattern of a difficult and ungrateful child. Two weeks later, Eleanor fires Carri
when she crashes the car after delivering the five-year-old to
school. Cocaine, taken the pervious night, registers in a urine test.
There are awful recriminations about failure to perform her
duties and threats of law suits.

Carri says she feels "too down" to make our next appointment. But Fran sees me. She is drawn, defensive, and looks ten years older than when I last saw her. She is quick to defend Carri, even before I speak. "Carri is a well-respected young woman in our community," she declares. "She wasn't treated well in London. She didn't behave well, but she wasn't treated well, either. She's only twenty. She's a good person."

It will take that conviction for Carri to retain her own sense of her goodness. As I prepare to leave Fran, Carri comes out to meet me. She will talk to me, after all. "I keep going over what happened. I keep asking, 'How did I do that stuff?' I loved the kids, I really did, and I keep thinking that if Guy had been in the car, I would've been more alert, you know? Anyway, I messed up, but I didn't hurt him. So I was lucky, because Guy wasn't in the car and didn't get hurt. You get confused, living in a family, but not being a kid. And I began to feel so bad, and I just didn't expect anything of myself anymore. And I didn't have a lot of luck with my boss."

Lucky and not lucky. Moral luck. The moral hazard of being young and taking on responsibility while one's adult judgment is still in a fledgling stage. I look at Fran, who takes Carri's arm as she grows confused by what she's saying. No longer a child, she will never forget this. But as a thresholder in a forgiving environment, she will be able to move on.

ACCEPTING THRESHOLDERS' LIMITS

The common assumption today is that children grow up fast: but an important problem facing thresholders is that they are in some ways grown up and in many ways retarded in their growth compared to previous generations. New communication methods in our culture have provided them with a great deal of information.

As a result, their awareness is both wide-ranging and superficial. Moreover, parenting styles today foster certain kinds of maturity but leave deep pockets of immaturity. The increased time demands parents face at work link up with an ethos of trusting a child's best judgment: It is both convenient and ideologically sound for parents to allow children to be responsible for themselves while at home, to choose their own clothes, their own meals, their own friends. At the same time, because we value their achievement and potential, we push them into a multitude of activities and chauffeur them from gymnastics to music lessons. We organize their schedules and we protect them from the outside environment. These are not bad parenting practices: They make sense in today's world where parents need jobs and the neighborhood is unsafe. But they result in uneven maturities in our children, who in some areas are used to having full control, and yet in others, are used to being controlled.

Some parents believe that the solution is to push thresholders into the wide world. Barry feels uneasy about offering his twenty-two-year-old son bed and board and takes every opportunity to nudge him out of the nest—not because he does not want to help his son, but because he believes that the best help is to push him away. Fran believes that responsibility will make a grown-up of her daughter. Eleanor believes that the only option, in working with what she sees as a new generation of helpless young adults, is to make a bargain with them: She will tolerate some of their immaturities as long as they do their job.

But thresholders sometimes cannot take on the mantle of adult responsibilities. Parents can assess and encourage their capacity to take on a responsible position:

1. Monitor their awareness of others' expectations.

This means being clear about what is expected. Parents should discuss the implications of these responsibilities. Employers should give young people a precise description of a job. Reminders of these expectations should be given automatically and neutrally, and assessments should be frequent. Employing young people is itself a responsibility.

2. Offer support.

Make your offer of support known. Remarks such as "Now you're on your own" are often made light-heartedly by parents, but thresholders take them seriously. Asking for a parent's (or employer's) advice or help should not be humiliating. Requests for clarification and confirmation ("Is this okay?") should be answered clearly. Remarks such as "You should know this by now" should be avoided.

3. Learn from mistakes.

The consequences of mistakes can be learning points. No one likes dwelling on their mistakes, but parents and employers can put them in the context of "learning to improve." If a young person is late, forgets an appointment, fails to complete a task she promised to do, we need to make sure she knows the full story of what happened. The point of the discussion is not to blame her but to make sure she understands what role she played in the mistake. Instead of thinking, "I really messed up," the thresholder can identify what made the situation difficult, such as, "I didn't have enough guidance or support." She should also identify the part she played in the problem, such as, "I didn't insist on clear instructions" or "I didn't know I would get so tired or how tiredness could affect my work." With this perspective, she learns what to avoid and correct in the future. When thresholders can learn from their mistakes, they are ready to manage adult responsibilities.

CHAPTER SEVEN

THRESHOLDERS ON THE FAST TRACK

SHADOWING every thresholder who meets a bump on the road to adulthood is the fresh-faced woman or man who gets it all right. The model thresholder leaves the protected worlds of family and school and steps through the open door to independence and success. While the people they grew up with still live like kids in a parent's home, those on the fast track are the high-profile twentysomethings who work and play hard, and then go home to high-rent apartments with good views and a ground-floor gym. Parents of these young people glow in the light of a task completed and turn their thoughts to other things, since their children (in their view) no longer need them.

Thresholders who make a good start in the adult world are lucky, but many find unexpected difficulties that they can barely name and for which they get very little support. They often feel abandoned as their parents assume they are just fine on their own. On the one hand, they feel powerful in their luck and skill and on the other, as though they are walking on ice. Rushed into a competitive work environment, under constant assessment, the phrase "looking after yourself" takes on new meaning. Employers are pleased to give them opportunities—but they also give them hell.

They drive them hard, ask them to prove themselves on every front, and capitalize on their ambition and their insecurity.

Many successful young adults exhibit symptoms close to those of manic depression:

1. They cannot regulate their moods or their energies.

Needing to unwind, but unable to relax, many thresholders in fast-track careers take the drugs that, in high school and college, they knew to refuse. Those who were careful and respectful of themselves and others as teenagers become young adults who engage in sex as recreation. They party hard and run on nervous energy.

2. They feel cut off from their families but are unable to forge a relationship with a peer.

Many parents mistake a thresholder's financial independence for emotional independence. They make decisions about their own lives based on the assumption that they are no longer needed as parents. These young people then believe that their own need for their families is inappropriate, but they have no satisfactory substitute.

3. They lose the capacity for reflection.

Teenagers constantly reflect on the value of adults' lives and constantly revise visions of their own futures. Young adults caught in this fast-track syndrome, however, describe their futures as "a blank." They say they "don't have the vaguest idea" where they will be in ten years' time.

3. They experience early burn out, and their careers stall.

The Financial Fast Track (Emma)

As Emma buzzes me into her Near Northside Chicago apartment, I smell the distinctive wax-and-polish perfume of a well-tended building. The ride in the elevator is fast and smooth. She greets me in the hall. Her handshake is dry and firm. I am led briskly along the carpeted corridor. Even with her high heels she keeps a step in front of me. She dismisses my enthusiasm for the lake view from her living room with a shake of her head: "It's a selling point." If, at twenty-three, she is excited and surprised by the possession of such surroundings, she does not let it show.

Emma is on the fast-track to adulthood. Two years out of college, she has a good job with a high income. She is financially independent from her parents and respected by her employers. She has the life most twentysomethings crave and a promising future. Why, then, did she contact me when she heard I was studying the rocky transition from adolescence to adulthood? Did she want to put herself forward as an exception?

I begin as I usually do, with questions that focus on her day-to-day life, before going on to talk about large-scale hopes and regrets. She answers briefly. Her job is "fine." Her colleagues are "mostly okay." When I ask Emma what achievements she is most proud of, she speaks about being independent, not relying on her parents, and being "okay with work routines and stuff like that." When I ask what she regrets, she talks about loss of personal contacts: "I meet lots of people, but I don't get to know them." When I ask her how she sees her future, she pales and her composure crumbles. "My dream was to be perfectly happy. I always believed there was a point at which I would definitely be happy, when I would become myself, instead of just trying to impersonate who I thought I should be. And now I feel that moment's passed me by, that I'll never find it, and that I'm already at the end of my life."

RULES OF THE ROAD

The move away from home or school affects young people in unexpected ways. For some, the crucial step is away from their family home to managing their emotional and practical lives in college. But many thresholders still feel supported in college, with the dorms, the classes, and the teachers and other staff providing an infrastructure of care and control. Many of these young people experience the adult environment outside college as a wilderness. Bewildered by expectations that they can function on their own, they feel small and stranded.

One way of coping is to polish the facade of maturity: If I look grown up, the reasoning is, I'll be okay. They are then quick to learn the rules of their adult environment. They appear self-assured. They know how to walk into a room full of grown-ups and behave as though they were one of them. They know how to hold a conversation, equal to equal, with other adults. They present their ideas to others, well-packaged and apparently secure. According to the maturity myth, these young people are on track. In their early twenties, they appear to be really grown up. But as they take on one aspect of adult life, they are at sea in many other respects.

In their first grown-up job, many young people feel they are playing a role they're not quite worthy of. They see themselves, still, as a teenager, a non-adult, and then feel a wave of panic as they realize they are now dealing with adults as an adult. Feeling like a child, still, they cannot believe they belong. For many young people, the sense of being an impostor is occasional—something like the comic mental asides in the TV series *Ally McBeal*, when the hotshot lawyer Ally, in conference with other lawyers, imagines herself as a tiny little girl, talking in a squeaky little girl's voice, sitting in an enormous adult chair.

This dissonance usually eases with experience. Gradually young people realize that it is, after all, possible to take on adult roles.

But a significant number of thresholders see themselves as running on luck, which may give out at any time. They are unable to see what they have done right and therefore do not know how to keep doing it. Emma constantly expects some imminent disaster: "I guess this is what's called living on the edge. There's this second before I open my eyes in the morning when I wonder whether I can really bear to wake up. The whole world seems dreadful. But then I do get up and I go to work and I do things I have to do and I just stay in that gear and don't think about anything else."

Emma's apparent successes alienate her from her family. Her mother, Paula, speaks of Emma in terms of pride and relief. "We've done a good job," Paula tells me, and Emma too picks up on the implication that the parenting job is over. As she follows the outward forms of adulthood, she feels that her real self—the self she has known since childhood—is being abandoned.

In watching her easy and unassuming competence, I can see why her employers have promoted her twice in the past six months. As I spend a day shadowing her at her work, I see she has a good memory for what's been promised to clients and what clients have said they require. Her unostentatious suggestions pave the way to solutions of several problems. She checks the paperwork on orders. She is meticulous in writing down messages. While many people in her company tend to raise the emotional tension during a crisis, she stays calm. Yet she barely seems to know the value of what she does. She feels her position is fragile: "I may be the flavor of the week, but lots of people who look okay for a while suddenly disappear."

She looks around and takes note of who advances quickly and who is left behind. In her quiet way, she is taking a crash course in the sociology of success. She notes that even her coworkers who are on the way up can fall to earth in the bat of an eye. She knows her progress has been charmed, so far, but as soon as she ceases to please her boss, she will be cast out of the magic circle: "They say you have to watch your back, but I just feel I have to watch my step. Things seem civilized here, but beneath the surface things are really cruel."

This increases her anxiety and informs her day-to-day behavior. Her employer asks whether she can get a report done or get him some sales figures by the morning, and she says she can even though this means staying at work well into the night. She feels she has no power to negotiate terms or to decline a request. "My heart starts pounding when I hear he wants 'a word' with me. I know whatever it is I'll have to do it."

Each day at work she is anxious about her performance. She seldom leaves the office before seven, and some days it is later. In the two full days I spend with her I see her eat one meal. Her stylish clothes hang loosely on her, as though she has lost weight since buying them. She has a habit of biting loose skin off her dry lips. Her hands, too, are chapped, and she holds them two inches above the desk, as though she were about to play a chord on a piano. There are simply no pauses, no relaxation points throughout the day.

She cannot keep up her guard outside work. In the past year she has had three boyfriends and several other sexual partners. She had an abortion the week before contacting me.

Finding it difficult to switch off, she turns to a common set of recreational tools for those in their early twenties—cocaine, Ecstasy, and LSD. Never before a drug user, Emma now uses cocaine regularly. "I can't relax, but I can escape. Some days it's just me, just once, in the late evening when I feel really alone and know I won't sleep. Mostly, though, it's a sociable Friday night thing. And when I use it, I feel I'm friends with everyone I'm with. I don't worry about the same things. Most of all, I don't worry about life."

Emma wishes that she would wake up and find that she had suddenly turned thirty. In her view, thirty is a time when you are really grown up, and you won't have the needs she has. Under the shadow of the maturity myth, she feels she should not have these needs.

Young people unaccustomed to the pace of adult life, who find themselves without the support to steady themselves, may follow a pattern of intense activity followed by periods of leisure. Emma tries to conform to proper adult roles in the workplace, and after work she tries to enjoy the twentysomething culture. The escapist lifestyle can become more addictive than the drugs taken. There's the freneticism of discos, raves, drugs, and drinking. During this all too common early-twenties breakdown, young people who have unblemished records may develop problems with drugs. The hectic pace of work and play disguises other needs that are devalued by the maturity myth.

FEAR OF SUCCESS

Over and over again, I hear from young people, who seem to be thriving, that their experience of success is confusing and punishing.

Success is something we strive for and something we expect will make us happy. It is a proof of our abilities, hard work, and perhaps our luck. Success is expected to make us feel better about ourselves. Some sense of ourselves as successful is necessary just to get by each day of our lives. Someone who cannot name any personal success in the present or recent past is bound to be depressed. Our craving for success starts early. The two-year-old crows with delight when she places the last block on her tower. The four-year-old cries with frustration when she is not able to paint just the picture she wants. As we go through school, our grades mean far more to us than marks on a specific exam. We read in them signs of our current and future worth. And when we step into our first job, a whole new set of possible failures and successes opens before us.

At this stage, young people begin to experience their successes in new ways. Suddenly, it appears that success does not always make us feel better. It can arouse anxiety, guilt, and fear. Success can set one apart from others. Young women, in particular, fear the social consequences of success.[2] They may worry that successes will make them unattractive or threatening. They may worry that it impossible to be both "nice" and successful. Though the pressure to hide intelligence or tone down their motivation in the name of femininity is easing, some girls and women continue to worry that success will expose them to mockery and envy.[3]

Another very different fear concerning success is the expectations others have of us when we have a good run of successes. Maybe they will expect more of us than we think we can deliver. We may feel lucky rather than competent and worry that soon our luck will run out. In such a state of anxiety, a young person can mess up just to get the failure over with. Young people sometimes handicap themselves to provide an excuse for failing. They may oversleep on the day of an important interview or get drunk rather than complete an assignment. Hiding behind the "alibi" of their bad habits, their real abilities are not actually questioned.

But something a little different, and more puzzling, has been observed in young people—particularly in thresholders who mature "on time," and who succeed in early adulthood. Emma displays this common and commonly overlooked fear: Success will disguise her as an adult who does not need to be cared for and loved. Success will deprive her of having her child-self needs fulfilled: "You leave home and suddenly there's nothing holding you up. It doesn't matter that you seem to be doing okay. Inside, I'm frightened. Every day I'm frightened." She is also reluctant to change too much, to move away from the person she was as a child.

It is not a mere coincidence that so much as been written about the "child within,"[4] just at the time at which the myth of maturity is at its height. For the myth of maturity declares that childlike bonds should be severed by the close of adolescence. The child-within approach is a counter move. It confirms the need to keep faith with childhood memories and feelings. But the child-within approach also falls prey to the maturity myth because it directs us to supply these needs ourselves. The stories of thresholders, however, show that they cannot keep faith with their needs all by themselves. They need to stabilize themselves through continued relationships with those who have helped them grow.

Young adults who look competent are often the ones who are likely to be left alone. At home Emma had family and friends. In college everyone she met was a potential friend. "You expected the other guys to be friendly. You could start up a conversation, and then go on to have coffee, or go on from where you'd got to next time you met. Here I see the same people every day on the el, but that doesn't give me the right even to say 'Hi.' And I can't make head or tail of the people I work with. One day they'll be really friendly, and the next day, they're blocked off, all preoccupied. You don't build up a relationship."

Emma goes through the motions of being a competent and independent adult. Inside, she feels unacknowledged and uncared for. The routine of her job, and the impersonal conditions at work, confound her. "I never knew you could see people so often and spend so much time with them, without being the least bit close to them." She is surprised, too, that she now has sex "sometimes with friends, and sometimes with guys I meet, just because it's sometimes nice. It's weird when I think about it, and maybe I shouldn't be so slutty, but I can't see that it really matters."

Both thresholders and their parents act in accord with the myth that the thresholder can function as an isolated unit. Parents assume that a daughter or son no longer needs the symbols and forms of stability and connection. It is when the children are "old enough" that many couples decide to separate, move, or travel. Many "down nest" when their children leave home, choosing a smaller and less expensive home. While this timing is understandable, it can also have emotional consequences for their children.

Emma's father, Doug, has wanted to retire for the last three years. After a hernia operation, he is looking forward to leaving the strains of work. He tells me about his conflict with his boss and the humiliating day-to-day negotiations at work. "I had my eye on the door, but with one of the kids still at home, I didn't leave." He and his wife, who had been "going their separate ways for many years," now decide to separate. The family house in a Chicago suburb is sold, and he moves to upstate Michigan, which he has always loved. Emma's mother moves downstate to be with her sister.

Emma feels abandoned: "They gave away my old crib. They threw out a lot of my old toys. I don't even know where my high-school yearbooks are." She can never again look at the backyard where she played as a child or trace the familiar sidewalks to the neighborhood park. At a time when she needs special reassurance of her childhood connections, it is assumed she will accept being cut off from them. Her parents' decision is rightfully their own, but whereas they would have expected these changes to disturb Emma as a teenager, they now think she is "all set up now" and "all on her own." She is left out of the small negotiations and flow of information that protect many daughters and sons from feeling cut off and out of control when a family undergoes the process of divorce.[5] Yet how can her parents key into her needs when the maturity myth holds such power over expectations and norms?

Emma tries to tell her mother how she feels but says she meets a brick wall. Both her parents persist in seeing her as a successful adult and do not see the daughter in need.

"When I was getting ready to go back last time, my mom gave me that look-over. You know how mothers look at you? and she said she envied me. She told me what a fine woman I was and how satisfied I was with my life. It was so weird. She's looking at me and telling me how I feel. And I wanted to tell her she'd got everything wrong but somehow I couldn't. Maybe if she says these things it's because she really needs to think I'm happy. I want her to know how I feel, but I guess she thinks I'm starting my life and I've got a good road ahead and I've done everything right. It would upset her to know the truth."

Emma wants to meet her parents' expectations. She cannot, then, expose her own needs. To have their support at this crossroads, both Emma and her parents would have to shatter the maturity myth.

But what is the truth that would upset Emma's mother? It is what thresholders constantly confront in their bewilderment: that they still have many of the needs they did as a child. They seek love and focus from their parents and reassurance that they are embedded within their family.

What could Emma do to make her good life as good as it should be?

1. She could tell her parents how she feels.

Often parents are much quicker to hear the message, "I don't need you anymore," than they are to hear messages about continuing needs. Young people can take the initiative and prod a parent into a new awareness. "I'm not going to stop being your kid, just because I'm grown up," Emma could say. After all, her parents are not withdrawing from her because they no longer love her. They are withdrawing because they see themselves as no longer necessary to her. (To strengthen her argument, she could persuade them to read this book.)

2. She needs to take new lessons in relaxation.

Like many young people on their own, Emma has lost the knack of relaxing. She needs to discover what does relax her. What does she enjoy? She could start with something comforting—like a good meal. With their natural stores of energy, young people often do not notice how much a sensible diet actually affects them. Her nightlife is a distraction, not relaxation. The trappings of that lifestyle—especially the drugs—add to stress because she has to run on caffeine to counter the aftereffects.

3. She could revise her strategies for dealing with stress.

When Emma has one of her three P.M. headaches, she could drink water (since headaches are often a sign of dehydration, and alcohol and caffeine are dehydrating) and sit quietly for fifteen minutes—rather than heading for Starbucks. To avoid the dread of opening her eyes in the morning, she could start relaxing early in the evening and go to bed early—instead of using her evenings to rev herself up.

4. She could practice self-assertion at work.

Employers may not intentionally exploit young people, but many are unable to resist taking advantage of their eagerness. An employer may need reminding that his or her request is unreasonable. Emma could try saying "no" to an additional assignment when it's too much. This can be done in a positive way: "I'll get that done as soon as possible, but to do it by the end of the day would not do it justice" or "If this has to be done by the end of the day, I could do a good job with someone to assist me."

Having the power to decline or negotiate an employer's requests will itself decrease stress (since nothing is more stressful at work than being out of control). If she does this successfully, then she will also feel more valued at work.

Parents can help a thresholder, whatever her job status and income. Here is what Emma's parents can do:

1. They could increase their awareness of their daughter's need for connection.

Parents can show respect for a son's or daughter's adult achievements without denying her status as their child. Financial independence does not switch off the emotional need for parents.

2. They could give reminders that this connection is valued and intact.

They could keep her up to date with the gossip of her familiar environment. They could talk about her childhood, using photographs, journals, or their own memories. If they move, they could make sure she feels at home in their new home. If they separate, they should explain the situation to her as carefully as they would to a younger child.

3. They could ask about her life.

Thresholders (just like teenagers) need parents to be interested in getting to know them in their new adult skin. They could carefully replace conversation-blocking statements such as, "Things are going so well for you," with conversation-opening questions. The more specific these are, the better. "How are you?" or "How was your day?" are vague and seldom draw people out. Find out more about their current projects, what movies they've seen, what their friends are doing.

4. They could pose self-monitoring questions about time control and leisure control.

They could ask how busy she is or whether she feels tired. They should not be put off by an "Oh, Mom/Dad. I'm grown up now." She still needs a parent's concern, which will focus her concern for her own well being. Also, these questions can focus on her coping skills. Instead of treating her as a child who needs a parent to take care of her, they could ask how she is managing her time, and what she does when she gets tired.

5. They could encourage personal pleasures.

Sometimes young people know how to work and to party, but they lose touch with things they actually enjoy. Her parents could ask Emma about an activity they know she enjoys—such as cycling or hiking or debating. They could urge her to take up these activities again. Even if she rejects the suggestion, she may start to reflect on her choice of activities.

They could provide occasional opportunities for personal pampering. As a birthday present, she could be given a one-day pass to a health club or a weekend home, when she is cared for just like a kid.

A parent's concern at this stage of a daughter's or son's life should be practical and positive. We can coach them to think about their own well-being, and we can tell them we are confident that they will get it right in the end.

SHORTCUTS TO MATURITY: THRESHOLDER MARRIAGES

THERE are a thousand different routes from adolescence to adulthood. Most involve persistent challenges, difficult choices, and a creative vision. Above all, most involve uncertainty and some risk. How one will change and develop along the way is an unknown. Some young people find this uncertainty intolerable. To avoid it, they take on an adult persona, pretending they already know the answer to the question: "Who will I be as an adult?" But because, at this early stage, they cannot develop their own answer, they adopt ready-made images of the grown-up. The familiar format gives them a false sense of knowing their future.

A grown-up is settled and responsible, with a spouse or even a child. A grown-up has well-formed ideas about commitments and values. Thresholders who want to be grown-ups reject the longer, slower route most young people take today in preparation for a complex and demanding adulthood.

In describing this foreshortened path from adolescence to maturity, Erik Erikson used the term "foreclosure." The term for a bank closing on a loan is linked to a psychological decision to close off the time-loan on youthful learning and exploration. The threshold years should come with a permission slip for slow-paced development, for scouting the adult world, for making gradual decisions and commitments. When young people find this developmental space too confusing and too open-ended, they turn down the opportunity for real, deep growth. They do not want to make the payments (of search and exploration) on this time-loan. This leads them to choose a preformed and limited identity.

Foreclosure on personal development is signaled by

1. The belief that at the entry point to adulthood, one's adult self—with its preferences and needs—is already formed.

2. The declaration of maturity, usually with some public form, such as marriage or parenthood.

3. The assumption that maturity can be achieved through a conscious decision.

Thresholders who follow this pattern ignore the opportunity to expand their horizons. They are hoping, by assuming the outward form of adulthood, to take a shortcut to deep personal change. This strategy invariably fails. Even the well-tried forms of adulthood that these thresholders opt for involve real life and real-life problems. While such thresholders believe themselves to be sensible and committed, they are unable to deal with the problems that arise. Many of these young people aim for security and certainty but end up bewildered by the mess around them.

Foreclosure is less common today than it was forty or fifty years ago. Once, what is now "early" was "timely." When the markers of adulthood—a stable job, a steady income—could be achieved by the age of twenty-one, that was seen as the time to settle down. Young men felt under pressure to take a job and look for security. If they did not, other young men would climb ahead on the career ladder. Common views about the appropriate age for bearing children put pressure on women to become mothers in their early twenties. Pregnancy after the age of twenty-six was seen as "late." Some of these beliefs were simply norms of fashion, but some were grounded in the reality that risks to the baby do increase in later pregnancies. In addition, many women felt social pressure to marry. Since most men married young, they chose young women. Waiting would result in diminished options on available men. At twenty-five, a woman was "on the shelf," and by twenty-nine, she was an "old maid."

This social pressure to buckle down to a career and to marry in what is now the threshold phase has been lifted for two reasons. First, a "career ladder" is now an outmoded model. Steady jobs are only temporarily steady. There are also more opportunities to jumpstart a career at any time of life. Second, getting married can no longer reasonably be called "settling down." Good marriages may end in divorce. People who marry before the age of twenty-four have a 60 percent chance of divorcing by the time they are thirty.

Real life cannot be controlled by yesterday's formulae. Nevertheless, some thresholders want to "settle" their lives. While this strategy is meant to avoid the risks of an unknown future, it actually increases risk. As thresholders make a preemptive bid to enact adult roles, they find themselves in situations that, as apprentice adults, they simply cannot manage. Moreover, having taken on those roles, they may then be encumbered by responsibilities that make any second shot at development more difficult. When they should, as modern thresholders, have the time and energy to prepare for their futures, they are caught up in situations that block opportunity. In particular, thresholders who become parents have immutable responsibilities to others. At the same time, they need skills and experience for long-term financial viability.

These complications present thresholders' parents with a dilemma. Should a thresholder's parent say: "This is your life. These were your choices. You face the consequences yourself"? Or, should a parent say: "My daughter or son has taken on more than she or he can manage. To give her a good launch into adulthood, I will have to provide the kind of day-to-day help she or he needed as a child"? The first alternative endorses the maturity myth: Young people will do better if they are independent. The second alternative acknowledges today's realities: Thresholders who have emotional and practical help from parents are the ones who thrive.

The mistakes our sons and daughters make in the threshold years can have profound effects on our own lives. Thresholders who think they are full-fledged grown-ups may become distraught and disoriented children when they divorce or separate. Parents of thresholders may also have to decide whether to take on parenting roles again—this time as grandparents. When they do take on these burdens and pleasures, their daughters and sons can have another chance to thrive in adulthood.

An Old-Fashioned Marriage (Mike and Joni)

Thresholder marriages face many special problems. The expectations of the couple are usually high—and untested. They are unaware of how much fantasies have formed their hopes and their love. They often feel they have to prove something to their parents, who in all probability warned them that they were too young. They have to stabilize their relationship at a time when their lives and their interests are rapidly changing.

When I first meet Mike, he is a few days away from leaving for college in Cleveland, three hundred miles away from the junior college he has attended for the past two years. "Upgrading" to a four-year college is a significant achievement. "Lots of my friends planned to do this, but couldn't manage it." When he talks about his future, he swings from talking about the next few months, counting the weeks before he will be able to see his girlfriend, Joni, again, to ten years down the line, when he looks forward to being responsible and settled. But he speaks with pleasure about possibilities opening before him, about enjoying this phase of his life. He hopes to have the opportunity to travel and study before he is, as he puts it, "locked into a job and tied down to family responsibilities."

His junior year—his first year away from home—is much harder than he expected. He finds the amount of material covered vast, compared to what he had in the past. He admires the other students for their intelligence but describes them as unfriendly and spoiled. Above all, he finds them immature. He describes them as "adolescent." He describes himself as "in many ways much older" than his fellow students and more serious about life. While he is reluctant to say he is depressed, he says that others look down on him and don't give him a chance. He misses Joni with an intensity that takes him by surprise. "With her I'm someone," he explains. They decide to marry after Christmas.

Joni displays a well-matched polish when I meet her. She has been living at home and attending a community college while working. She says she is glad to marry Mike. They were going to marry anyway, so what difference does it make when they marry? Apart from her and Mike's parents' reluctance to see them married so young, everything will work out. "Being single really doesn't suit us. Things are more straightforward this way. There's not that uncertainty about who you'll be with next year or the year after. We don't know what jobs we'll have, but at least we know we'll be together."

For these young people, "maturity" is a kind of playacting.

Mike and Joni naively think that being able to *act* mature is the same as *being* mature. Their strategies for dealing with struggle are less creative and certainly less critical or searching than they had been one year before. They opt for clarity. The questions they confront during the next eighteen months make their futures less clear than they ever were.

HOW INEXPERIENCE SHAPES "MATURE" STRATEGIES

Young adults are at a vulnerable stage. There is still a vital need for close emotional support to help them withstand the challenges of risk and uncertainty. They also benefit from other adults' wisdom¹ but may consider themselves "too old" to listen to a parent's advice. Mike's father, Frank, feels helpless and frustrated: "Mike's going back to a time that seems archaic. He's going right into that niche that my generation rejected—marrying young, having kids young, and having to gear your whole life to meeting those responsibilities. Most of my friends are tearing their hair out because their kids are swearing off marriage, and aren't producing [grand] kids because they think they're too young to be parents at thirty. Here's my son saying he can't be a junior in college without a wife by his side."

Mike looks coolly at his father. "This is a decision I've made after a great deal of thought," he replies. "What kind of thought?" Frank demands, and then the exchange passes into mutual recriminations: "You never take me seriously"/"You never listen to me"; "You're always trying to put me down"/"I'm trying to help";"You refuse to listen"/"Why should I listen to you about this?"

It is not only Mike's clothes that reveal his admiration for retro styles. He wants a life that harkens back to the 1950s and dislikes what he calls the irresponsibility of the Me Generation. He believes that his parents' marriage did not last because they were "immature and they could only think of themselves and what they wanted." He thinks that one reason his parents divorced was that they did not marry until they were thirty and had by then developed in different ways. They always wanted to do their own thing. They fought over things like giving each other space and respecting each other's autonomy. They made their lives, Mike concludes, "too complicated."

With the path to adulthood longer than ever, people are marrying and having children later.[2] In less complicated times, young people could grow up more quickly and could step into adult roles at the close of adolescence. Mike and Joni try to buck the modern trend.

They then confront the problems of any young marriage. Even when they were the norm, early marriages were difficult. Romantic ideals have not been modified by experience, and young people coming into a marriage inevitably expect too much. Being a couple has never been easy. But in the past, there was a social order that supported the outer frame of a marriage. When the relationship became difficult, there was still some inevitability about it that made sense of sticking with it. Now—especially in early marriages—there is more interference than support. Ending them is easier, and being unmarried is easier.

In addition, Mike and Joni face the special problems of student marriages. Mike and Joni live and think in different contexts. They organize their work and their leisure according to different frameworks and find themselves out of sync.[3] Joni takes a job at a department store downtown. Mike is sometimes asleep when she leaves in the morning. When she comes home, he is working at his desk or, more frequently, in the library. She would like him to share the job of cooking dinner. She has been at work all day, and she is tired. But he says he has been studying all day, and *he* is tired. They argue over who is the real worker. Is it Mike, who is upgrading his skills for their future? Is it Joni, who is earning money now, money that they need for their food and apartment?

In Joni's view, Mike does not understand how tiring her work is. Often she does not mind coming home and, after giving her feet a rest, starting dinner. She likes cooking for him. But it would be nice, sometimes, to have him do the same for her. What she finds most distressing is his preoccupation in the evenings. She comes home from work and wants his company and attention. "He doesn't talk to me. He finishes eating and runs back to his books." Mike says Joni does not understand how much being a student absorbs him. It is not something you can just switch on and off. He has to think, read, write papers. He cannot stop in the middle of a term paper. She can switch off as soon as she comes home. She wants his company. She wants to talk and relax with him. He is still thinking about the next day's class. Not that Mike never relaxes and never wants to talk or to party. But his timing is linked to exams and the due date of an essay. After these, he wants to party or slump for a few days. Joni cannot take the all-night celebrations. Her time is measured by working hours.

Joni feels sidelined by his student preoccupations and rhythms. When Mike tells her his grades are sliding and that he hasn't been working, she feels betrayed. She has put off her need for his company so that he can study. Instead, he has been seeking other students out. Suddenly he finds their society congenial. She feels that her gift of allowing him time alone has been misused. He feels she does not understand how difficult college is and how much is at risk with each paper or exam. "You're entire worth is on the line."

They married to create a secure base in which each would feel valued and from which they could show others how serious and committed—and mature—they were. Instead, they now seek comforts away from one another. Instead of shoring up the other's ego, each feels devalued by the other. They married to avoid the challenges of a changing, outside world. Instead, these challenges pull them apart.

GIVING THRESHOLDERS A SECOND CHANCE

Thresholders who take a shortcut to maturity are often difficult to help. They tend to be calm and confident on the surface. What we don't see is that their confidence is kept intact by a determination to limit their lives. They will give up, as Mike does, ideas of traveling and extending their studies or training in order to make do with what they have and who they are at present. Their calmness would give way to an overwhelming anxiety if they were pushed to develop themselves further.

It is often very difficult to get through to thresholders who take shortcuts to adulthood, because they are well defended. They themselves do not want to confront their doubts—that's why they're foreclosing their options. It is difficult, therefore, for parents to prevent a thresholder foreclosing on his or her life, but they can help them recover from disappointments and get back on track. They can:

1. Anticipate problems.

When a thresholder wants to declare her maturity with some dramatic action (such as marriage), hold discussions of possible outcomes. Keep these discussions as neutral as possible. Remarks such as "You're too young" and "No one can tell you anything" will be counterproductive, since the thresholder blocks off self-awareness. Instead of "forbidding" such moves or punishing them ("You won't a get a penny from me if you marry now"), propose alternatives. For example, suggest a delay of marriage. Suggest they try living together. But don't expect too much from efforts at this stage.

2. Avoid humiliation.

Humiliation is the greatest threat to the child/parent bond. "I told you so" and "Why can't you just grown up?" may seem like mild expressions of exasperation when spoken by a parent, but they can chill a daughter or son to the bone.

3. Tolerate returns.

When young people make false starts, they need second chances. Their families are the best providers of those second chances. Remember, most young people who "leave home" at the end of adolescence return home for prolonged periods throughout the threshold years. Thresholders should be able to experience returning home as normal.

When young people make false entries into adulthood, they need to retreat before they make another start. Mike is too ashamed to seek his family's support. "It never occurred to me that I was as young and foolish as people said I was. I made this mess. I have to work it out." Joni, less bound by the maturity myth, goes home to her family. "It's the most humiliating thing that's happened to me. And now my whole future is just a blank. I always thought I'd be Mike's wife. That was one thing I was sure of. Now I'm not sure of anything." She is sitting on the sofa in her mother's house. Hair unwashed, wearing baggy sweats, she is the perfect picture of the depressed young woman. There is even an empty carton of chocolate ice cream on the coffee table in front of her. Joni's mother hears her daughter's voice rise as we talk. She comes into the room and sits beside her daughter. There are a hundred things she could say: Joni hears them in her mind, even if her mother does not speak them. I see the daughter's second guessing of what the mother might say: A combination of

"I warned you this would happen" and "Don't worry, Mom's here."

When Thresholders' Parents Are Grandparents
(Rosanne and Faith)

Sometimes thresholders make choices—or mistakes—that engender other children. They may feel old enough, or want to declare themselves old enough, to take on the responsibilities of being a parent. This is a trump card in the bid to appear grown up. How can anyone deny that they are grown up if they are themselves a parent? How can anyone tell them what to do if they are in charge of their own children? Parenthood is an instantaneous marker of adult status.

Sometimes parenthood seems to provide an answer to questions about the direction and meaning of one's adult life. Parenthood, after all, gives one, ready-made, a significant adult role. The child becomes a willing supporter of the parent's ego, and few mothers of babies feel worthless or alone. Parenthood, then, seems to some young people, a magic bullet.

Parenthood also shapes each and every aspect of a young person's life, but few acknowledge this beforehand. Young people routinely minimize the amount of time and energy and money parenthood entails. They speak of being able to study while the baby sleeps. They speak about being able to move around freely because "it only takes one arm to hold a baby." When experienced parents hear thresholders speak about parenting, their response often is, "You don't have the slightest idea." But young people who choose to foreclose on the threshold phase are not good at listening to more experienced adults.

Once they are parents, their responsibilities are immutable. The realities of parenthood then strike hard. These are:

1. a twenty-four-hour job, with no pay

2. diminished employment and training opportunities

3. diminished earnings throughout their lifetimes

Parenthood—especially motherhood—is often perceived by young people as more negotiable than it turns out to be. What you feel a baby needs when you are not a parent is very different from what you want to give your own child. The demands of this love, combined with the daily routines of child care, are not accurately predicted by most parents. Once they realize the strength of those demands, they have no choice but to do their best to meet them.

Parenting tasks incur enormous costs on a young woman's career. Though most women now expect to work while they have children, the tactics of this are still hard to manage—and even harder at entry-level jobs. They are hard in the studying or training phase, when young people need to concentrate and be alert. The sleepless nights of parenting young children do not mesh well with these demands. The impact on an adult career is likely to last far longer than a child's infancy. A woman who has a child at twenty-one is estimated to forgo more than double the earnings of a woman who has her first child at twenty-nine.[4]

The best protection a thresholder has from long-term impediments of early parenthood is through the practical support given by her parents.

Normally we think of the role of being grandparents as being able to enjoy young children and then hand them back to their parents. But ever increasing numbers of midlife people are becoming more involved with the rearing of grandchildren. Some are as actively involved in this care as any parent. A report by the U.S. Census Bureau in 1999 showed that 4.7 million grandparents live with and participate in the care of their grandchildren.[5] Millions more are caring for grandchildren without actually living with them.[6]

Grandparents tend to live longer, to be healthier longer—and so are able to play an active role in caring for grandchildren. This trend is fortunate for their daughters. Whereas once the outlook was gloomy primarily for *teenagers* who became parents,[7] now a thresholder who becomes a parent loses out on that crucial development of what is called "human capital" or the development of the skills, training, and experiences that make her attractive to employers. Nothing sets back a career, as clearly as losing out on the early learning about work cultures.[8] For any parent, the typical structures of work, career, and mothering are unforgiving. For a single and extremely young woman, economic and social realities are more like barbed wire fences than windows of opportunity. But if a young parent has the support of her parents, she may be able to ameliorate the damage caused by this setback.

THE SELFISH/SELFLESS DIVIDE

At twenty, Faith had had enough of school. She had had enough of worrying about her future according to the rules of sensible forward planning. Aware of new risks in a world where "there are so many jobs and so many people competing for them, and nothing to guide you through," she has a nostalgia for past certainties. Faith looks back on a time she imagines as being "so much more simple. You knew what things were going to be like. You knew you were going to work for a while and then get married. You knew your husband would support you. Now you just can't see your life as a whole. My mom's been married twice, and she's had a few boyfriends, but I never know what she'll be doing next, what job she'll have, whether she'll have a boyfriend. It's stupid to agonize over these decisions. It's stupid because there's no telling what I'll be doing later on."

When she discovers she is pregnant after "one careless after-noon," she takes a positive view. Declaring that she is as grown up as she will ever be, she feels ready, now, to have a child. "I think it will be good for me," she explains. "It will be a focal point, you know, and a way of knowing who I am, and a purpose."

Ten months after the birth of her son, I see her again. She is no longer with her boyfriend "full time," but he still visits regu-larly. She has given up evening classes at the community college because she is too tired. In fact, she says, "It's like a tiredness I've never felt before. I just become a different person." Activities she once took for granted now involve strategic planning: "I can't do anything without thinking about the baby. Everything takes so much longer. Just getting out of the house is a chore." She is lonely but also is uncomfortable when friends visit: "You're so totally different once you have a kid. I see my friends looking around this place and their noses wrinkle up and I know I look like a mess. I feel totally and utterly depressed about the mess I've got myself into."

Yet she also says, "Drake is really the best thing that ever hap-pened to me. He's so beautiful, the most beautiful thing I've ever seen. And now he's more and more responsive. And when I look at him I feel a really different kind of love, and I know whatever happens, it's all worth it."

A young mother's feelings are full of contradictions—love, excitement, the thrill of being important, as well as the frustra-tion of self-sacrifice, social isolation, and the ravages of fatigue.[9] Faith looks into her baby's eyes and sees herself anew. She is not just someone who messed up but a source of wonder and delight. She also feels anger at what's happened to her and anger at her boyfriend for being so apparently unencumbered by this bond. She is dazed as to how she could have accepted this situation without understanding its consequences.

Faith's mother, Rosanne, revisits the dilemmas of mother-hood. She, too, has to balance her own wishes against the needs of another. She is entering a phase of life during which she expected she would have more time to do her own thing. As she reflects on what to do, she has to slay the maturity myth: "I warned Faith she was too young. Now maybe she has to sort things out herself. You can't sort out their problems when they're grown-ups themselves. But it's hard for her, and such a waste, when you think of her whole life—and you think about what kids her age are doing—all sorts of things—and she can't. And I love being with Drake. And it will give her a chance to get on her feet. She's talking about law school now, and I think she could really do it. I think she really could if she had the chance." Rosanne argues away the maturity myth in favor of her knowledge that she can help her daughter.

The enormous advantages of a grandparent as caretaker are:
1. The child is cared for by someone he will love and trust.
2. The care is likely to be stable and trustworthy.
3. There will be an easy changeover when Faith does have more time to do more parenting.
4. It is costless for the thresholder/parent.
5. It maintains family bonds.

The disadvantages are largely notional. The argument against is: Faith is an adult who should take responsibility for her own actions.

Indeed, Faith must learn to take responsibility for her actions. But, as I have already argued, young people learn more readily when their responsibilities are managable. With too much responsibility, they may learn how to cope, but they seldom thrive. What are the costs of this responsibility? Faith can become a nonworking single mother, which may force her into poverty, or a working single mother who puts her child in day-care, which may not be adequate and cannot be as satisfactory as a grandmother's care.

Of course, responsibility remains an important issue for thresholders. In these situations, however, Faith's responsibilities should be reframed. They are:

1. To take steps toward improving her future, showing commitment and direction.

2. To participate as much as possible in raising her child.

3. To acknowledge the help a parent is giving her.

A new cross-generational extended family is emerging. This new family pattern has profound importance to the well-being of future generations. Parents may become active parents a second time around. All this is against expectations today's parents grew up with—expectations that their children would become, in their early twenties, independent adults. As this becomes less and less likely, young parents will need co-parents. Few social networks outside the family will support a thresholder—especially a single one—who becomes a parent. The well-being of two generations is at stake, and their best resource is the grandparent. As Rosanne reflects, "My sister says, 'You're nuts. You should be enjoying life now.' But where's the enjoyment in seeing my daughter cut off from all the opportunities she still deserves? Okay, she has a baby. But she's still my kid, you know, and I'll look after her if she needs me."

CHAPTER NINE

THRESHOLDERS IN A
MATERIAL WORLD:
MANAGING MONEY

MONEY is one of the most common bones of contention between parent and thresholder. But arguments between thresholders and parents about money are never just about money. They are about gratitude, responsibility, and independence. Parents worry that their daughters and sons may be taking them for granted. They are concerned that "things come too easily to young people these days." A son or daughter sometimes believes a parent who can afford to help out financially, and doesn't, is being stingy. In refusing to give money, it seems they are refusing to give love. Given these out-of-sync responses, parents see their young adult children as selfish and irresponsible. Their response is: "See what comes of helping you. You're spoiled. I've helped you too much. You have to get by on your own. I'm not always going to be around to bail you out."

Over the years parents give much to a son or daughter in practical and financial terms. They practice self-denial so that a child will have more than they can easily afford. When a daughter or son asks for more than is necessary, parents are hurt: "Doesn't she think I've given her enough?" or "Can't he show gratitude by being more careful with money?"

Arguments over money can go on for years, without either parent or thresholder realizing what is actually at stake. Twenty-four-year-old Annette borrowed money from her mother and stepfather to buy a car when she was twenty-one. They are still arguing about the payments of the loan. Her parents accuse her of being "spoiled" and "ungrateful." She feels that she is being unfairly condemned.

Rene's mother, Jessie, demands an instant repayment of a loan she had made her daughter when, at twenty-one, she was unemployed. Two years later Rene has been working for eighteen months and buys her own apartment. Jessie declares: "If you can afford this chic studio, you can afford to repay me." Rene says her mother is being "controlling." Jessie reminds her that she had to forgo a vacation to offer her daughter the loan.

Ned asks his parents for a loan when he is earning more than they are. His father calls him "inconsiderate." His mother is hurt and puzzled: "Whatever happened to my thoughtful little boy?"

Long after the actual money is forgotten, anger rages over questions about how much is given and what has been valued.

Spirals of accusation and resentment can be prevented through awareness that:

1. Managing money as a thresholder is far more difficult than managing money as a teenager.

Accurate budgeting, money management, and repaying debts are daunting tasks. Even when a thresholder is not aiming for financial independence in the short-term, the long-term prospect of being on one's own financially looms large in her or his approach to money. Young people are often confounded by the cost of living and by the size of their debts. They may deny themselves essential things, such as food or a warm coat. Or, they may believe that there is no point in trying to be careful with money, since they cannot imagine ever settling their accounts.

2. The environment presents persistent temptations to spend money.

Advertising is universal. It carries messages that expensive items will offer us an attractive identity and will prove our worth. Thresholders have been raised in this culture to be consumers. As they reach their twenties, they are an advertiser's prime target. In this environment, sensible financial restraint can seem like real hardship.

3. Out-of-control spending may have symbolic meaning.

Shopping can be a distraction from unhappiness. Temporarily, buying something can compensate for being lonely. It is a way of giving oneself a gift and showing love.

Shopping can also make someone feel powerful, when he feels powerless in other areas of his life. When shopping meets these needs, it can become addictive.

4. Financial arrangements should be clear and consistent.

While some renegotiations can be reasonable, this is an area in which firmness is very effective. Parents can offer practical advice (about how to earn, how to save or to structure repayments), but bailing a young person out of a self-made financial problem is a precedent to avoid.

How Money Can Divide Thresholder and Parent (Jo)

Quarrels about money can distort a parent/thresholder relationship. These quarrels are often fuelled by the maturity myth according to which parents should keep a daughter or son at arm's length, emotionally as well as financially. The thresholder then feels rejected—and angry and uncared for. The arguments may be based on good principles and good intentions, but they are counterproductive. This is clear as I witness the conflict between Jo and Serge, daughter and father who, by arguing about love and gratitude, threaten the attachment they both value.

I first meet Jo in her parents' spacious Chicago apartment overlooking the lake. The windows are large, the drapes heavy, the furniture solemn and substantial. She sits on the sofa, shaking with anger after "another horrible blow up" with her father. When I ask whether she would like me to come back at a better time, she shakes her head and mutters, "There's never a better time."

Jo is in the midst of late college preparation. She had applied to several private East Coast colleges, but her applications were rejected. Her grade average was not high enough to gain admission to the places her parents had expected. Her father was initially supportive during this disappointment. "It's really only one rejection," he told her as she wept over the pile of rejection letters. "If you're accepted by one, you're accepted by all of them. If you're rejected by one, you're rejected by all of them. They're like one school." Her safety school had put her on the waiting list, and she recently heard she had been admitted. It has been a tense summer: "They've been really hard on me, especially Dad. He keeps making suggestions about what I should do. When he asks if we can talk I get butterflies in my stomach. He doesn't know the difference between talking and lecturing. Whenever he wants to talk to me I know he's going to sit down and order me around. He has this list of jobs I was supposed to try for this summer, and he also wanted to hire a tutor to polish up my math. When I wasn't gung ho on something he'd just turn around and say, 'You're lazy.'"

Jo's father, Serge, is polite but edgy as we speak. His annoyance with Jo still plays upon his nerves. The causes of, and solutions to, her problems seem straightforward to him. He frames them in the context of the myth of maturity and the myth of the spoiled child: "She's had things too easy. She's a smart kid, and could have made it anywhere if she'd just put in that little extra effort. But why work for three hours for an A, when you can get a B with half an hour's work. That's how she figured it."

He believes he has been too indulgent and let her stay his little girl for too long. Now it is time for her to go out in the world and find that "it is a tough place, and that even smart, pretty girls have to work to get what they want. When she comes whining to me for something now, my message is 'Grow up.' She has to learn to sort things out herself."

The quarrel that was interrupted by my arrival was about money—but of course it was not just about money. It was about ingratitude ("She doesn't appreciate all I've done for her") and irresponsibility ("She can't handle a budget") and inadequacy ("She didn't bother to get a job this summer"). As with all quarrels, timing is just as much an issue as are high principles. Jo returned from a trip to the Watertower Place Mall with shopping bags full of clothes just as her father was going through the credit card statements. In this tense preparing-to-leave-time, he is watching for signs of readiness. He expects her, as someone about to leave home, to be serious and restrained. Instead, she is being self-indulgent.

"How," he asks, "will she ever learn what's what unless she's forced to learn?" He feels under pressure to give her swift lessons, to use up "the short time I have left with her"—referring to what he sees as the brief time he will be actively involved in parenting before she grows up and is on her own. He announces that he is going to establish a "new regime." He cuts her college budget by a quarter of what they had previously agreed and decrees that some payment of her fees will be a loan, which she will have to repay by working during the summer.

Like many parents who are financially well-off, Serge worries that Jo has more than is good for her—but he then curtails emotional support alongside financial support. He presents financial restriction as a way of showing his disapproval, and this is what Jo focuses on in her tirade against him: "I hate the way my Dad says, 'Grow up.' It's the most maddening thing, like he knows what being grown-up is and I don't know anything. In my parents' eyes I'm hopelessly immature. This money thing is *pathetic*. I went out this morning with the credit card. This was fine with him then. Believe me, this morning he was saying, 'Get what you need.' Then I come back to this palaver about nothing. I don't mind working. I don't mind paying back some of the tuition. But I hate it when he comes over like the big man who's making me do this as a punishment. And believe me, it's not just today. This has been going on since graduation. I go through every day thinking, a hundred times each day: 'I'm going to show them. I'm going to have to make it without their help.'"

Jo believes that her father gives her money grudgingly. She finds this humiliating, and tries to punish him with her coldness. "I don't talk to him like I used to. He really doesn't know what's going on in my life now." Like most thresholders, Jo puts "being judged at the top of my hate list." She feels that Serge thinks he is perfectly justified in humiliating her and that he wants her to feel bad about herself.

Jo and Serge are caught in a vicious cycle. Serge assumes that his daughter's task is to "grow up." "Growing up" means being capable of managing on her own, without any financial indulgence from him. But, paradoxically, he thinks she wants to separate from him. Like many parents, he confuses being responsible, on the one hand, with being independent (and separate), on the other hand. Like many parents, he confuses financial indulgence with emotional support and appreciation, which are greatly needed.

Serge does not realize that responsibility is best learned with a parent's help. It is best practised in an emotionally supportive context. And it is best learned, at this stage in life, when parents use their resources (their wisdom and their practical knowledge) to help solve problems. He does not realize he can give emotional support without giving financial support. Confused by the clash between his genuine responsiveness to Jo and his misguided principles, he is overgenerous one moment and overly-guarded the next. A better approach would involve:

1. Working out the arrangement of financial support and then explaining it carefully to his daughter.

2. When money problems arise, acknowledge the difficulty of learning how to manage money. Focus on the challenge, not on her "irresponsibility" or "immaturity."

3. Ask how she plans to address the problem. Encourage her to develop the plan and work on the solution herself.

4. Praise her for her success when she does manage her budget.

The New Materialists (Ned)

Young people are at risk from the consumer culture. As children, they are under pressure to establish their identities with clothes and gadgets and accessories. As teenagers, they develop a sense of belonging by having the same shoes their friends have. They assert a sense of value by flashing a designer logo.

The materialism of adolescence often eases by the thresholder phase. A nineteen- or twenty-year-old is far less likely to badger parents about buying the latest gadget or up-to-date designer clothes. They are more likely to show concern for their family's expenses. Many thresholders speak regretfully of the financial burdens they place on their parents. They at least try to manage a budget. Newly employed, however, many young people vacillate between awe at the immense wealth of a regular paycheck and amazement at the real cost of living. They often have to relearn money management.

Money becomes an obsession with thresholders usually not through greed, but through debt. Watching out for their own living expenses comes as a shock. There is a huge difference between managing an allowance and managing one's livelihood. One hundred dollars seems an awful lot when saved up in allowances, but in the real world of rent and food and replacement of clothes, it doesn't go far. When these young people start to earn a good salary, they can lose all financial sense.

Until he was twenty-two, Ned managed on what he borrowed and what he earned in part-time work in a coffee house. He knew his parents had to scrimp and save to send him to college. In his senior year, he started to pay them back. As he worked in his first poorly paid job, he was meticulous about repayment. This restraint dissolved when, at twenty-three, he took a highly paid job in a new technology firm. Suddenly, what had been unthought-of luxuries became necessities. The question, "How can I earn enough to get by?" turned into the question, "Am I earning enough to keep up?"

Young people start out as idealists, but when they navigate their adult worlds they can regress. The simple common sense that they could be relied on to have as teenagers suddenly deserts them. This seems to be a response to their fear of being adults. They want to send out the message: "I'm not really grown up."

When I ask Ned what achievement he is most proud of, he looks at me in surprise. "What do you think?" he demands and gestures toward his sleek sound system and designer furniture. He lives in the same building as Emma,[i] who has introduced me to him. While she put herself forward as someone having difficulty with the transition from adolescent to adult, Ned is talking to me "because Emma asked." He does not see himself, when I first speak to him, as anything but in the right place, at the right time.

Ned calls himself a new materialist. This is how he describes a new generation of yuppies. They differ from the yuppies of the 1980s in that they do not see themselves as on a stable upward curve but merely at a comfortable oasis. Their duty, Ned explains, is to make the most of things now: "I don't expect things will be as good as this forever, but I'm going to enjoy it while I can."

In fact, new materialists do not want to spend their entire lives working hard to earn high salaries. They would rather earn less and "have a life." They are highly critical of what they see as the rat race. However, they have been raised in the consumer culture and taught that material things are important—and so they experience contradictions.

Like many young people, Ned feels ambivalent about his job. He is afraid of losing his job, which has so many perks; but he is also afraid of keeping it for too long and feeling bored and stuck. He tries to manage his anxiety by buying proof of the reality of his success: "Is this real?" is answered as he spends money to prove its reality. In spite of his high salary, he is in debt.

The process of buying and choosing gives Ned a sense of power. "I like going into a store and showing I have money to spend. And I like deciding whether something's right for me." He keeps up with his coworkers with higher salaries and big bonuses. He goes with them to their clubs, their restaurants. He gets into debt, which for a while he manages by juggling his clutch of brand-new credit cards. When the cards are cancelled, he asks to borrow money from his father.

Ned's parents are taken aback when he asks to borrow money. He is earning more than his father. Adam is confused, and a little hurt, and then angry when Ned does not pay back fifty dollars a month as they arranged. And the question they deal with as they deal with money is, "Who has my son become?" The issue of a few hundred dollars tears son and parents apart.

Ned's mother, Janet, speaks reluctantly but clearly. "I never thought I'd say this about him, my own son, but I'm not sure I like what he's becoming. Sometimes I hope he'll fall in love and—you know, get a little softer. He was such a generous boy, really, and so careful with money. When he started working in high school, I practically had to force his allowance on him. He'd say things like, 'Don't worry Mom. I'm earning now.' But he was earning nothing compared to now—and we were better off then—and now he's asking Adam for money! And all he thinks about is how much money he earns and what things he can buy."

Out-of-control spending is often a substitute for the goals that can't be reached: gadgets can be purchased, but the real goods in life aren't.[2] And after all, thresholders have been raised as consumers. They have come under pressure to adopt a lifestyle as part of their identity: who they are can often be seen as linked to what they choose to buy. Ned's own unease emerges as he speaks of his future as a full-fledged adult: "I've jumped in at the deep end, and all I can do is keep going. I'd like something else, something a bit more satisfying, and I'd sure like less stress. But I don't see how. My dad would throw a fit if I gave up now, and Mom would think I was losing it. They're disappointed with me enough as it is. I have to keep earning like this to pay back what I owe, but then I have to spend a lot to look the part I have to take in my job."

Reflecting on his lack of management, the maturity myth seems true: Adam and Janet feel they have been too obliging to Ned, that he has not learned the importance of independence, that they are wrong to give him signals of their continuing support, that the best way to help him develop is to leave him to clean up his own mess and learn to live without their help.

But support does not have to come in the form of financial support. Adam and Janet can give Ned advice and encouragement as he rethinks his lifestyle. They can help him assess consequences of his compensatory spending habits. They can force home consequences by requiring repayments and refusing further loans. They can do this neutrally, without judging him for making a request. Ned can feel the power of his parents' support, even when no money comes with it.

Shopping Addictions during the Threshold Years (Jasmine)
Increasing numbers of young people are finding themselves with debts that to them are unimaginable. Some even opt for bankruptcy as the only way of freeing themselves from the relentless pursuit of creditors. Young people, not yet employed, are offered ten-thousand-dollar bank loans. Twenty-three-year-old Jasmine has debts of fifteen thousand dollars. At twenty, she bought a car for six thousand dollars, and that is now sold. The rest of the money was spent "on a bunch of other things—mostly makeup and clothes." The more depressed she gets about debt, the more she cheers herself up by shopping.

A common way of distracting oneself from self-doubt and loneliness is shopping. Buying something expensive can seem to mark one's importance. It is like presenting oneself with a gift ("I deserve this") when one is feeling down. When this compensation becomes an addiction, it can also become one's main problem—which one escapes from by more shopping.

A shopper makes decisions about what and whether to buy something. Some shopping addicts enjoy exercising their power to make decisions. Some young people shower themselves with material gifts to provide the tokens of love no one else gives. Jasmine explains her mounting debts: "I always liked shopping, but now it's different. When I'm doing it—you know, buying something—it seems like I really, really need it. I've always been careful with money—really responsible. No one ever tagged me 'extravagant.' My mom always trusted me more with money than anyone else. It was my brother who kept wanting his allowance early. But now I get so low that I think, 'I'll just go look around co-op.' It's a chance to get out—you know, take a break? But even though I'm enjoying myself just looking, I feel this—this hole right in the pit of my stomach, and I guess I feel sorry for myself, but it's deeper than that, it's really trying to save myself, and I look at something I like. I mean, it can be a book or a notebook, it's not necessarily a whole lot of money, and I buy it because I think I'm so unhappy I deserve something."

Unhappiness becomes expensive. Jasmine's notion of what is or is not "a whole lot of money" founders on her general inexperience with money. Spacing out costs (or budgeting) can cause problems for anyone. For Jasmine, the problem is that what she experiences as "need" is skewed. Desperate for comfort, she makes impulsive decisions. Her behavior reveals a common pattern: The thresholders who were unhappy and who felt lonely were far more likely to fall into debt through extravagance than were thresholders who felt well grounded in family and friends.

Addictions are habits that have destructive consequences, that the person practicing those habits may long to break, but cannot. A shopping addiction involves:

long hours shopping
buying things even when you have determined not to
buying things you never use
buying even when you know payment will be immensely problematic

All addictions are linked to poor self-management, and self-management becomes an altogether more complex affair in early adulthood. The so-called executive processes—the mental skills of organizing oneself in day-to-day life—are slowly and painstakingly established. What seems like "just common sense" once it is learned, is actually an accumulation of experience about oneself, one's stamina, one's productivity, one's response to temptations and stimuli. Jasmine says, "I used to know how to balance a checkbook, but it's weird how so many small checks can amount to so much. I never had a check bounce in college but now it's a regular thing. Everything mounts up. I get so many parking tickets in the city, and they make me feel stupid so I just toss them aside, and then I get late fines and so I feel even worse. It's not just the big things in life—it's the little things too I can't keep together."

Her mother helps her pay off one month's demands, but three months' later she is badly in debt. She takes out another loan.[3] "I was desperate. Then, suddenly, I had all this money again. There was this warm glow inside. I felt safe. I felt special. People couldn't make me feel inferior. And I thought it didn't matter if I bought a few things because nothing I bought really cost a lot. But now I have these debts, and I can't imagine ever paying them back."

Overcoming shopping addictions requires both self-determination and support from others.

Jasmine's first rule is to avoid temptation. This means she avoids shops. She finds an alternative form of entertainment. She cuts up all credit cards (so she has no easy means of buying things on credit).

The second approach is to ask herself what she gains from the purchases: entertainment, power, company? She needs to find other ways of getting these. She should also ask herself how long the pleasure from her purchases actually lasts? She could write out a list of consequences from her debts: Whom has she hurt or disappointed?

To avoid money troubles in the early threshold years parents should

1. Make the financial position clear.

From the outset these things should be clear: how much the parent is contributing, how much is part of a loan, and what must come from other sources of funding. These can be broken down by month or term to give a more managable focus. If a young person knows the budget from the outset, then expenditure can be monitored, and needs for supplement income assessed before things get out of hand. If a parent's financial position changes unexpectedly, then the thresholder should be made aware of this, and its implications, as soon as possible.

2. Be consistent.

If parents offer and then withdraw their offers, or declare limits and then exceed them, the thresholder's own incentive for consistency is decreased. What often happens then is that the daughter or son focuses on managing a parent's mood rather than on managing the budget.

3. Don't bail out.

While I urge parents to help their sons and daughters in all sorts of ways, I argue for tough love when it comes to money troubles. Help a daughter or son plan repayment of loans or other debts but do not make them go away.

Generosity is perfectly acceptable when parents can afford it, but this should be in the context of trust and appreciation. It is not for settling unnecessary debts.

CHAPTER TEN

CLOSING THE DOOR: SUICIDE AND SELF-HARM DURING THE THRESHOLD YEARS

WHEN most parents think about a suicidal thresholder, they think of someone else's son or daughter. Yet suicide is the second most common cause of death in young adults.[1] Approximately 5 percent of college students speak seriously about suicide when they seek a counselor. Among thresholders not in college, the rate of suicide and attempted suicide is even higher. The total number of suicides among thresholders has risen fourfold[2] during the past twenty years. Young men are four times more likely to kill themselves than are young women, though young women are more likely to practice self-harm, which can be as alarming and as physically damaging as attempted suicide.

If young people at risk could be clearly identified, the task of helping them would be far easier than it is. But most young people who attempt suicide are not mentally ill in any clear, formal sense. The feelings and experiences suicidal thresholders describe are shared by most young people at some time. These are:

1. Loneliness

During the early stages of adulthood, young people are sometimes convinced that no one really cares about them, and no one will notice whether they live or die. Parents and friends insist that they are "always there" for a child and that they care deeply, but this may not prevent the thresholder herself from feeling totally alone.

2. Feelings of worthlessness

Young people at risk of suicide feel that they will never amount to anything. They may reject others' attempts to bolster their spirits because they feel that any interest or concern or hope on their behalf will be wasted. They respond to praise with confusion and sometimes with anger, thinking that the person who speaks well of them is making fun of them or being blatantly insincere.

3. Feelings of hopelessness and helplessness

Some young people are overwhelmed by their problems and believe that nothing they do will make anything better. They do not bother to seek help. They view their situation as hopeless and therefore believe that nothing and no one can help.

4. Disappointment

When a close friendship or romance ends, when they cannot settle into college, when they lose a job, young people can feel like total failures. Those who have been high achievers, in particular, may see their success in early adulthood as crucial to their personal identity. They may feel ashamed, unloved, and unworthy of love.

5. Stress

Young people often juggle a variety of things. They may be learning the ropes of day-to-day independence, while at the same time taking on a range of new activities and responsibilities. They have to learn to organize their time and energy as they switch from one thing to another. They can easily suffer stress from overload.

6. Anger

Sometimes a thresholder is so angry (usually at being rejected or humiliated) that he or she can act impulsively. Suicide is sometimes an act of revenge.

7. Use of alcohol and drugs

Alcohol and drugs are used by young people for self-medication. They use them to moderate their stress and unhappiness. But sometimes alcohol or drugs magnify feelings of helplessness, worthlessness, and anger. With rational argument suppressed, they attempt suicide on impulse.

A young person who attempts suicide thinks of dying as a way to get relief from what he or she is feeling. What can be so confusing to others is that the young person's unhappiness does not seem so terrible. Breaking up with a girlfriend, messing up a job interview, failing an exam—are little bumps along a long road. When a thresholder talks about his despair or draws up a series of plans for killing himself, other people often dismiss what he says as absurd. "Don't be such a drama-queen," he is told. "You don't really mean that," or "Come on, things aren't really that bad." Even worse, he may be accused of "trying to get attention" or "trying to guilt trip" someone.

When a young person we care about speaks so negatively, he is likely to arouse deep anxieties in us. Sometimes we rush to protect ourselves and deny he can possibly mean what he says. Instead of starting a conversation, we batter it to the ground. "You can't possibly mean that!" we cry in disgust. The most effective approach, however, is to take any threats of suicide seriously:

1. Ask.

If we are concerned about the extent of someone's depression, we should ask whether he is thinking of taking his life. Many people are reluctant to pose this question because they do not want to "put anything into his head." But asking if a person feels suicidal is very unlikely to give him an idea he did not already have.

2. Listen.

It is difficult to listen to someone who speaks so negatively about himself and his situation. But when he feels someone really wants to understand him, he feels less isolated.

3. Discuss.

Young people who attempt suicide are not able to think long-term. Discussing problems will not solve them but can put them in perspective. The point of discussion is not to offer solutions but to talk through alternatives. This can be hard work because, in a negative frame of mind, young people reject every positive suggestion. Persistence in getting a discussion going can help reframe this outlook.

4. Be practical.

Usually a suicidal person sees his problems as overwhelming and intractable. If specific problems can be identified then at least they can be addressed in practical terms. Perhaps he needs an extension on a deadline, or more training at work, or a less rigid schedule. Even a small improvement can improve his outlook. Because he operates on the assumption that nothing can improve, solving even one problem can persuade him that larger problems, too, can be managed. But while you offer help don't promise him more than you can give. A person who is suicidal does not need further disappointment.

5. Refer.

A suicidal thresholder is too great a responsibility for any parent or friend to handle on her own. A referral to someone with objectivity and experience is essential. But such referrals should never be substitutes for the attention and support of a friend or parent.[3]

Losing the Self (Greg)

My first introduction to Greg came through his suicide note: "I let everyone down. I'm not going to make it. I can't go on."

He is twenty-three, thirteen months out of college. He describes his last two years in college as "the high point of my life—and the edge of a cliff." Each day of his final semester as editor of the university newspaper he spent in the cluttered newspaper offices, which were always warm with activity. The room buzzed as he entered. People broke off conversations to jump at him with questions. He had to make ten decisions from the time he got through the door to the time he got to his desk. Twice a week before the paper was printed, he stayed until five in the morning. Yet he also graduated *cum laude*.

Everyone expected him to land a plum job after graduating. He sent out résumés all over the country. The boxes of books and winter clothes stayed packed in his bedroom in his mother's home. Why unpack, he reasoned, when he was so soon to be on his way? By August, his neighborhood friends had gone their separate ways—back to school or to jobs either in the nearby city or across the country. He no longer has anyone he "can just hang out with. If I want to go to a movie, I have to go alone."

From sixty applications sent out in June, he was offered two interviews. Unsuccessful in these, he is still living at home, jobless, in September. His view of himself and his place in the world becomes defeatist: "You have to fight so hard to be anyone in this world. I could just about swing it in college. I'd do well in something, and I'd think—great, this is great, I'm really something. I felt competent and important. Leaving college I had to start all over again. You get this sense that you're so small and just don't matter. You discover how helpless you really are."

Each morning, he stays in bed until he hears his mother leave for work, and he tries to be busy in the evening. He learns to greet her with a shake of his head, which means, "No job today." He knows what her question will be: "Everytime I see her I know what she wants to ask. She really expects a hopeful answer." He declines to take phone calls from his father. "The conversations are so tired. He wants to give me a pep talk and a lecture rolled into one."

Six months is a short span in the life of a person, but it is time enough to discover that one may be exceptional in one setting and easily overlooked in another. Depressed young people do not necessarily have more problems than other thresholders, but they feel more confused by them, and their problems signal a loss of control. Greg explains, "It never occurred to me that I wouldn't get any job. I thought I had a great record. At first I was really puzzled and hurt, then I just came to accept it—like, you know, that's the sort of thing that's happening to me."

In February, he lands a job with a large city paper. At the time he celebrated with family and friends and hyped it as a big deal. Even before he received his first paycheck, he signed a lease on an apartment. He knew even then, however, that the position was insecure and that, for most of the new recruits, the job would be temporary.

"It sounded much better than it really was. Here's this paper that's a household name, and you're a journalist on it at twenty-three. But what happens is they hire lots of people at the same time. You're not on a salary. You get paid if you get an assignment. And of course there's only a small chance of a completed assignment actually running in the paper. So you turn up in the morning and if someone gives you a story or likes your idea for a story, you get the assignment and you have a job for that day. To get that far you have to make sure people there know you and what you can do, and convince them that you're the person who should write the piece they want. After a few months most of the new people are gone, because they're sick and tired of turning up and not getting a story and not getting paid. But when I got a story, I'd make a thousand dollars in one week. I was like . . . (he pants like an eager puppy). I worked at giving my stories a spin. It didn't matter that this was crap, not journalism. Because 90 percent of the stuff written doesn't get printed anyway. What stunned me was that even crap could get beyond the fact checker. And I was getting these pats on the back, getting to be known in the place. My dad phoned me when I had a byline—'Well done, kid!' I was desperate to keep going."

Many thresholders learn very quickly that in the wide world, they are easily replaceable. Yet the need to feel unique and special is so strong that without it, they can feel annihilated. The shock of these experiences can distort their way of thinking. Greg talks about his parents only in terms of their disappointment or pride in his job. He comes to believe that any failure to complete the "task" of this phase—to launch himself as an independent young man in the job market—will make him dispensable in their eyes, too.

Nothing creates more insecurity in young people than thinking that their connection to others depends on their ability to be a successful adult. When a piece Greg writes is shunted aside in favor of another's work, he suffers an asthma attack. "It was ridiculous. I felt like a heel. But what I was feeling is: They're trying to crush me to death."

His increasing irritability with his coworkers stems from anger common to young people who feel they have been driven by promises and expectations that now seem to dissolve. The routine criticisms that any young employee gets go to the very core of his being. He snaps back defensively, or he crumbles. He believes that everyone at the paper is waiting to catch him out. When he is "let go," he throws a tantrum in the editor's office. "I could see myself doing ridiculous things. I was shouting, and then I went to clear out my desk and I threw everything on the floor. I just lost it."

As he left the office he remembers thinking how lucky it was that this was the middle of the day: his roommate would be out, he would have the apartment to himself. He thought he was lucky because it was a Tuesday, and he did not expect a phone call from either of his parents until Friday. He remembers thinking that he was being sensible, seeing his first priority as calming down. But the apartment seems strangely hot and dusty, unwelcoming, as though it does not want him to be there. He shouts at the room to "stuff it," and takes some marijuana from his roommate's stash. Instead of relaxing him, the cannabis makes him groggy. He looks at his bank statements to see "how long he can last." A blinding headache is the last straw. It is proof that everything will always go wrong. He reflects on the "string of broken promises" that has formed since his twenty-first birthday. Believing he has failed because he is behind some notional schedule of where he should be at the ripe age of twenty-three, he tries to hang himself. Tucked into his checkbook, he leaves the note: "I let everyone down. I'm not going to make it. I can't go on."

A CRY FOR HELP

A suicide is sometimes called a cry for help. This means that a person attempts suicide but does not actually want to die. Instead, he wants to make a statement, loud and clear, that things are not well with him, and he needs help. But for most young people, motives for suicide are highly mixed. There is the motive for revenge, as young people see suicide as a means of punishing parents and friends who have abandoned them in some way. At the same time, suicide can be a self-sacrifice—atonement for letting people down.

Suicide is a bid for control in a context in which a young person feels powerless, and it is the ultimate escape into rest and sleep, a final draining away of responsibility and anxiety. Greg does not anticipate, as a teenager would, funeral eulogies and weeping friends. He imagines his death as relief. "When I was hooking that rope up, it seemed like I was doing a reasonable thing. I thought I was seeing things clearly for the first time in a long time. I thought it was a brilliant way to stop the pain. It was so scary—the way death seemed the best solution to all my problems. On one level I knew this was mad, but on another it seemed the most logical thing in the world."

Recovery from a suicide attempt is a slow and grueling process. A suicide attempt disrupts the entire family and creates a flood of new problems as people deal with their own guilt and anger. Greg's mother, Cathe, reflects, "Greg was the greatest kid. I trusted him, always, and he worked hard, and he was bright, and he always did so well. He talks about all the pressure that everyone put on him. I didn't mean to pressure him. I always thought he was the one pushing himself. But I guess it was me, too. I'll never forgive myself." Greg's roommate, Charles, who found him and saved his life, moves out immediately, leaving Greg responsible for the entire rent. Charles is questioned by the doctor, the police, and Greg's parents. "They keep asking, 'Weren't there any signs? Didn't you see something was going on?' Well, I didn't. Greg's just a stupid kid and I never want to see him again."

Cathe lives in terror that he will make another attempt. His father is angry and uncomprehending. "These kids have everything going for them, and they just mess up. I don't get it."

Greg, then, experiences a new set of problems from the effects of his suicide attempt. "I thought it was a way out. I wanted to avoid letting people down. At the time, it really seemed a very good solution to all my problems. The worst thing was coming to and remembering what I did and realizing I'd messed up this thing, too. You don't get pity. You don't get help. You're branded a failure, and you disappoint everyone. Nothing's changed. Your problems haven't gone away, but everyone now knows about them and wants to talk about them. Everyone you care about is blaming you, and blaming themselves, too. It's the worst mess I've ever seen."

In a lighter moment of our discussion, Cathe tells me about Greg's twentieth birthday: "It was when Greg was a teenager that my hair turned gray. On his twentieth birthday, I said, 'You're no longer a teenager. My hair will turn brown again.' It was a joke, but I didn't realize then how silly it was. You really do expect the worst of things to be over when your kid hits twenty. But," Cathe concludes abruptly, "it's not."

RECOVERIES

Depression, which is at the root of most suicide attempts, is the quintessential experience of low self-esteem, of having no control over one's life at present, and of having no hope in one's future. It involves a profound disruption in the way one sees the world. There are two different but related routes to recovery.

1. The first involves reframing one's experiences.

This involves modifying expectations. We should bring into our culture the realization that early adulthood can be so challenging and confusing that extra supports are needed. In this context, young people could be coached to deal with common disappointments, such as the failure to get or keep a job. They could learn to expect these setbacks as normal events. Therefore, the disappointments would not be experienced as reflections on their personal lack of worth.

2. The second recovery track involves improved problem-solving skills.

Hopelessness is a key feature in depression. Young people sometimes feel unable to identify different problems that confront them. Their problems may be nothing out of the ordinary, but because they are unable to name them, they seem insurmountable. Practice in identifying different problems and thinking about a number of possible solutions can make an apparently impossible situation managable.

3. A crucial factor in recovery is parental responsiveness.

Parents' awareness of their long-term influence on a child's well-being often leads them to blame themselves for every setback a daughter or son experiences. It is time to shift the focus from parental blaming (a person's deep unhappiness is related to what a parent did) to parental responsiveness: "There is much you can now do to help a son or daughter."

One of the most striking features of depressed young people is the withdrawal of parents' emotional support, guidance, and expressions of affection. This withdrawal is not the initial cause of the young person's depression. It is a response to depression—which then makes the depression worse.[4] What seems to happen is that depressed young people are so negative and irritable, particularly to parents, that their parents withdraw. They mistakenly think that a daughter or son "doesn't want me and doesn't need me," or is now "old enough to sort things out for himself." A parents' responsiveness and affection remain crucial supports for self-esteem.

Self-Inflicted Pain as a Mask for Emotional Pain (Lydia)

Self-mutilation is practiced primarily by young women in a frenzy of self-hatred. In teenagers, it is often associated with eating disorders or experiences of sexual abuse. Some girls describe how they punish themselves for being fat or breaking a diet by burning their skin or pounding the parts of their body they judge to be "too fat."[5] The comfort of food (or of sex or masturbation) is followed by the punishment of self-inflicted cuts or burns or punches.

The threshold years can witness a different kind of self-harm, born of anxiety about potential assaults on one's identity. One purpose of cutting or burning or freezing oneself is to drain away intolerable feelings of shame or loneliness. Young people who self-harm say that seeing the blood flow from a wound or the blister develop from a burn calms them like a caress. Often, they say they feel no pain. Convinced of their insignificance and disconnection, they inflict a physical assault to assure themselves of their physical reality.

While these young people are sometimes accused of trying to get attention, they are primarily trying to:

1. express their pain
2. deflect their anxiety
3. confirm their reality

Lydia's last few days at home are subdued. She and her father, Jim, move with care, coordinated in their avoidance. He watches her carefully (hoping he'll catch a smile) but tries not to intrude. His gentleness toward her makes me aware of her vulnerability. "Are you going to take the travel iron?" he asks. She shakes her head: "There will be one in the laundry room." He wonders whether she should take the fisherman's sweater hanging in the back of the cupboard: it will be cold in Maine. His voice catches, grows husky. She hesitates for a moment, then replies, without feeling: "That's not my sweater."

Now Lydia is preparing for her second leave-taking. She left her state college after two semesters and said she needed time to "sort herself out." Though she is not eager to start school again, she is afraid of being stuck at home forever. Finding a college that would accept her after her shaky start involved a difficult and disheartening search. She is relieved she has, as she puts it, "another chance," but is worried that her parents are giving her more than she deserves, more than they can easily afford. Each day, she obsesses about the cost: "I feel it in the pit of my stomach—all that money they're forking out." She hopes to justify her parents' expense, but, still depressed, she has low expectations: "I'm not sure whether I'll be able to cope this time. I'm really worried. I don't even remember whether I was worried before. I can't remember what I was thinking about this time two years ago. I try to look back and think: Was I worried? What was I expecting? But I can't remember anything about what I was thinking."

But she does not settle in her new college, either. The classes are too large, the students not what she expected. She isn't rushed by any sorority. "It's the loneliest place on earth," she tells me. "No one likes me or finds me interesting. You know something? No one *sees* me. I get some perfunctory 'hello' from this girl passing me in the dorm, and then she'll squeal 'Hello-it's you—*Wonderful!*' when she sees anyone else. The classes are either too boring or too difficult. There are some nice kids there, but they seem like they are from a different planet. There is nothing there I could link up with."

Her sense of being a misfit becomes almost paranoid: "I think everyone here had a meeting where they decided they wouldn't talk to me."

At home during the winter vacation, Jim says, "My daughter's more of a worry to me since she hit twenty than she ever was as a teenager. Sometimes she goes around like some wild animal. Maybe she looks quiet, but you never know when she's going to bite. I know she's done drugs—weed, at the very least, which she wouldn't touch in high school. I'm terrified of losing her to this depression. I hear her weeping in her room at three in the morning and I just hang outside her door, waiting for it to stop. I don't know what it'll take for her to get back some of her old spunk."

A few months later she is still in school, but her grades are poor. She is worried about the up-coming exams—worried, but unable to study. Sitting in her room, brooding over her textbooks, she suffers an anxiety attack that leaves her feeling shaky and breathless. In the early hours of the morning, she walks outside and buries her bare feet in snow drifts. She sets up competitions with her own endurance. Then she comes inside and presses lighted cigarettes into her frozen feet and ankles. The pain, she says, "soothes" her. It is a "distraction."

This fills her morning. First there is the sting of the wounds, and then the careful tending of the blisters, which makes her feel cared for. The capacity of her body to heal itself reassures her and fills her with pride. The pain calms her: the physical marks transform the problematic and intolerable emotional pain into a more managable discomfort. Strangely, she feels "in control" when burning herself—and she feels alive: "I used to feel everything. And now all I feel is dull and bored. When I burn myself I feel real."

Lydia grows tearful as she sees from my blanched face that her behavior is not as logical and simple as it seems to her in the early hours before first light: "I know no one's happy all the time. People say, 'You just have to get through these first years.' But these years are nothing but unhappy, that's all it's been—unhappy, and I don't know if I can make sense of thinking it's going to go away. It's my own fault, but I can't change it."

For many people, the steps toward growing up that are normally exciting are traumatic. They can manage themselves well, as long as their emotional life has familiar structures, with daily feedback from friends and family. The smooth-running systems of the high-school student can be run off the rails when the emotional supports are gone. As Lydia explains: "I knew my high school like the back of my hand. I knew my way around. I knew the teachers. I knew the kids. I felt part of things. I could never say of college, 'This is my college.' I could only say, 'I go to this college.' Whenever I do stuff now I feel I might as well not be doing anything. There was this weird space around me. No echo. I feel totally unreal."

Without the feedback—or echo—from her family, school, and community, Lydia feels in a state of meltdown. What she does no longer matters.

The increasing cases of self-mutilation among young people occur in the vacuum between adolescence and adulthood, as they suffer a sense of lost identity and lack of human connection. When self-harm occurs, the following steps should be taken:

1. Identify the mental pain.

Self-harm is an expression of one's sense of being harmed inwardly. Identifying the real problem would make its destructive symptom disappear.

2. Manage anxiety in more positive ways.

Self-harm is an expression of acute anxiety. Young people need to develop positive techniques for relaxation and distraction.

They could begin with simple breathing and muscle-relaxing exercises that control the body's response to anxiety. Then they could identify activities they enjoy, such as reading, watching a film, walking, having a good meal, talking to a friend or parent. Some pleasures or comforts will be passive (such as eating, having a bath or sauna), but some will involve active participation (such as reading or drawing or sewing or writing). Passive comforts provide a sense of self-care. Active pleasures exercise one's sense of power or efficacy.

Learning to provide oneself with minor, short-term pleasures of both kinds can supply a far better sense of one's reality than watching a self-inflicted wound bleed.

3. Reframe problems.

Young people who mutilate themselves blame themselves for their problems. They believe they are unhappy because they are "worthless" or "bad." Self-punishment therefore seems appropriate. They need to replace the blaming response ("It's all your fault") with one oriented to problem solving ("Here is a problem. It could be solved in various ways").

One day, our culture may change to reinforce rather than threaten young people's sense of reality. As parents revise unrealistic expectations of young people and correct inappropriate responses to them, they set in motion much-needed change.

CROSSING THE THRESHOLD

THE myth of maturity is harming our daughters and sons as they make the crossing from adolescence into adulthood. Parents, teachers, employers, and young people themselves, buy into this myth, which idealizes independence and self-reliance. Maturity is thought to be marked by separation from childhood loves and needs.[1] Dependence is seen as a weakness. Parents, acting in the name of love, may withdraw emotional or practical or financial support, thinking it best for a daughter or son to solve her or his own problems—even to suffer alone the consequences of mistakes or misjudgment. Unrealistic expectations crush thresholders' confidence and prevent the adults who care for them from providing the support necessary to a smooth crossing.

The maturity myth distorts our vision, so that we hear rejections from our daughters and sons more clearly than we hear their pleas for connection and support. We assume that thresholders want to separate from us, both psychologically and physically. But human development is relational. We are born into relationships of dependence and love. We grow within such relationships, which change as we grow, and which most of us continue to live in and through throughout our lives, however much we, the people we love, and our relationships with them change. The conclusion many of us come to, because we continue to feel strong bonds (both positive and negative) with our own parents, is that part of us remains stuck in adolescence.[2] We feel there is something wrong with us if we have not "achieved" psychological separation from our parents. In parallel, we repress the impulse to remain close to our children. We believe that it is selfish and unhealthy to cling to them.

At one time, the maturity myth may have had some use. It helped highlight the value of individuality and self-direction. It encouraged us to expect young people to think for themselves and to choose their own future paths. But as family traditions and social networks erode, it is dangerous to emphasize independence to the exclusion of relationships. Self-reliance is now not so much a virtue to be fostered as a necessity in the midst of a world that does not inspire trust. "You have to look after yourself because other people won't," thresholders tell me. The myth that promotes the supreme importance of self-reliance and independence has outlived its rightful life span and emerged as a half-truth.

The transition from teenager to adult has become fragmented and unpredictable. Schooling is now more complex because young people can choose to study a wider range of subjects and courses. They can earn advanced degrees in more fields and at more institutions. They can select among a wide variety of programs and strategies for financing their education. Career choices are more complicated because there is a wider variety of jobs and a more uncertain economy. There are many more flexible careers without well-established career tracks. Yet lack of resources—from parents, teachers, employers—is damaging young people's ability to navigate these complex pathways.

THRESHOLDERS' EXPECTATIONS
AND THE REAL WORLD

While the paths have become increasingly difficult to navigate, young people's expectations are on the rise. Today's "ambitious generation" expects a great deal from adulthood. They want to have jobs that are satisfying, well-paid, and prestigious. They want to live comfortably, have friends, and lots of fun. These expectations will not always be met.

Today, 90 percent of high-school seniors expect to attend college. While most plan to get a degree in four years, very few actually do. Only 34 percent of young people starting at a four-year college or university complete a bachelor's degree in four years, and only 5 percent of those entering a junior college complete a bachelor's degree in four years (and 7 percent in five), though 70 percent planned to.[3]

Looking further ahead, more than 70 percent of young people expect to work in a professional job. They want to be executives, engineers, health professionals, lawyers, athletes, artists, and entertainers at a rate much greater than the number of such jobs currently available. The number of young people wanting to become lawyers and judges is five times that of the projected number needed. The number who want to be writers, athletes, or entertainers is fourteen times the anticipated openings.[4]

Young people's ambitions are full of paradoxes. They expect success but are haunted by fears of disappointment and failure. They see themselves as striving in a world plagued by the difficulty of making a comfortable life. Whether or not they articulate it, they are shadowed by the pressures and compromises of their parents. They feel anxious about their place in this world and wonder what personal costs they will incur if they resist this hard-work culture, with its contradictory aims and its imbedded hypocrisies. Above all, thresholders worry about being lonely. They worry that the independence expected of them will cut them off from family and friends and community.

Ask thresholders how they see themselves in five years' time, and they reflect cautiously, seriously. They worry they will have unexciting, uninteresting jobs. They worry about being trapped in the demands of work, without adequate rewards. This is the first generation in living memory to expect to be worse off financially than their parents.[5]

The concrete outcome for each thresholder depends on many things. Success is always possible, whatever the odds against it. Lifelines can come in the form of schools or mentors, friendships, families, community networks, and new opportunities. But grown-ups have to offer these lifelines. As Robert and Beverely Cairns discovered in their research on two thousand young people, "The idea that parents can remove themselves from responsibility for their child's education and development at some magical age is misguided."[6] In this study, it was the young people who described their parents as highly supportive who were the most likely to experience this passage positively.

THRESHOLDERS PAST AND PRESENT

The challenges of this transition are not new. The crossing from teenager to adult has always been difficult. But as society has changed, this transition has become so difficult that we can no longer afford to ignore it. As possible pathways into adulthood multiply, young people have to be creative and flexible in their lifestyles. Do they want more personal time—perhaps at the expense of financial rewards? they ask themselves. Do they want the financial perks that will only come with high-pressure jobs? While they hope to establish long-term friendships, family networks, and a satisfying career, they learn about the realities of competition, insecurity, and daily routine.

At one time, children moved fairly rapidly into adult life, taking on adult roles, earning wages, and marrying. Even in the middle of the twentieth century, there were many opportunities to find a safe niche, with a job, a family, and a community. Today young people reach different stages of adulthood at different times. Some will be high earners before they think of having a family. Some will have children while still being supported by their own parents. Some will have higher degrees, but be forced by economic necessity to live in a parent's home. Some will be pampered in school, and then face great responsibilities once in a job. There are now no clear markers along this road.

The status of young adults is undefined. Because we have no term for this phase, we do not understand it. Thresholders appear as a hybrid, neither teenager nor grown-up, yet both. They grow up quickly in the sense of being made aware, at an early age, of the problems and secrets of the adult world. They mature physically at an early age. They develop their own tastes, their own material needs, and their own culture. But their ability to thrive as independent adults comes much, much later.

THE IMBEDDED FAIRY TALE

Long ago, the idea of learning what one needed to know outside the family took root in the human imagination. In a fairy tale referred to as "The Three Languages," the youngest son is seen by his father and two older brothers as stupid and worthless.

After several attempts to educate him, his father is at his wits' end. "This boy will be a foolish man," he cries in despair. Nonetheless, he decides to give his youngest son one more chance to prove himself. He sends him to study for a full year with a master teacher. After a year, the young son returns home and is questioned by his father and brothers: "What did you learn?" The son replies, "I learned that dogs barked." The brothers laugh and the father despairs at this nonsense. Declaring that it is time this simpleton son learn to fend for himself, the father orders the boy out of the home. As the young man wanders through the world, he comes across a town besieged by dogs that bark so loudly that none of the town's inhabitants can rest. They are dying of fatigue, but the dogs do not allow them even a minute's sleep. Using the knowledge he gained with the master, the young man talks to the dogs and tames them into silence. He restores peace to the land, is honored by the townspeople, and returns in triumph to the father.

The model has taken root in our imagination: Alone, cast out by his parent, a boy proves himself and becomes a worthy man. His rite of passage is through a forest or wilderness into which he is cast by an unappreciative family. This model of leave-taking and making one's way in the world stays with us. It shapes parents' responses to their own sons and daughters. It shapes young people's expectations of themselves.

The original tale of separation and triumph emerged in a very different society. The ideal of leaving and returning as a rite of passage emerged in a time of greater family cohesiveness and control. The transition from child, with its associations of need and dependence, to adult, with its associations of knowledge and power, has changed over time. Before the Industrial Revolution, the transition from parent's home to one's own was often protracted. Even as young people took on adult roles, they lived in a culture that honored family connections. Often, when they became wage earners, they entered intermediate households as apprentices, or boarded with surrogate families. Even in leaving home and making their way in the world, they were recognized as youth who needed to be treated as part of a family.[7]

After World War II, new patterns emerged. Going away to college gradually became the acceptable intermediate phase. But in college, young people were still recognized as needing care and control: the college acted in *loco parentis*, which meant the college exercised parental authority. Marriage was seen as crossing over from youth to adulthood. In marriage one formed one's own family, which then became the primary unit of companionship and support. But even after marriage, ties between parent and daughter or son were often very strong. Adult children continued to live close to their parents and to see them frequently.[8]

During the 1950s and 1960s, the transition from dependent adolescent to independent adult was, at least on the surface, the most condensed and clear. Many young adults left home, married, and started families in a pretty short space of time. It became common to describe the parents whose children left home to work or study as having an "empty nest": once chicks learn to fly, they leave for good. Those young people who didn't leave the nest were struggling in a twilight world between child and adult. Prolonged dependence on a parent was considered an abnormality brought about by a parent who was too selfish to let go. The 1955 Oscar-winning film *Marty* depicts a young man's inability to find a mate as a consequence of his being unable to leave a mother who uses her son's love to guilt trip him into staying home. In the 1960s, the image of the clinging parent was branded on the culture by Philip Roth's novel *Portnoy's Complaint*. Parental involvement was seen to be a dangerous thing. Therapists worked with patients to help them distance themselves from their parents. Family therapists talked about "enmeshed families" in which members were "unhealthily" connected to one another. While these patterns could explain real problems in some families, the image came to haunt many perfectly healthy parents and children who worried about "blurred personal boundaries" and "overdependence."[9]

Parents are now quick to key into a daughter's bids for "her own space" or a son's "need for autonomy." They teach themselves to "bite their tongue" or "keep silent" or let their children "make their own decisions." They neglect to hone skills in maintaining connection and offering support.

The high value on independence is reflected in institutions outside the family. Colleges now pay tribute to the maturity myth. The policies they adhere to are based on the premise that young students are grown-ups. According to most college policies, it would be retrograde to have curfews, work checks, routine pastoral care. The notion that a college is in *loco parentis* is dead, since college students are no longer thought to need parents. These assumptions are also reflected in the workplace. Employers do not take on thresholders as apprentices to be taught and tended. They hire them as workers who have to make a contribution or leave.

REVISING THE FAIRY TALE

The transition from teenager to adult is a long and often zigzag process. Today young people need continuing support as they find their footholds in the adult world. As their futures appear before them more like a maze than a set of paths, they need others' focus and involvement. During this passage, young people are more or less forced to become navigators who negotiate opportunities and risks. Those who succeed in tolerating risks and change and navigating this passage successfully are those who continue to have a parent's responsive care, attention, and support.[10]

Questions abound about this new vision of the process of maturity. The first question parents ask is: **"How can young people develop as individuals if we keep them close?"**

There is a common confusion between the concepts of individuality and separation. Without being aware of it, many parents think their children can only develop their individual identity through psychological distance or separation from the parents. But in fact, people gain an identity as much through their sense of belonging to a person or family or religion or locality or nation as they do from refining their points of difference. And indeed, being different from someone is not necessarily the same as being separate.

Human development is relational. As soon as we are born, we are aware of our connection to others. An infant watches the face of a parent and fastens on the range of facial expressions. From week one, infants focus on voices and touch and movement. Infant and parent engage in an interpersonal dance, through which their sense of self and the world around them grows.[11] We come to know ourselves as much through our ability to love and hate others as we do from knowing ourselves apart from others.

It is nonetheless true that as our daughters and sons grow, we allow them greater control over their lives. By the time they are thresholders, we cannot be with them in the way we were when they were children. And so the next crucial question is, **"How do I parent a thresholder?"**

We barely have any point of reference for parenting an adult daughter or son. Parenting is often presented as an all or nothing affair: we look after children, and then we let go. These assumptions should be revised.

1. As teenagers stand on the threshold of adulthood, they may fear losing their parents and panic in the face of pressures to be grown up and independent. Parents can reassure their daughters and sons that the bond between them is strong.

Thresholders thrive on messages of care, concern, and readiness to help. These can come in down-to-earth exchanges of family information. They can come in general assurances about "always being there." They can be communicated by alertness to depression or stress. If these messages are given clearly and consistently, they will counter the maturity myth.

2. A thresholder needs to feel that her parents want to get to know her as she changes. A parent's continuing appreciation for the person she is and the person she will become helps maintain confidence. But appreciation has to be grounded in reality. No thresholder wants to be a known quantity to parents. As we listen to our daughters and sons we show that we really do want to get to know them as adults. We can do this by posing questions and then paying attention to their replies. We must be prepared to hear about changes in their plans and in their views.

3. Thresholders may be independent in many ways, but a parent's practical help will ease anxiety and create more possibilities for them. The details of day-to-day living are hard to sort out. Some young people will be adept at handling their bank accounts but hopeless at arranging to see a dentist. Some will fail to get an important application in on time. Some will make an appointment for a job interview and then be at a loss in following through with travel arrangements.

As we accept that young people mature quickly in some ways, and slowly in others, we will be more tolerant of these lapses. Parents' assistance is a way of teaching. It can be presented in the form of instruction ("This is how you go about this sort of thing"), but denigrating messages ("You're old enough to do this yourself," "I can't believe you forgot this") are definitely to be avoided. Humiliation comes quickly to thresholders, who would rather save face than get the required help.

4. Thresholders benefit from grown-ups' input in forming coherent plans. While I am often told by parents, "He doesn't want to hear from me" and "She never listens to a word I say," I have found that practical help from parents is highly valued. Young people do not like "being ordered around" or "lectured to," but they crave a supportive forum in which they can explore possible solutions to present impasses and paths to their futures. Over and over, they expressed a wish for more personal guidelines and safety nets.

5. While young people are quick to resist a parent's rigid ideas about their futures, they crave acknowledgment of their hopes. This acknowledgment can be expressed by helping them develop plans to realize their hopes. Thresholders benefit from parents' wisdom and experience in aligning their ambitions with their current choices. Parents can help get information about possible routes to various careers and about requirements for various careers. Research repeatedly shows that young people who are able to see their ambitions through and recognize opportunities spend a significant amount of time with their parents discussing actions and strategies to help them reach their ambitions.[12]

"But can't we ever say, 'My job is done. You're on your own.'?"

It is understandable that, after the stressful teenage years, parents look forward to a well-deserved reprieve. But we have to change our expectations of the time line of parenthood. The assumption often is that we spend time with kids and, when they grow up, our time is ours. This assumption has to be modified as the time frame of growing up expands. If we—and our children—are very lucky, we will be able to say, "My time's my own now"; but this is not some special right we have. Only in the rarest cases can a parent reasonably say, "Enough is enough." There will always be questions about how much and what kind of parental input is appropriate—but this is a question parents have to ask at every phase of a child's life. It should not, therefore, be too daunting to address it at the threshold phase.

Children may not need us forever, but parenting time is for longer than we ever thought. Continuing to offer our practical help (and sometimes our money) to young people may seem costly—but the long-term costs of not helping them are far higher than the costs of helping them.

"Won't my continued help undermine their initiative or independence?" parents ask. They worry that keeping a close eye on their children and retaining the parental emergency alert system will harm their children. They assume that thresholders' needs are a weakness that they must overcome.

This concern is formed by the assumption that the real adult stands alone. Instead, we have to revise our notion of what the "real adult" does. The real adult knows how to be responsive, knows how to use her or his knowledge and practical skills to help others. We help our children by setting a good example of how to behave toward another family member, how to show continuing care.

A question some parents ask is, **"Does this mean we shouldn't expect young adults to be responsible?"**

We must expect responsibility, and we need to give young people opportunities to be responsible. But we have to expect that young people will sometimes let us down, and we have to be forgiving. We have to be ready to help them, sometimes, just as we

did when they were children. But, more important, we can prevent putting young people into situations they cannot handle. By
anticipating problems, we can avoid them.

We may have to curtail the responsibility we give young people. Colleges could revise their expectations that the young people who enter them are already grown up. The curriculum should
change its shopping mall displays to a clearer system of choices
and provide intensive course counseling. Employers should have
special programs for training young people. They, like parents,
should be alert to problems of responsibility overload. In each
place of work or study, thresholders should find a forum for discussion of young people's personal passages without a sense of
shame, isolation, or diminished worth.

Thresholders sometimes listen to me and ask, **"Are you saying
that even at age twenty-two or twenty-three, I'm not a grown-
up?"** And I respond with my own question: "What do you
think?" and then, "Is that really so bad?"

Thresholders are well aware of their fears of becoming adults.
They live with the anxieties of making the right choice and
worry how the choices they make will affect their futures, both
tomorrow and ten years from now. They worry about being lost
in the maze of adult paths or stranded in boredom and useless-
ness. They panic at the prospect of being on their own. But they
also balk at the notion of still being a kid.

If we open up a new vision of the thresholder, who is not a
kid but a young person still attached to parents—a novice
adult—we can sustain their dignity and contain their fears.

Parents, teachers, and employers then ask me, **"Why are
things so difficult for thresholders today?"** Young people have
so much going for them. They have more technological help with

their work, more access to entertainment, more access to education. Why do we need to give them even more?

Today's thresholders are growing up amid decreasing social capital.[13] Since the 1960s there has been a sharp fall in social networks: The connections of friendship, reliance, and trust are so valuable to society that political scientists call them "social capital" because they indicate the net worth of a society.

The fall in social capital can be seen across a range of activities. As it becomes more and more common for both parents to work outside the home, there are few adults available to children after school. Family time is diminished by increased working hours. Family connections fragment with persistent divorce.[14] Thresholders are likely to live at some distance from other relatives and are more likely to have parents who think it is wrong to "interfere" in their lives.

Thresholders are increasingly less likely to have a stable and substantial network of friends. They will change friends frequently as they change jobs and move.[15] Neighborhoods are less likely to be community networks. Children's movements outside the home are restricted by fears of crime and accident. During the past decade, many facilities like recreational parks and after-school programs have closed, depriving young people of opportunities to build networks. As the environment becomes less supportive and more dangerous, people place increasing value on self-reliance. Such distrust is difficult to alleviate. It prevents people from engaging with others and therefore getting to know and trust them. Even worse, it can lead to behavior that bolsters distrust. A vicious cycle forms: As the trust in other people diminishes, the quality of society deteriorates. Crime and fraud increase, as does mutual suspicion. Slow to trust others, we are slow to make friends. Being alone seems the safest option.[16]

It is this fragile society into which young women and men in their late teens and early twenties are entering. There is a real danger that people will become more and more isolated, more lonely, and will have lifestyles that do nothing to decrease their or others' isolation. We have to think about what repair-mechanisms we can set in place to make up for the shortfall of social capital.

The social capital we lack in our society can be replaced by close family ties and frequent communication. My call to arms is to prevent the breakdown of networks extending to the parent/child bond. Young people need significant and continuing help from the bonds that still remain. For all that has changed in the family during the past four decades, the parent/child bond is still strong. It will have to remain strong to get people through the threshold years.

But this vision of continued care and responsibility is threatened by the maturity myth, which denies the need for social capital as it declares the grown-up person should stand alone. Depriving young people of help does not foster true independence.[17] To "let them go" just at a time in social history when there are fewer and fewer networks outside the parent/child relationship[18] is a terrible option. Instead, we must perform that delicate dance between moving close and giving room. It is mandatory that parents see helping their daughters and sons across the threshold to adulthood as their responsibility. In so doing, we will establish a richness of relationship that will last a lifetime.

My proposal may sound radical, but in many ways it is modest. It simply makes use of the love and concern that is already in place. Instead of clinging to our ideals of independence and maturity, we can respond to our children's needs. If we listen and learn, we can foster their slow-growing spirits.

ENDNOTES

INTRODUCTION

1. Erik Erikson, 1980, *Identity and the Life Cycle* (New York: W. W. Norton), p. 100.

2. There is implicit recognition of this in the fact that many academic courses on adolescence deal with young people until the age of twenty-eight. Parents' and teachers' expectations—and young people's own expectations, however, are based on adolescence ending in the early twenties.

3. Michael Rutter and David Smith (eds.), 1995, *Psychosocial Disorders in Young People: Time Trends and their Causes* (London: John Wiley).

4. Personal communication, Bob Harris, Berkeley Business School, Dec. 1997.

5. C. M. Young, 1984, "Leaving Home and Returning Home: A Demographic Study of Young Adults in Australia." *Family Formation, Structure, Values*, vol. 1 (Canberra: Australian Family Research Conference Proceedings), pp. 53–76.

6. A. Schnaiberg and A. Goldernberg, 1989, "From Empty Nest to Crowded Nest: The Dynamics of Incompletely-launched Adults." *Social Problems*, vol. 36, 251–269.

7. Elizabeth King Keenen, 1997, "When You Can't Afford to Leave Home: Clinical Implications of Economic Realities." *Child and Adolescent Social Work Journal*, Aug., vol. 14(4): 289–303.

8. Daniel Levinson, 1996, *The Seasons of a Woman's Life* (New York: Ballantine), p. 71.

9. Jeffrey Jensen Arnett, 1997, "Young People's Conceptions of the Transition to Adulthood." *Youth and Society*, Sep., vol. 29(1): 3–23.

10. See Daniel Levinson, op. cit., p. 94.

11. John Bynner, Elsa Ferri, and Peter Shepherd (eds.), 1998, *Twenty-something in the 1990s* (Brookfield, Mass.: Ashgate).

12. Economic and Social Research Council (Great Britain), 1997, *Agenda*.

13. "30% in Teen-Ager Survey Considered Suicide," *New York Times*, September 14, 1988.

14. Only 34 percent of young people starting at a four-year college or university completed a bachelor's degree in four years. And only 5 percent of those entering a junior college completed a bachelor's degree in four years (and 7 percent in five), though 70 percent planned to. Statistics cited in Barbara Schneider and David Stevenson, 1999, *The Ambitious Generation* (New Haven: Yale).

15. These young people were aged between eighteen and twenty-two when I started the interviews. They lived in Chicago (9), Washington, D.C. (7), Michigan (6), northern California (6), and southern California (4). This was an opportunity sample, drawn from the younger brothers and sisters who participated in my 1990 study *Altered Loves: Mothers and Daughters during Adolescence* and the daughters and sons of women who participated in my study of midlife women (*Secret Paths: Women in the New Midlife*, 1995, New York: W.W. Norton). I met with each thresholder at least twice but also communicated by other means—primarily phone and email, and sometimes letter. At least one meeting was in their family home (where I also met a parent or parents) and, if they left home, another meeting took place in their new territory— college, apartment, or workplace.

16. See also *Youth, Citizenship and Social Change Research Programme*, Economic and Social Research Council (Great Britain), 1997.

17. Ruthellen Josselson, 1992, *The Space between Us* (San Francisco: Jossey-Bass) identifies and describes these dimensions of relationship.

18. R. R. Koback and A. Sceery, 1988, "Attachment in Late Adolescence: Working Models, Affect Regulation, and Representations of Self and Others." *Child Development*, 59, 135–146.

CHAPTER ONE

1. Peggy Orenstein, 1994, *Schoolgirls: Young Women, Self-Esteem, and the Confidence Gap* (New York: Anchor); Mary Pipher, 1994, *Reviving Ophelia: Saving the Selves of Adolescent Girls* (New York: Ballantine); Joan Jacobs Brumberg, 1997, *The Body Project: An Intimate History of American Girls* (New York: Random House).

2. Sherry Hatcher, 1994, *The Narrative Study of Lives*, vol. 2. (Thousand Oaks, Calif.: Sage), p. 177.

3. Joan Jacobs Brumberg, 1988, *Fasting Girls: The Emergence of Anorexia Nervosa as a Modern Disease* (Cambridge, Mass.: Harvard); L. K. G. Hsu, 1980, "Outcome of Anorexia Nervosa," *Archives of General Psychiatry*, 37; Naomi Wolf, 1990, *The Beauty Myth* (New York: Morrow), p. 149. Psychotherapist Sarah Greaves has even higher estimates:

She says that between 12 percent and 33 percent of university women have eating disorders. Ten percent of these women die. See Sarah Greaves, 1998, "Student Counselling and Brief Dynamic Psychotherapy: Brief Encounters in the Rite of Passage of the Student." Unpublished paper.

4. D. Goldstein et al., 1995, "Long Term Fluoxetine Treatment of Bulimia Nervosa." *British Journal of Psychiatry*, 166, pp. 660–666.

5. Ruthellen Josselson, 1992, *The Space between Us* (San Francisco: Jossey-Bass); Terri Apter, 1990, *Altered Loves: Mothers and Daughters during Adolescence* (New York: Ballantine); David Bell and Linda Bell, 1983, "Parental Validation and Support in the Development of Adolescent Daughters." In Harold Grotevent and Catherine Cooper, eds., *Adolescent Development in the Family* (San Francisco: Jossey-Bass).

6. Pauline Bart, 1971, "Depression in Middle-Aged Women." In Vivian Gornick and Barbara Moran, eds., *Women in a Sexist Society* (New York: Basic Books).

7. If the parent's despondency were actually a response to the thresholder's independence or lack of need for a parent—as the empty-nest theorists believe—then parents whose child had less separation anxiety would have more empty-nest problems. For them, the sense of losing one's significance as a parent would be greater, because the child's need for the parent was less. But in fact, the most severe empty-nest loneliness was in parents whose children exhibited the greatest ambivalence about leaving and being separate. What is often seen as a parent's selfish sense of loss is really a reflection of the child's continuing need.

8. Pat Allatt, 1996, "Conceptualising Youth: Transitions, Risk and the Public and Private." In J. Bynner, L. Chisholm, and A. Furlong, eds., *Youth, Citizenship and Social Change* (Aldershot, U.K.: Ashgate), p. 92.

9. Jeremy Hazell, 1976, "The Problem of Pointlessness—A Challenge for Counseling." *British Journal of Guidance and Counseling*, 4 (2), pp.156–170.

10. Binge drinking is common and indeed is an expected part of college life. Abercrombie and Fitch Company, in their autumn 1998 brochure, welcomed students back to campus with a guide to drinking games and recipes for potent cocktails. Nearly half of U.S. college students surveyed had engaged in binge drinking within the previous two weeks. (Henry Wechsler et al., 1996, *Binge Drinking on Campus: Results of a National Study*, Bethesda, Md: U.S. Department of Education, Higher Education Center for Alcohol and Other Drug Prevention). See also, "Drug Use Rises Again in 1995 among American Teens," *University of Michigan News and Information Services*, Ann Arbor, Mich., December 11, 1995.

CHAPTER TWO

1. Sigmund Dragastin and Glen Elder, 1995, *Adolescence in the Life Cycle: Psychological Change and Social Context* (New York: John Wiley). "As new social identities are pressed on [the new college student], and as he is given the structural opportunities to practice and enact their behavioral implications, the student may well begin to conceive of himself as being a different person from what he once was. Changes in overall self-conceptions are intertwined with changes in a variety of more specific personality and attitudinal attributes, including expectations, aspirations and perceptions.

"It may turn out that the 'identity' construct is particularly useful in the study of the transition to college. High school students have expectations, aspirations, and perceptions in a variety of substantive areas; and many of these change as individuals enter and begin their progress through college." (pp. 166–167)

2. Erik Erikson, 1998, *The Life Cycle Completed* (New York: W. W. Norton), p. 10.

3. Erik Erikson, 1981, "The Problem of Ego Identity." In Laurence Steinberg (ed.), *The Life Cycle* (New York: Columbia), p. 192.

4. Ruthellen Josselson, 1987, *Finding Herself: Pathways to Identity Development in Women* (San Fransco: Jossey-Bass). "Identity is the interface between the individual and the world, defining as it does what the individual will stand for and be recognized as." (p. 8)

5. Lyn Mikel Brown and Carol Gilligan, 1992, *Meeting at the Crossroads* (Cambridge, Mass.: Harvard), p. 176.

6. Jane Loevinger observed that many young people, in particular young women, seem to regress when they enter institutions of higher learning: "A disturbing possibility is that for some significant fraction of students, particularly women, college is a regressive experience." See Jane Loevinger et al., 1985, "Ego Development in College." *Journal of Personality and Social Psychology*, 48, 947–962. She suggests that college "may affect dramatically and negatively young women's experiences of themselves."

7. David Elkind and Robert Bowen, 1979, "Imaginary Audience Behavior in Children and Adolescents." *Developmental Psychology*, 15, 38–44.

8. Sherry Hatcher, 1994, *The Narrative Study of Lives*, vol 2 (San Francisco: Jossey-Bass), p. 192.

9. David Riesman, 1949, *The Lonely Crowd*, uses the term "other-directed" to describe a personality that keys into other people's responses and values as a control mechanism. I see this more as a phase of personality than as a fixed personality characteristic, but Riesman's description of the other-directed personality remains compelling.

10. Similar cases are discussed in Hadas Wiseman, 1995, "The Quest for Connectedness: Loneliness as Process in the Narratives of Lonely University Students." In *The Narrative Study of Lives*, vol. 3 (Thousand Oaks, Calif.: Sage), pp. 116–152.

11. Sigmund Freud noted this common belief and named it "the family romance." This was the story (or romance) that some children told themselves: They were really born of a royal family, but were adopted by their more mundane parents.

12. See Erik Erikson, *The Life Cycle Completed*, p. 192: "The rudimentary strength developing at this stage is *competence*, a sense that the growing human being must gradually integrate all the maturing methods of verifying and mastering *factuality* and of sharing *actuality* of those who cooperate in the same situation."

13. According to Erikson, isolation is the essential core pathology of early adulthood. See chapter 1, "Youth: Fidelity and Diversity," in Erik Erikson (ed.), 1963, *Youth: Change and Challenge* (New York: Basic Books).

14. M. Kovacs and L. J. Bastiaens, 1995, "The Psychotherapeutic Management of Major Depressive Disorders in Childhood and Adolescence: Issues and Prospects." In Ian Goodyer (ed.), *The Depressed Child and Adolescent* (Cambridge, U.K.: Cambridge University Press).

15. For the positive role that quarreling often plays in teenage/parent relationships, see Terri Apter, 1991, *Altered Loves: Mothers and Daughters during Adolescence* (New York: Ballentine).

CHAPTER THREE

1. Many prestigious engineering and science colleges have no prerequisites for any course, and students have to use both common sense and sources of unofficial knowledge to decide in what order to take courses.

2. The curriculum in many American colleges is excessively unstructured. Some have no requirements. Each student can design her or his own course. On the assumption that young people are adults and can construct their own education program, they are offered choices. In reality, these young adults have little basis on which to choose and so, in a sea of opportunity, they flounder.

3. Daniel Levinson in collaboration with Judy Levinson, 1996, *The Seasons of a Woman's Life* (New York: Ballantine), p. 233.

CHAPTER FOUR

1. Harriet Bjerrum Nielson, 1998, "Gender, Love and Education in Three Generations." In K. Weber (ed.), *Life History: Gender and Experience* (Denmark: Roskilde University).

2. See also R. Coles and G. Stokes, 1985, *Sex and the American Teenager* (New York: Harper and Row).

3. Sharon Thompson, 1995, *Going All the Way: Teenage Girls' Tales of Sex, Romance and Pregnancy* (New York: Hill and Wang).

4. Sharon Thompson, op. cit., and Sharon Thompson, 1990, "Putting a Big Thing into a Little Hole." *Journal of Sex Research*, Aug. 27, no. 3, 341–361.

5. Deborah Tolmam, 1990, "Just Say No to What?: A Preliminary Analysis of Sexual Subjectivity in a Multicultural Group of Adolescent Females." Paper presented in April at the annual meeting of the American Orthopsychiatric Association, Miami.

6. Forty-seven percent of thresholders in the United States do not live in a nuclear family. See Carol Samms, 1995, "Global Generation X: Their Values and Their Attitudes in Different Countries." The Seven Million Project. Working Paper 8 (London: Demos).

7. Rostyslaw Roback and Steven Weitzman, "Grieving the Loss of Romantic Relationships in Young Adults: An Empirical Study of Disenfranchised Grief." *Omega Journal of Death and Dying*, 1994–1995, 30 (4): 269–281.

8. For a discussion of these gender differences see Nancy Chodorow, 1978, *The Reproduction of Mothering* (Berkeley, Calif.: University of California Press).

9. Glenn Good and Phillip Wood, 1995, "Male Gender Role Conflict, Depression and Help Seeking: Do College Men Face Double Jeopardy?" *Journal of Counseling and Development*, Sep.–Oct., vol. 74(1): 70–75.

10. Ruthellen Josselson, 1987, *Finding Herself* (San Francisco: Jossey-Bass). Josselson found that some thresholders felt they blended with others. One woman she interviewed said: "I sort of bend towards people. But I have such varied friends that there's always opposition pounding at me." (p. 136)

11. Melanie Thernstrom, 1996, "Diary of a Murder." *New Yorker*, June 3, pp. 62–68.

12. Jane Gallop, 1997, *Feminist Accused of Sexual Harassment* (Durham, N.C.: Duke University Press). Gallop writes: "at its best teaching is a consensual amorous relation—outlawing it restricts and chills pedagogic relationships." (p. 56)

CHAPTER FIVE

1. Barbara Schneider and David Stevenson, 1999, *The Ambitious Generation* (New Haven: Yale). Terri Apter, 1991, *Altered Loves: Mothers and Daughters during Adolescence* (New York: Ballantine). James Youniss and Jacquelline Smollar, 1985, *Adolescent Relations with Mothers, Fathers and Friends* (Chicago: University of Chicago Press).

2. Mark Phippen, quoted in "A Helping Hand," by Pauline Hunt, *The Guardian Higher*, April 21, 1998.

3. Ted Hughes and Frances McCullough (eds.), 1982, *The Journals of Sylvia Plath* (New York: Ballantine), p. 176.

4. Colette Dowling gives a powerful account of her high-achieving daughter's college burnout. Dowling links the drive to perfection to women's hidden fears of inadequacy. She believes that mothers, fearful of their own inadequacies (implicitly) ask their daughters to be perfect in compensation, so the cycle of high achievement/inner terror and burnout is repeated. I see this syndrome as occuring across gender and being located primarily in a developmental phase, rather than in a woman's state. I also have found that parents are quick to revise their expectations of a daughter's or son's achievements when they see how their own expectations are out of sync with a child's well-being. See Colette Dowling, 1988, *Perfect Women: Hidden Fears of Inadequacy and the Drive to Perform* (New York: Summit).

5. See Terri Apter, 1997, *The Confident Child* (New York: W. W. Norton).

6. Ruthellen Josselson, 1987, *Finding Herself: Pathways to Identity in Women* (San Francisco: Jossey-Bass), p. 31.

7. The argument is that celebrities sell things—books, tickets, clothes, even pension plans. The market economy then has incentives to sustain the celebrity culture.

CHAPTER SIX

1. Kate Purcell, 2000, *Moving On* (Coventry, U. K.: Institute of Employment Relations, Warwick University).

2. One in ten young people aged thirty to thirty-four has yet to leave home. *Social Trends*, 2000 (London: Her Majesty's Stationery Office).

3. *(London) Sunday Times*, January 30, 2000, Section 1, p. 21.

4. Erik Erikson, 1981, "The Problem of Ego Identity." In Laurence Steinberg (ed.), *The Life Cycle: Readings in Human Development* (New York: Columbia), p. 197.

5. *New Scientist*, January 22, 2000, pp. 22–27.

6. In the 1990s, one third of people between the ages of fourteen and nineteen had some kind of paid job. See Matthew Wald, "In New England Especially, Low Employment Spurs a New 'Child Labor'." *New York Times*, April 4, 1992, p. 7.

7. Some researchers believe that the transition from child to employee is too swift, one of the many means of truncating youth today. See Matthew Wald, "In New England Especially, Low Unemployment Spurs a New 'Child Labor'." *New York Times*, April 4, 1992, p. 7.

8. Whether or not Louise Woodward was in any way responsible for a baby's death,

the psychological profile of people responsible for such incidents is that of an immature person who suffers from fatigue.

CHAPTER SEVEN

1. Ecstasy and the new forms of LSD (only half the strength of the LSD commonly taken in the 1960s and 1970s) create a lifestyle of partying. Several million doses are taken each weekend. The addiction is not so much to the drug as to the lifestyle.

2. For further discussion of this see Matina Horner, 1969, "Fail: Bright Women." In *Psychology Today*, 3(6), p. 36; and Terri Apter, 1994, *Working Women Don't Have Wives* (New York: St Martin's).

3. The difference in motivation between girls and boys is now seen to be negligible. Robert Cairns and Beverley Cairns, 1994, *Lifelines and Risks: Pathways of Youth in Our Time* (New York and London: Harvester Wheatsheaf).

4. Emily Hancock, 1989, *The Girl Within* (New York: Ballantine); Gloria Steinem, 1991, *Revolution from Within: A Book of Self-Esteem* (Boston: Little, Brown).

5. Patrick Johnson, William Wilkinson, and Keith McNeil, 1995, *Contemporary Family Therapy: An International Journal*, June, vol. 17, pp. 249–264.

CHAPTER EIGHT

1. Anthony Giddens, 1991, *Modernity and Self-Identity: Self and Society in the Late Modern Age* (Stanford, Calif.: Stanford University Press).

2. *Social Trends.* 1997. London: Her Majesty's Stationery Office.

3. See Michele Schienkman, 1998, "Graduate Student Marriages: An Organizational/Interactional View." *Family Process*, Sept., vol. 27(3), 351–368.

4. *Women's Incomes Over a Lifetime.* London School of Economics, reported in *The Guardian*, February 21, 2000, p. 5.

5. U.S. Census, 1999; see also Michael Young and Jean Stogdon, January 12, 2000. New Age Travails. Society. *The Guardian*, pp. 2–3.

6. Out of the 4.7 million grandparents who live with their grandchildren, 3.7 million are raising grandchildren in their own home. One million others are living with grandchildren because they need to play an active part in supporting them. U.S. Census, 1999.

7. N. Cambell, 1999, "Older Workers and the Labor Market." In J. Hills (ed.), *Persistent Poverty and Lifetime Inequality: The Evidence.* CASE Report 5 (London: London School of Economics).

8. K. Rake, 2000, *Women's Incomes over Their Lifetimes: A report to the Women's Unit, Cabinet Office*. London: Her Majesty's Stationery Office.

9. Jane Weaver and Jane Ussher, 1995, "The 'Twenty-Four Hour a Day' Job: Discourse Analysis with Mothers of Young Children." Women of Psychology conference, Leeds, U.K.

CHAPTER NINE

1. Emma is described in Chapter 7.

2. Katherine Newman (*Declining Fortunes: The Withering of the American Dream*, New York: Basic Books, 1993) argues that the generation that reached their twenties in the 1950s see themselves as frugal and as having more material comforts because they save more and the people who reached their twenties today buy the newest appliances and equipment (because, relatively speaking, such items are less expensive than they once were) on impulse, unable to save money. However, the utmost frugality would not allow them to purchase the housing that their parents were able to purchase. Hence, Newman notes that the difference in spending patterns is not so much a matter of younger people being unable to delay gratification and save for a better future but of the younger generation's rational assessment of what they can and what they can never afford.

3. This debt is facilitated by current marketing practices. Not only do store cards offer the opportunity to collect debt, they also provide young people with shopping therapy—not only having material things, but also putting them in a position where they can act out being grown-ups, having power to choose and take. After all, this is part of what they have learned—that growing up means buying things for yourself and satisfying material needs.

CHAPTER TEN

1. The first most common cause is accidents.

2. Don Foster, M. P., 1995, "A Report on the Level of Student Stress and Suicide Rates." House of Commons Library, London, U.K.

3. Cambridge University Counseling Service, 1998, "Responding to the Risk of Suicide—A Guide for Those with Welfare Responsibilities," Cambridge, U.K.

4. M. Kovacs and L. J. Bastiaens, 1995, "The Psychotherapeutic Management of Major Depressive and Dysthymic Disorders in Childhood and Adolescence: Issues and Prospects." In I. Goodyer, *The Depressed Child and Adolescent* (Cambridge, U.K.: Cambridge University Press).

5. Morag MacSween, 1993, *Anorexic Bodies: Perspective on Anorexia Nervosa* (London and New York: Routledge).

CHAPTER ELEVEN

1. For a full discussion of this point see Terri Apter, 1991, *Altered Loves: Mothers and Daughters during Adolescence* (New York: Ballantine), pp. 57–108.

2. Peter Blos, 1979, *The Adolescent Passage* (New York: International Universities Press); and Anna Freud, 1958, "Adolescence." *The Psychoanalytic Study of the Child*, vol. 13 (New Haven: Yale), pp. 255–278.

3. Barbara Schneider and David Stevenson, 1999, *The Ambitious Generation* (New Haven: Yale), p. 217.

4. See Barbara Schneider and David Stevenson, op. cit., pp.77–78.

5. Carol Samms, 1995, "Global Generation X: Their Values and Attitudes in Different Countries." The Seven Million Project. Working Paper 8 (London: Demos), p. 10.

6. Robert Cairns and Beverely Cairns, 1994, *Lifelines and Risks: Pathways of Youth in Our Time* (New York and London: Harvester Wheatsheaf), p. 259.

7. Peter Laslett (ed.), 1972, *Household and Family in Past Time* (Cambridge, U.K.: Cambridge University Press).

8. For example, see Michael Young and Peter Willmott, 1957, *Family and Kinship in East London* (Glencoe, Ill.: Free Press).

9. There is a large body of literature on blurred boundaries and blended identities. Theories about blurred identity boundaries as a sign of immaturity became an issue in feminist psychology, since women were judged more susceptible to this than were men. Blurred boundaries and blended identities then became the cornerstone of feminist psychological theories, and their status as immature mechanisms was challenged. The most influential and brilliant discussion of this is in Nancy Chodorow, 1978, *The Reproduction of Mothering* (Berkeley: University of California Press).

10. Barbara Schneider and David Stevenson, op. cit.

11. Daniel Stern, 1985, *The Interpersonal World of the Infant: A View from Psychoanalysis and Development Psychology* (New York: Basic Books).

12. Barbara Schneider and David Stevenson, op.cit.

13. James Coleman, 1990, *Foundations of Social Theory* (Cambridge, Mass: Harvard University Press).

14. Divorce and remarriage also create extended families of step relations. These sometimes adapt to needs for support networks.

15. Toni Antonucii, cited in *The (London) Sunday Times*, April 18, 1999, Section 1, p. 5.

16. Robert Putnam, 2000, *Bowling Alone: The Collapse and Revival of American Community* (New York: Simon and Schuster).

17. Robert Cairns and Beverely Cairns, op. cit.; Barbara Schneider and David Stevenson, op. cit.

18. For all the change there has been in the family, the parent/child bond (in particular the mother/child bond) has not decreased.

INDEX